The Political Environment of Economic Planning in Iran, 1971–1983

Also of Interest

The Problems of Arab Economic Development and Integration, edited by Adda Guecioueur

†*Rich and Poor States in the Middle East: Egypt and the New World Order,* edited by Malcolm H. Kerr and El Sayed Yassin

†*Local Politics and Development in the Middle East,* edited by Louis J. Cantori and Iliya Harik

†*The New Arab Social Order: A Study of the Social Impact of Oil Wealth,* Saad Eddin Ibrahim

OPEC: Twenty Years and Beyond, edited by Ragaei El Mallakh

†*A Concise History of the Middle East,* Second Edition, Revised and Updated, Arthur Goldschmidt, Jr.

Economic Growth and Development in Jordan, Michael P. Mazur

Mexico's Dilemma: The Political Origins of Economic Crisis, Roberto Newell G. and Luis Rubio F.

The Gulf and the Search for Strategic Stability: Saudi Arabia, the Military Balance in the Gulf, and Trends in the Arab-Israeli Military Balance, Anthony H. Cordesman

Industrial Progress in Small Oil-Exporting Countries: The Prospect for Kuwait, edited by Maurice Girgis

The Foreign Policies of Arab States, Bahgat Korany and Ali E. Hillal Dessouki

†Available in hardcover and paperback.

Westview Special Studies on the Middle East

The Political Environment of Economic Planning in Iran, 1971–1983: From Monarchy to Islamic Republic

Hossein Razavi and Firouz Vakil

Based on both research and first-hand experience, this book provides a politico-economic analysis of the operation of Iran's economy before and after the revolution of February 1979. The authors discuss the function and effectiveness of economic planning during the shah's tenure and relate the shortcomings of plan preparation and implementation to the explosive psycho-economic instability of the regime. They then discuss the institutional problems that the revolutionary regime has been facing in operating the economy and foresee the possible consequences of its failure to appropriately deal with these problems. Finally, analyzing the economic postures of important opposition groups, the authors outline future prospects for economic planning in Iran.

Dr. Hossein Razavi, a senior consultant at Ernst & Whinney in Washington, D.C., served as a bureau director at the Plan and Budget Organization of Iran from 1976 through November 1981. **Dr. Firouz Vakil** is currently a country economist at the World Bank. He held several positions at the Plan and Budget Organization of Iran, including that of under secretary for informatics, during the 1973–1979 period.

The Political Environment of Economic Planning in Iran, 1971–1983: From Monarchy to Islamic Republic

Hossein Razavi and Firouz Vakil

Routledge
Taylor & Francis Group
LONDON AND NEW YORK

First published 1984 by Westview Press

Published 2019 by Routledge
52 Vanderbilt Avenue, New York, NY 10017
2 Park Square, Milton Park, Abingdon, Oxon OX14 4RN

Routledge is an imprint of the Taylor & Francis Group, an informa business

Library of Congress Cataloging in Publication Data
Razavi, Hossein.
The political environment of economic planning in Iran, 1971–1983.
(Westview special studies on the Middle East)
Bibliography: p.
1. Iran—Economic policy. 2. Iran—Economic conditions —1945- . 3. Iran—Politics and government—1941–1979. 4. Iran—Politics and government—1979-
I. Vakil, Firouz. II. Title. III. Series.
HC475.R39 1984 338.955 84-3635

ISBN 13: 978-0-367-29499-1 (hbk)

ISBN 13: 978-0-367-31045-5 (pbk)

Contents

Tables and Figures

Tables

Figures

Acknowledgments

The major part of the material presented in this book is based on official and unofficial interviews and discussions that we have had with many employees of the Plan and Budget Organization of Iran. We are most indebted to these colleagues, whose names are too numerous to include here.

We have benefited from the comments of several scholars who reviewed earlier versions of the manuscript. In particular, we are grateful to Fereidun Fesharaki for his invaluable suggestions on the organization of the book and to Salah El-Serafy and Hassan Ali Mehran for their constructive comments on Chapters 3 and 5. However, the responsibility for any errors of fact and judgment is solely our own.

Finally, we want to thank Mary Murtha for her invaluable editorial assistance on several chapters of the manuscript and Libby Barstow of Westview Press for her meticulous editing of the entire manuscript.

Hossein Razavi
Firouz Vakil

1
Recent Political Events: An Overview

From 1941 to 1979 Iran was ruled by Mohammad Reza Shah Pahlavi, whose regime was toppled in February 1979 by a coalition of religious, nationalist, and leftist groups. During the course of the upheaval, the leader of the religious opposition, Ayatollah Rouhollah Khomeini, moved to the center of the opposition movement and headed the revolution against the shah. After the fall of the shah, Khomeini took control and appointed a provisional government to run the country. A referendum in March 1979 provided Khomeini with a mandate to establish an Islamic republic to replace the monarchy. Since then, the Iranian political environment has been subject to severe power struggles among those factions that had previously united to overthrow the shah's regime.

The political history of Iran during the nineteenth and twentieth centuries has been extensively analyzed.[1] Therefore, this chapter will neither repeat nor summarize the literature; nor will it evaluate or trace the historical roots of political events. Rather, our purpose is to highlight and analyze those political developments that serve to frame our discussion of the economy's management in other chapters of this book.

The Early Years of the Shah

Mohammad Reza Pahlavi's reign began in 1941 when his father, Reza Shah, abdicated under pressure from foreign forces (Britain and the Soviet Union). "The fall of Reza Shah ended the politics of state control; it had begun the politics of social conflict."[2]

Unlike his father, the young shah adhered to the provisions of the constitution, which provided for government by a cabinet responsible to a freely elected parliament. Many political prisoners who had been arrested during Reza Shah's tenure were now released from jail, and a relatively free press was revived.

An opposition group to the government, the pro-Soviet Toudeh party, was formed; its main center of activity was the northern part of Iran, and it advocated radical politico-economic changes. The British, on the other hand, encouraged Sayyed Zia Eddin, a former prime minister, to form the National Will party, a right-wing conservative party that often advocated a return to old Islamic traditions. Elections in 1943 resulted in a new political spectrum in the parliament: Both the right (National Will party) and the left (Toudeh party) were able to send representatives. Between these two groups was a nationalist group led by Mohammad Mossaddegh, who was known for his opposition to any foreign influence.

In 1945 a coalition of the Toudeh party and other leftist groups (with the support of the occupying Soviet army) formed provisional governments in Azarbayjan and Kurdistan, both of which declared their autonomy (not their independence). In 1946 the influence of the Toudeh party reached its peak, and the central government took three Toudeh ministers into its cabinet. After a few months, however, a tribal revolt backed by religious leaders and landlords forced the dismissal of the Toudeh ministers. Their dismissal signaled a change in the balance of power. Because the Soviet army had left the country and the Toudeh party had lost its force, the central government sent troops to put down the Azarbayjani and Kurdish autonomy movements. Thus, the Toudeh party had a limited role in the late 1940s and was finally outlawed in 1949, when it was alleged that a member of the party tried to assassinate the shah.[3]

In 1950 the issue of oil nationalization was raised when the new parliamentary election was held. A coalition of nationalist groups called the National Front, led by Mossaddegh, won the majority of seats, and in March 1951 the parliament approved the nationalization of the oil industry. In March 1951 Prime Minister Ali Razmara was assassinated, and the shah chose Hossein Ala to replace him. The parliament not only refused to approve Ala but also appointed Mossaddegh as the new prime minister.

During Mossaddegh's period as prime minister (1951–1953) there were serious economic hardships. U.S. and British oil companies had unofficially boycotted Iranian oil. Britain placed major restrictions on its trade with Iran and on the convertibility of Iranian sterling balances in Britain. In addition, the United States and Britain continuously attempted to overthrow Mossaddegh's government. Faced with all these difficulties, Mossaddegh's only source of support was his popularity with the people. In 1953, when Mossaddegh's popular base had somewhat weakened due to economic discontent and political division among his supporters, an Anglo-U.S. coup successfully overthrew Mossaddegh and brought back the shah, who had left the country when a previous coup against Mossaddegh in August 1953 had failed.

The Shah's New Rule

The shah began his new rule with a different approach than in his previous rule: His actions were more dictatorial. In addition, he had become interested in modernizing Iran's economy and in strengthening the military. Because of U.S. involvement in the fall of Mossaddegh and in the shah's new tenure, U.S. influence expanded in all political and economic dimensions, which changed the balance of foreign influence in Iran.

The shah's major concern was to prevent another Mossaddegh-type revolt. The shah thus began his evolving dictatorship by intervening in the 1954 parliamentary elections to ensure that the parliament was subservient to him. This intervention, of course, directly ignored the main thrust of the constitution, which provided for free elections.

When the election of 1960 approached, the shah and his U.S. advisers were convinced that a more democratic environment was required to make the elections more real. Consequently, the shah introduced a two-party system: The Melliun party was headed by Prime Minister Manouchehr Eghbal, and the Mardom party was led by Assadollah Alam, an old friend of the shah. Although there was no fundamental difference between the two parties, the official statements implying a free election encouraged opposition groups to take an active role in the campaign. The election results nevertheless disappointed many people, and open discontent over vote fraud grew rapidly. The shah disassociated himself from the election results, which had declared Eghbal the winner, by advising the elected deputies to resign and to hold new elections. The Eghbal cabinet was then forced to resign, and the shah appointed Jafar Sharif Emami as prime minister. Sharif Emami's government scheduled new elections, which were held in January 1961. These elections, though also viewed as dishonest by the opposition, resulted in the deputation of several independent candidates, including one from the National Front.

The new parliament became a scene of controversy regarding corruption in government and increasing politico-economic discontent in the society. Demonstrating before the parliament, Tehran's school teachers, led by Mohammad Darrakhshesh, announced a strike over pay. Two teachers were killed by the police and a new wave of demonstrations began.

At this stage, the shah was willing to relinquish some of his power by bringing National Front members into the government. No agreement could be reached between the shah and the National Front, however, and the shah invited Ali Amini to form a cabinet. Amini, who had previously held the positions of finance minister and ambassador to the

United States, was a critic of Prime Minister Eghbal and, implicitly, of the shah. Amini accepted the shah's offer on condition that the shah dissolve the parliament; it was dissolved, and he was appointed prime minister in April 1961.

Amini's appointment was to some extent supported by the United States, which was then pressuring the shah for more democratic political conditions. Amini launched an extensive economic program that included land reform, anticorruption, antiinflation, and budget-saving plans:

> In its fifteen months in office, the Amini government moved toward improving Iran's foreign exchange position via drastic cuts in non-essential imports, restrictions on foreign travel and purchases of foreign currency by Iranians. But serious problems came in April 1962 when Amini and his new finance minister, Dr. Jamshid Amuzegar, tried to get all ministers to reduce their budgets. The Shah refused to reduce the army budget, and so in July, Amini resigned, giving as his reason the inadequacy of American aid.[4]

Following Amini's resignation, Assadollah Alam was appointed prime minister. The National Front leaders asked Alam for free elections, but he rejected the request. Thus, in late 1962 the National Front began to attack the shah openly; the shah had the leaders arrested and tried to soften the general opposition by adding new reforms to the land-reform program of 1962. In early 1963 the shah called for a national referendum on a reform program that included land reform, the sale of government-owned factories to finance land reform, profit-sharing by industrial workers, giving women the right to vote, the establishment of a national literacy corps, and the nationalization of forests. The program, called the White Revolution, passed the referendum.

Also in early 1963, Rouhollah Khomeini, viewed at the time as one of the religious leaders, began to preach against the shah in the religious city of Qom. That March Khomeini was arrested for a short period, which added to his stature among the masses. After his release he continued to attack the United States for its support of Israel and to criticize the Iranian government for its close ties to the United States, though he did not object to the monarchy. Khomeini was arrested again on June 4, which led to a series of demonstrations in various parts of the country. The riots lasted for several days before they were crushed by army troops. Khomeini was released in August 1963 with the expectation that he would not interfere in politics, but he immediately asked his followers to boycott the parliamentary elections of October 1963. He was arrested again and held until May 1964. The following October he criticized the parliamentary bill giving diplomatic immunity to U.S. military personnel. This time he was exiled to Turkey. A year later he went from there to Iraq, where he stayed until 1978, when the Iraqis expelled him and he went to France.

A new party called Freedom Movement, emerging as a distinct wing of the National Front, had been formed in 1961. It was led by Mehdi Bazargan, who later served as the first prime minister of the Islamic regime (after the revolution of February 1979). The Freedom Movement party was a link between Islam and modern politics, its members mostly moderates with a genuine religious tendency. As will be described later in this chapter, the Freedom Movement played an important role in Iranian politics during and after the revolution.

From 1963 to 1977 there was only a little official change in political parties and leaders.[5] In the early 1960s a new political party called Iran Novin had been formed. The leader of the party, Hassan Ali Mansur, was appointed prime minister in March 1964. He was assassinated in January 1965, and another Iran Novin leader, Amir Abbas Hoveyda, was appointed prime minister; he held this post for about thirteen years. In March 1975, while Hoveyda was still in power, the shah announced that all Iranians should become members of one party. The Rastakhiz party was then formed with the understanding that all government employees were members. The Rastakhiz party was generally viewed as an imposition on the people's political beliefs and activities. As such, it generated more resentment than sympathy for the regime.

Despite the prevalent repression, new underground groups were formed. Among these, two groups that became active in the late 1960s turned into important guerrilla organizations: the Marxist People's Fedayian Organization and the Islamic leftist People's Mojahedin Organization. Both groups, choosing armed struggle as the appropriate strategy to fight against the shah's regime, carried out a number of assassinations and engaged in urban guerrilla activities. Many members of these two groups were executed by the shah's regime.[6]

The Revolution

Open opposition to the shah arose in early 1977. Many observers have attributed its appearance to the human-rights policy of U.S. President Jimmy Carter, yet as Nikhi R. Keddie has observed: "The influence of the human rights policy was not due to any significant American pressures, however, but to the belief by both the Shah and the opposition that the United States might act for human rights."[7]

At the initial stage the opposition took the form of circulation of open letters from secular activists concerning problems with the Iranian economy and violations of human rights. In this series, the most influential were the letter by Ali Asghar Haj Said Javady and the joint letter by National Front leaders Karim Sanjabi, Shapur Bakhtiar, and Daryoush Forouhar. Following these were letters by a group of well-known writers and by the newly formed Association of Jurists requesting freedom of the press and the observance of human rights. Also of major importance were the frequent meetings and gatherings of intellectual groups, in which the failures of the regime were discussed.

Facing a politico-economic crisis, the shah decided to remove Hoveyda from the prime ministry.[8] In August 1977 the shah appointed Jamshid Amuzegar as the new prime minister. Amuzegar and his so-called technocrat cabinet viewed inflation as the major politico-economic problem of the country. They therefore launched a deflationary program that resulted in mass unemployment, which in turn increased the public's discontent.

Adding fuel to the political fire was an article published in the semiofficial newspaper *Ettelaat* in January 1978. This article, later attributed to Information Minister Daryoush Homayoon, denounced Khomeini as a British puppet who had been opposing the shah in exchange for large sums of money received from England. The next day a massive protest was held in Qom, and a number of people were killed when they were attacked by the police. This was the breaking point, after which political activities turned into massive religious demonstrations.

Forty days after the Qom incident, another demonstration was held in Tabriz in which banks, theaters, and other Western establishments were destroyed and a number of people killed.[9] The forty-day-interval riots continued for several months, each leading to further violence and deaths. The opposition had begun to realize that the religious network and traditions provided a readily available establishment through which political activities could be carried out most effectively.

In May, June, and July 1978 several demonstrations were held in Babol, Qom, Esfahan, and Mashhad. However, the critical phase started on August 11, when demonstrations in Esfahan led to the imposition of martial law in the city. Adding to the problems of the troubled regime, a movie theater in Abadan was set on fire on August 19, and 377 people died in the blaze. Three days later, the funeral ceremony for these people turned into an antiregime demonstration that resulted in the positioning of army troops in Abadan.

On August 27 Jafar Sharif Emami was again appointed prime minister. The parliamentary debate over the approval of the new cabinet was televised nationally. Eighteen members of the parliament opposed Sharif Emami's cabinet, several of them expressing severe criticism of the shah's regime. Though Sharif Emami's cabinet was approved by the parliament on September 16, this approval had taken three weeks, and political conditions had changed significantly in the meantime. For one thing, a mass rally had been held in Tehran on September 7 in which the demonstrators had demanded the ousting of the shah. For another, on September 8 the government had declared a six-month period of martial law in Tehran and eleven other cities; on the same day, army troops had fired into demonstrators in Tehran, killing a large (still controversial) number of people. This incident had eroded whatever hope there had been for the success of Sharif Emami's cabinet. It had failed before it had been officially formed.

On October 6 Ayatollah Khomeini flew to Paris. There he was provided with easy access to the international media, so that his messages were then communicated to the Iranian people more effectively. As a result, a new wave of demonstrations and strikes began in late October 1978. Riots in the town of Gorgan on October 24 and in Rasht the next day resulted in the destruction of many hotels, banks, and public buildings. At the same time a new strike paralyzed the oil industry, and other government organizations followed suit.

On November 6 a military government was named by the shah, with General Reza Azhari as prime minister. The first step that the military government took was to arrest twenty-two prominent officials, including former prime minister Amir Abbas Hoveyda, the former head of SAVAK (the secret police), and six former ministers. All were charged with corruption.

On November 17 the opposition started testing the strength of the military government by organizing antiregime demonstrations in eleven cities. These demonstrations were followed on November 20–22 by bazaar riots that resulted in a clash with army troops. Ayatollah Khomeini then called on the armed forces to desert if ordered to fire on the demonstrators. This created a new concern for the military government. Knowing that the opposition was planning to hold demonstrations, the military government lifted the ban on processions for a forty-eight-hour period. The subsequent demonstrations on December 10 and 11 provided a clear signal of the regime's position among the masses. Millions of people demonstrated against the shah.

On December 12, the military government announced the resumption of martial law, which the opposition did not take seriously. The continuing strikes and riots reached a new peak by the end of December. In the meantime the shah began negotiations with the opposition groups to form a coalition government. National Front leader Karim Sanjabi rejected the offer and asked for the shah's abdication; however, another National Front leader, Shapur Bakhtiar, accepted the offer and presented his cabinet on January 6.[10] Ayatollah Khomeini called Bakhtiar's new government a "plot against the revolution" and asked the Iranian people to resist it.

On January 13, 1979, the two sides of the political struggle each formed a council. The shah formed the Regency Council to take over his duties while he left Iran for what he termed a vacation. Khomeini formed the Revolutionary Council that would be in charge of selecting and installing a provisional government after the fall of the shah. On January 16 the shah left Tehran for Aswan, Egypt, and Bakhtiar officially took charge.

Bakhtiar's tenure as prime minister lasted about one month. During this period, newspapers that had been banned by the military government started to publish again. A large number of political prisoners were released, and SAVAK was officially abolished. Bakhtiar also tried to arrange a meeting with Khomeini to discuss the future of the nation. Demonstrations and strikes nevertheless continued, many resulting in severe clashes with army troops.

On February 1 Khomeini returned to Iran. Hundreds of thousands of people lined the streets to welcome him. On February 5 he named Mehdi Bazargan to head the provisional government, despite Bakhtiar's assertions that he was still the legitimate prime minister of Iran. Pro-Khomeini demonstrations continued and extended to sections of the armed forces, resulting in a bloody clash between Air Force technicians and the Imperial Guard. The whole episode finally ended on February 11, when the Army Supreme Council announced the armed forces' neutrality in the political crisis. Bakhtiar disappeared, Tehran's military governor and other senior army generals were captured, and the commander of the Air Force was killed by the revolutionary forces. Khomeini supporters took over the state radio and television on February 12, and the provisional government of Bazargan officially took charge.

The Provisional Government

Bazargan's cabinet consisted of some prominent leaders of the National Front, most of whom came from the Freedom Movement party. These were mostly moderate individuals whose basic attempt was to start things moving again without imposing severe changes upon the structure of the system. However, Bazargan faced an increasing challenge from Islamic fundamentalists who sought to take the power away from the government.

These fundamentalists had influence in the Revolutionary Council and operated through four distinct arms: the revolutionary courts, the revolutionary committees, the Islamic Republic party (IRP), and the Hezbollah (the Party of God). The activities of the revolutionary courts were at the initial stage limited to trials of officials from the previous regime; after a few months, however, these courts took charge of trying members of the opposition. The revolutionary committees, which had been established to protect the peace and security of the cities, turned into executive organs that intervened in almost all public (and some private) affairs. The Islamic Republic party, the official organ of the fundamentalists, was very active in formal politics; it pushed for control over governmental organizations, as well as over the parliament.

The Hezbollah did not have any official organization. Acting as a crowd that appeared wherever an opposition group held a meeting, it physically attacked the meeting, sometimes killing or injuring a number of participants. At the initial stage, the Islamic fundamentalists disassociated themselves from the Hezbollah. At a later stage, however, when the fundamentalists had gained control over all governmental organs, they praised the Hezbollah members as "brothers who saved the Islamic revolution."

The first visible sign of conflict between the Bazargan cabinet and the Islamic fundamentalists was the argument over the execution of high-level officials of the shah's regime. These executions had started a few days after the revolution and had continued at an increasing rate. Bazargan publicly condemned these executions, but the fundamentalists supported them.

A more important source of conflict between the Bazargan cabinet and the fundamentalists arose from the revolutionary committees' interventions in public affairs. Although Bazargan consistently complained about these interventions, Khomeini made conflicting statements regarding his position. On March 7, for example, after the fundamentalists had accused Bazargan of being too liberal, Khomeini called the provisional government weak, but when Bazargan submitted his resignation the next day, Khomeini changed his stand by expressing his full confidence in Bazargan's cabinet.

Over time the power shifted from Bazargan to the fundamentalists. This shift was due by and large to Khomeini's support of the fundamentalists, a support enforced smoothly and intelligently. In fact, Khomeini did not publicly express his support of the fundamentalists for more than two years, but instead began eliminating those authorities who posed a threat to Islamic fundamentalism. On May 24, 1979, he announced that anyone whose direction diverged from Islam was an enemy of the revolution, an announcement clearly targeted at the secular nationalists, who did not believe in being ruled by the Islamic clergy. Hassan Nazih, a lay liberal who had become the director of the National Oil Company after the revolution, responded by offering his resignation. The process of elimination was continued until all nationalist leaders had been removed from high-level positions, with nationalism being denounced as an "anti-Islamic" attitude that should be suppressed.

Bazargan had numerous problems with Khomeini's interventions in government affairs, some of which were symbolic of Khomeini's intention to weaken the government. For example, in early July Bazargan's defense minister ordered the dismissal of the commander of the military police, but the commander refused to leave his post unless ordered to do so by Khomeini. A day later Khomeini told the commander to stay. Bazargan's reaction to this type of event was to submit a resignation and then to withdraw it after Khomeini had talked him out of it.

On July 19, 1979, a new agreement was reached between Bazargan and Khomeini. According to this agreement, four members of the Revolutionary Council were brought into the cabinet to unify the positions of the Revolutionary Council and the government. These four—Madavi Kani, Hashemi Rafsanjani, Abolhassan Bani-Sadr, and Javad Bahonar—later became important figures in Iranian politics. However, despite Bazargan's hope, the unification of the Revolutionary Council and the government did not solve the problems that the government had experienced with the Islamic fundamentalists' interventions in public affairs.

The conflict between Bazargan and the fundamentalists reached its peak in early November when the fundamentalists attacked him for his "friendly relationship" with the United States. Bazargan met with U.S. National Security Advisor Zbigniew Brzezinski on November 2 to discuss matters of mutual interest, only to have armed students occupy the U.S. Embassy on November 4. Bazargan denounced the occupation—but Khomeini expressed his personal support for it. As a result, Bazargan's provisional government resigned on November 6, and Khomeini ordered the Revolutionary Council to take charge of the government.

The Hostage Crisis

The hostage crisis, apparently a response to the admission of the shah to a U.S. hospital, provided the fundamentalists with an effective tool to force the liberals out of power. U.S. embassy documents were used extensively to denounce many nationalists and lay religious politicians, and each document was published with calculated timing. Depending on who resisted the fundamentalists' expansion of power, an embassy document was released to imply that the person resisting was the tool of the United States. Another major benefit gained by the fundamentalists was the rapid approval of the Islamic constitution, which would have faced much more resistance if this specific political environment had not prevailed.

The occupation of the embassy on November 4 occurred at a time when Bazargan and his foreign minister, Ebrahim Yazdi, were still being shown on television shaking hands with Brzezinski. Moderate politicians found themselves in such a line of fire that any who hoped to survive had to make a statement against the United States. Abolhassan Bani-Sadr, for example, who later denounced the student captors as "children who behaved like a government within a government," at this time declared his support for the embassy seizure and demanded the return of the shah, whom he called "the greatest criminal history has seen."

After the fall of the Bazargan cabinet, the Revolutionary Council assumed power and appointed new ministers. Bani-Sadr, taking charge of the foreign ministry on November 9, wrote a letter to United Nations (UN) Secretary General Kurt Waldheim requesting that the UN Security Council be convened and that an international inquiry be made into the shah's rule. The United States initially resisted the request. However, on November 25 Kurt Waldheim announced the preparation for an urgent meeting of the Security Council to deal with the hostage crisis. Bani-Sadr announced that he would go to the United Nations in New York the next day. Before he could depart, Khomeini announced that he did not believe in the Security Council meeting, whereupon Bani-Sadr resigned his post and Sadegh Ghotbzadeh was appointed foreign minister.

Ghotbzadeh, while coping with the prevalent anti-American passions in Iran, tried his best to solve the hostage crisis as fast as possible. On January 2, 1980, he met with Kurt Waldheim in Tehran to discuss preliminary actions toward a solution. On February 23 a UN commission of inquiry, consisting of representatives from Algeria, Venezuela, Syria, Sri Lanka, and France, arrived in Tehran. Bani-Sadr (who was now president) and Ghotbzadeh (still foreign minister) met with the commission and announced that it could see the hostages. Their student captors, however, said that there would be no plans for the commission to visit the embassy. The conflict between the government and the student captors over the hostages reached a stage at which Khomeini announced that the solution to the crisis lay in the hands of the parliament, whose members, he said, would be elected by the people.

Having seen a solution to the hostage crisis postponed, U.S. president Jimmy Carter announced a series of sanctions against Iran on April 7, 1980. They included the breaking of diplomatic relations, the invalidation of all visas issued to Iranian citizens for future entry to the United States, and the prohibition of exports from the United States to Iran. These were, of course, in addition to the freeze on the Iranian government's U.S. deposits and assets that he had ordered on November 14, 1979. President Carter added a few more items to the sanction list in mid-April and announced that the next step would be some sort of military action.

On April 22 the foreign ministers of the European Economic Community voted unanimously to impose economic sanctions on Iran. Canada and Japan shortly followed suit. The Iranian government's immediate reaction was to make trade agreements with those countries that would welcome such an opportunity.

On April 25 a U.S. rescue operation to free the hostages abruptly ended. Apparently, mechanical malfunctions in some part of the aircraft resulted in an order to terminate the mission. During the withdrawal, a helicopter crashed into a transport plane, killing eight U.S. servicemen.

That May the Iranian parliament convened. However, the hostage crisis, which the parliament was supposed to resolve, was not scheduled for discussion. After the shah's death on July 27, 1980, the members of the U.S. congress wrote a letter to the parliament urging Iran to resolve the hostage crisis. The letter was read in Parliament on July 30, but the members still did not raise the issue, waiting for guidelines from Khomeini.

On September 12, 1980, Khomeini issued a statement outlining the conditions for freeing the hostages: (1) the return of the shah's property in the United States, (2) the cancellation of U.S. financial damage claims against Iran, (3) the freedom of all Iranian assets in the United States, and (4) a guarantee of political and military nonintervention in Iran. The United States agreed with all conditions except the first, since the return of the shah's property was not within the jurisdiction of the U.S. government.

On September 16 the Iranian parliament decided to set up a commission to study the hostage crisis issue. The commission's report, submitted to the parliament on November 2, was basically an endorsement of Khomeini's conditions. On November 3 an interministerial committee was appointed to arrange the freeing of the hostages according to the approved conditions. Thereafter, the hostage crisis was handled solely by the cabinet; the prime minister, Mohammad Ali Rejaei, did not discuss the issue with Bani-Sadr, the president.

Early that November the Algerian government started to play an intermediary role between the United States and Iran, both of which had announced several times that a solution was near. The final agreement was reached on January 19, 1980, and the hostages were released during the last hours of Carter's presidency.

Power Struggles in the Islamic Regime

Power struggles in the Islamic regime began shortly after the provisional government took charge. At the initial stage, the Islamic fundamentalists succeeded in weakening Bazargan's provisional cabinet. During this period the fundamentalists' general purpose was to solidify their rule by establishing their own institutions and by undermining rival political groups.

A referendum was held on March 31, 1979, allowing the people to choose between the monarchy and the Islamic republic, though the latter was still undefined. The Islamic republic overwhelmingly won the referendum, and Khomeini declared April 1, 1979, to be "the first day of the Government of God."

On May 8, 1979, Khomeini ordered the formation of the Islamic Revolution Guard Corps, a special armed force, to protect the Islamic revolution. This organ was quickly established and it expanded rapidly, providing a major force against the activities of opposition groups. Since then, it has launched numerous armed attacks on various political groups and has captured thousands of their members.

In August 1979, the draft of a constitution was presented to an elected assembly of experts dominated by clerical and pro-Khomeini forces; the document gave total power to the leader (Khomeini in his lifetime). Twenty political groups announced their decision to boycott the upcoming referendum on the constitution, and the opposition both to the draft of the constitution and to the members of the assembly became so strong that Bazargan decided to dissolve the assembly. Before he could implement this decision, his cabinet fell. The constitution was then put to the vote on December 2, 1979, and received the approval of about 70 percent of those who participated in the voting.

The undermining of rival political groups by the Islamic fundamentalists was undertaken by suppressing the freedom of the press and the freedom of speech. First, the Tehran newspaper *Ayandegan* was attacked by the fundamentalists on May 12, 1979, after Khomeini had called it depraved. The paper ceased publication, and its facilities were later confiscated. That July 22 the *New York Times* correspondent in Tehran was ordered to leave. Shortly afterward, five European journalists were expelled, the Associated Press was ordered to close its Tehran bureau, and the correspondent for the *Wall Street Journal* was sent packing. On August 20 a total of twenty-two newspapers were shut down, leaving only a few proregime papers in circulation.

Physical attacks on political group meetings were a routine activity of the Hezbollah. As early as April 20, 1979, Hezbollah members assaulted the headquarters of the People's Fedayian Organization in Abadan. Among other political meetings, that of the newly formed National Democratic Front on August 12 was attacked and hundreds of people were injured. The Hezbollah's activities were especially intense during Bani-Sadr's presidency.

After the fall of the Bazargan cabinet in November 1979, the Revolutionary Council appointed another transitional government to take charge until the constitution had been approved and the new president elected. One of the members of this transitional government was Bani-Sadr, who was appointed minister of economics and finance (as previously mentioned). He was presumably a theorist of Islamic economics and had kept close contacts with Khomeini since the early 1970s, when Bani-Sadr and Khomeini were in exile in France and Iraq, respectively. During the final months of the revolution, when Khomeini was in Paris, Bani-Sadr had served as his close adviser.

After the revolution, Bani-Sadr served as a member of the Revolutionary Council. He also spent considerable time giving speeches about the organization of the ideal Islamic government, most of which were broadcast on the state radio. His views on the Islamic system, however, were in sharp contrast to those of the Islamic fundamentalists, and in foreign-policy matters he was known as a follower of Mossaddegh, who was opposed to any foreign influence, including that of the Soviet Union.

Following his resignation as foreign minister, Bani-Sadr ran as an independent candidate in the presidential election of January 1980. His principal rivals as the campaign began were Jalaleddin Farsi from the Islamic Republic party (IRP), Massood Rajavi from the leftist People's Mojahedin Organization, and Admiral Ahmad Madani, known as a secular nationalist. Massood Rajavi was eliminated by Khomeini because Rajavi had not voted for the constitution. Farsi withdrew from the election because he was not an Iranian by birth, and the IRP then introduced another candidate, Hassan Habibi. He got less than 4 percent of the vote. Bani-Sadr won the election with 75 percent of the vote.

Bani-Sadr's rise to the presidency coincided with the time that Khomeini had been hospitalized for a heart attack. Shortly afterward, Khomeini appointed Bani-Sadr commander of the armed forces, which was one of Khomeini's own tasks according to the constitution, and at the same time also appointed him to head the Revolutionary Council.

Having lost the presidential elections, the Islamic fundamentalists put all of their efforts into the parliamentary elections of May 1980 and won the majority of seats in Parliament. This started a new wave of conflicts between Bani-Sadr and the IRP, whose leader, Ayatollah Mohammad Beheshti, later became a personal enemy of Bani-Sadr. Beheshti was the chief of the Supreme Court, through which he controlled the judiciary branch, and the members of his party dominated the parliament, through which he controlled the legislative branch. Beheshti's next goal was to take over the executive branch by pushing Bani-Sadr out of power.

Bani-Sadr's first task after Parliament convened was to introduce a cabinet. His choices for prime minister were all viewed by the parliament as "not sufficiently Islamic" or "not sufficiently revolutionary." After a long quarrel, he reluctantly introduced Mohammad Ali Rejaei, who was shortly approved as prime minister by the parliament. Bani-Sadr maintained, however, that Rejaei had been imposed on him and that he could not work with Rejaei's cabinet. The conflict between the president and the prime minister became so severe that Khomeini appealed to all authorities, from the president on down, to end their differences and to serve the interests of the nation. The executive branch nevertheless remained for all practical purposes under the control of the IRP, and Bani-Sadr, even while he still held his title as president of the country, was becoming the leader of the opposition.

The outbreak of the war between Iran and Iraq in September 1980 changed the form of the power struggle between Bani-Sadr and the fundamentalists. Now serving as the commander of the armed forces, Bani-Sadr spent most of his time in the south of Iran, and Rejaei ran the government. Bani-Sadr counted on the popularity that he was gaining in the armed forces and pictured himself as a national hero, but Rejaei and his party were at the same time strengthening their grip on the government.

The power struggle between Bani-Sadr and fundamentalists erupted throughout the country in the form of political meetings and demonstrations. Clashes between the supporters of Bani-Sadr and of the Hezbollah intensified at an increasing rate. The leftist People's Mojahedin Organization declared its support for Bani-Sadr; in addition, many nationalist and liberal groups, having seen all other alternatives eliminated, now supported Bani-Sadr in opposition to being ruled by the Islamic fundamentalists. On the other hand, the pro-Soviet Toudeh party and a fraction of the leftist People's Fedayian Organization supported the fundamentalists.

The war atmosphere provided the government with a new mandate to prohibit all activities on the part of opposition groups. On March 8, 1981, all political meetings were declared illegal, many newspapers were banned, and Khomeini himself recommended that the politicians make "no more speeches until the end of the war." The People's Mojahedin Organization continued its demonstrations, however, and Bani-Sadr continued to criticize the incompetency of Rejaei's cabinet, the dictatorial acts of the IRP, and the treason of those who had handled the release of the hostages. On March 16 Khomeini set up a three-man reconciliation committee to study the problems between the two sides. This committee rebuked Bani-Sadr for having made inflammatory speeches.

On June 2, 1981, Chief Justice Beheshti proposed that Bani-Sadr be tried for having violated the constitution. On June 9 a rally in support of Bani-Sadr was attacked by the Hezbollah, and on June 10 Khomeini dismissed Bani-Sadr as commander of the armed forces. When another demonstration was held in support of Bani-Sadr on June 20, members of the Islamic Revolution Guards Corps opened fire on the demonstrators, killing at least twenty-four and injuring no fewer than two hundred people. On June 21 the parliament declared Bani-Sadr incompetent, and on June 22 Khomeini formally removed Bani-Sadr from the presidency.

After the fall of Bani-Sadr, a Presidency Council was formed to take charge until a new president was elected. The members of this council were Beheshti, Hashemi Rafsanjani, and Rejaei, all from the IRP. It now appeared that the IRP had reached its goal and was prepared to silence the remaining opposition. In less than two days, thirty of Bani-Sadr's supporters were executed. On June 28, however, a bomb exploded in the headquarters of the IRP and more than seventy IRP leaders were killed, including Beheshti, four cabinet members, six deputy ministers, and twenty members of the parliament.

The Islamic regime spent the month of June reorganizing itself. That July it was ready for a new start. It held elections to name a new president and to fill forty-six parliamentary seats, many of which were vacant because the members had been killed in the June 28 bombing. Throughout July the Islamic regime executed more than 250 of its opponents.

On August 3 the new president, Rejaei, chose Javad Bahonar (the new leader of the IRP) to serve as prime minister—and both men were killed in a bomb explosion on August 30. This led to a new presidential election that October, through which Ali Khameneii was named as president. He introduced Mir Hossein Mousavi as prime minister.

Meanwhile, Bani-Sadr, who had gone into hiding after his dismissal from the presidency, and Massood Rajavi, the leader of the Mojahedin Organization, had escaped to France on July 30, 1981. There, they announced the formation of the National Council of Resistance, aimed at toppling the Khomeini regime and returning Iran to a democratic path.[11] Inside Iran the council launched severe attacks upon Islamic fundamentalists, killing (according to the Islamic regime) more than one thousand government officials. In turn, Khomeini's regime executed (according to the council) more than twenty thousand of the council's supporters, most of whom were members or sympathizers of the People's Mojahedin Organization. One of the heaviest losses to the council occurred in February 1982 when their ranking leader, Musa Khiabani, was killed in an armed raid on his house by security forces of the Islamic regime.

The power struggle within the Islamic regime continued even after the IRP had taken charge of all public institutions. The struggle was now characterized by disagreements among the fundamentalists themselves—due in large part not only to the issue of which economic system to choose, but especially to that concerning the status of private ownership in an Islamic society. These disagreements, along with their consequences, are discussed in Chapters 5 and 6.

Here, it should be mentioned that in late 1982 the right wing, which advocated moderate economic policies, acquired enough power to attack the leaning of the system toward communism. On November 7, 1982, the speaker of the parliament called the pro-Soviet Toudeh party "a disreputable party with a filthy record" and charged that it had penetrated the administrative structure of certain public institutions; this was a clear indication that the Islamic regime had changed its attitude toward its relations with the Soviet Union. In January 1983 the Islamic regime blamed the Soviets for their support of Iraq in the war and expressed the hope that Afghanistan would be "freed of foreign troops." Shortly afterward the government refused to renew the visa of the Tehran representative of the Soviet news agency, TASS. Finally, in early February the leaders of the Toudeh party were arrested on charges of spying for the Soviet Union; they confessed in a televised interview that they had spied for the KGB (the Soviet intelligence agency) and that all of their activities were financed and managed by the Soviet Union. Following the interview, hundreds of Toudeh members were arrested, and eighteen Soviet diplomats were expelled from Iran.

The deterioration of Iran's relations with the Soviet Union coincided with the Islamic regime's campaign for improved relations with the West. In the meeting of the seven major powers held in Williamsburg, Virginia, in May 1983, Hans-Dietrich Genscher, the German foreign minister, said he believed that Iran wanted very much to increase its economic, political, and cultural dealings with the West. Other foreign ministers at the meeting expressed the same belief, and they agreed to welcome Iran back into the family of noncommunist nations.

Notes

1. For recent sources, see E. Abrahamian, *Iran Between Two Revolutions* (Princeton: Princeton University Press, 1982); and Nikki R. Keddie, *Roots of Revolution: An Interpretive History of Modern Iran* (New Haven: Yale University Press, 1981).
2. Abrahamian, *Iran Between Two Revolutions,* p. 165.
3. The Toudeh party became very active again in 1952–1953 when Mossaddegh's premiership allowed for open political activity by all groups. The

Toudeh party supported Mossaddegh at the early stage, but turned against him in the final days of his premiership. For a political history of the Toudeh party, see ibid.

4. Keddie, *Roots of Revolution,* p. 155.

5. The major changes of this period were economic. These changes, together with their impacts on the politico-economic conditions of the country, are discussed in Chapter 4.

6. For a history of the People's Mojahedin Organization and People's Fedayian Organization, see Abrahamian, *Iran Between Two Revolutions.*

7. Keddie, *Roots of Revolution,* p. 231.

8. The economic crisis of this period is discussed in Chapter 4.

9. Gathering of friends and relatives on the fortieth day of death is a Shiite-Moslem tradition.

10. Bakhtiar was expelled from the National Front; the next day he announced his acceptance of the shah's offer.

11. The National Council of Resistance has published a program for its provisional government. This program, together with the economic position of the council, is discussed in Chapter 6.

2
The History of Planning in Iran

Introduction

According to UN Economic and Social Council Resolution 1494 and General Assembly Resolution 2681 (Section 25), the unified approach to development analysis and planning implies efforts (1) to leave no sector of the population outside the scope of development; (2) to effect those structural changes that favor national development and activate all sectors of the population and all social organizations, ensuring their participation in the development process; (3) to aim at social equity, including the achievement of an equitable distribution of income; and (4) to give priority to the development of the human potential, including providing employment opportunities and providing for the needs of children.

The history of planning in Iran reflects an evolution in thinking toward the above definition. Moreover, it accepts as a premise that government intervention in the affairs of the economic ship of state is a necessity if the less-developed countries are ever to take their rightful place among the community of nations. This strategy of economic development, consciously begun by Reza Shah upon his accession to the throne in the mid-1920s, was modeled after Kemal Attaturk's etatist model.

The etatist model in turn assumed a convenient complementarity between politics and economics. The visionary ruler, in the twentieth-century context, needed to reign over a prosperous nation if his rule were ever to mean anything to the history books. Yet the world was divided between the haves and have-nots, the less-developed and the industrialized nations, or—as Raul Prebische defined it—the center and the periphery. The less-developed nations were constrained by the vicious circle theory—a country is poor because it is poor—and were hindered in their growth prospects by a lack of human and physical capital. Under such circumstances it was difficult to envision a development process in the Third World whereby the natural forces of capitalism could on their own contribute to social and economic development, as they had to a great extent done in the nineteenth century for the now-industrialized world.

The inevitable conclusion was that any nascent progressive capitalist forces needed to be encouraged, prodded, and indeed fostered by state intervention and guidance. In the context of Third World countries, where the political superstructure often implied a one-man show, this meant that the ruler would have to be the main protagonist of state intervention in order almost single-handedly to haul the national entity into the modern industrial world. This was certainly the view expressed by Reza Shah (and Attaturk in nearby Turkey) in pre–World War II Iran.

The First Development Plan: 1949–1955

Although the etatist model of industrialization served Reza Shah well through the 1930s, it did not provide for anything more than a series of ad hoc actions taken by the various ministries and coordinated at the top, again in an ad hoc fashion, so as to be in line with the ruler's vision. The postwar attempts at state intervention were gradually to become, under Mohammad Reza Shah, more coordinated and more reflective of the need to come up with a strategy of economic development that would be implemented by the government's administrative machinery and guided by the ruler. This process was eventually formalized along the lines of a functioning planning system (discussed in the next chapter), albeit heavily weighted in favor of the ruler's preferences.

As the history of the period (1925–1979) has shown, the planning process in Iran gradually evolved from a series of ad hoc actions in the direction of economic development into a formal and complex system, one in which the aims were to achieve unified, comprehensive development through a unified and comprehensive planning approach. In this, it was rather similar to the approach defined by UN Economic and Social Council Resolution 1494.

The First Seven-Year Development Plan, enacted by the Iranian parliament some six months after its inception, represented a first attempt at organizing the national allocation of public resources according to a predefined national strategy of development. Moreover, it formalized economic and social development as a national goal, a situation that had existed de facto under Reza Shah's reign and was now to be de jure with his son Mohammad Reza Pahlavi.

The plan recognized that although Iran had gained economically through the etatist industrialization of the pre-war years, the impact of

Table 2.1. Planned and Actual Public Expenditures, First Plan--1949-1955 (billion rials)

Sector	Estimated Expenditure	% of Total	Actual Expenditure	% of Estimated Expenditure
1. Agriculture & irrigation	7.3	27.8	5.7	78.1
2. Transport & communications	7.7	29.3	3.5	45.5
3. Industries & mines	5.3	20.1	4.1	77.4
4. Social services	6.0	22.8	.8	13.3
5. Regional development	-	-	-	-
6. Others	-	-	-	-
7. Total development	26.3	100.0	14.1	53.6

Source: Plan and Budget Organization, Tehran

US$1 = 67.5 rials

World War II had undone much of that industrialization and weakened the central government's control, due to foreign occupation. It was therefore natural for the government to attempt to redress this situation by launching a reconstruction effort. This was to be done (1) by developing a seven-year plan designed to guide the government specifically in its expenditure allocations throughout this period, and (2) by setting up a Plan and Budget Organization (PBO) to oversee and control these expenditures according to the predefined national objectives. With the help of the U.S. State Department and the International Bank for Reconstruction and Development (IBRD), the Monidson Knudsen Construction Company and subsequently the U.S. consulting firm Overseas Consultants were chosen to aid Iran in this endeavor. By September 1949 a seven-year plan had been drafted and the Plan and Budget Organization had been set up.

Table 2.1 summarizes the planned and actual expenditures of the First Development Plan. The figures indicate a plan that fell far short of expectations, given that only 53.6 percent of the planned expenditures were actually spent and that the expenditure pattern favored agriculture over industry and transport. The intention when the plan was drafted had been for a fairly even distribution of expenditures between agriculture, industry, and transport. Yet the oil nationalization act of 1951 changed the total picture, since oil funds dried up and the flow of foreign exchange to the planning machinery was cut off.

The total plan had called for development expenditures amounting to 26.3 billion rials, of which 14.0 billion rials were to be provided by the public sector. "In the event, adequate funds were denied to the Plan Organization due to internal conflict, problems with the Anglo-Iranian Oil Company over the nationalization of the Iranian oil industry and the failure of the country to raise foreign loans."[1] The political turmoil of the early 1950s overshadowed the nascent development efforts, and in fact the First Development Plan was for all practical purposes suspended.

Nothing much can be said about the success of this plan. The PBO was a new organization, and much effort had to go into building it. Setting up an efficient planning machinery proved much more difficult than the government had been led to believe by the original consultants; indeed, it was almost impossible to recruit Iranians qualified by education to fill sensitive planning positions, and planners qualified by experience were scarce even in Western countries. Thus, even if the political equation had allowed for a smoothly functioning planning process, much energy would still have been siphoned off in order to build the PBO and set up that process.

From a structural point of view, the First Development Plan was hardly a plan. It did not take the total economy into account (possibly because of a lack of data), and it did not even cover the whole of the public sector. It was simply a list of investment projects that were broken down by major sectors and unrelated to one another. Although the basic game plan was an industrialization strategy, it was difficult to discern this from the thrust of the document. The First plan thus achieved essentially no more than the setting up of a planning machinery and the renovation of industries established under Reza Shah's reign.

The Second Development Plan: 1956–1962

Because of the serious disruptions following the nationalization of the oil industry, the First Plan was shelved in favor of a new development plan that was to take effect in 1956 and last for seven years. Like the first, the Second Development Plan emphasized agriculture and transport, as shown by the planned and actual expenditures data in Table 2.2.

The Second Development Plan was drafted on the basis of the October 21, 1954, agreement between Iran and the international oil companies, for it was already recognized by the Iranian planners that oil revenues would fuel the plan. Thus, based on oil-revenue projections and on promised loans from the United States and from the IBRD, as well as on funds provided from the mobilization of domestic resources, the Second Plan provided for a total outlay of about 81.1 billion rials. Of

Table 2.2. Planned and Actual Public Expenditures, Second Plan--1956-1962 (billion rials)

Sector	Estimated Expenditure	% of Total	Actual Expenditure	% of Estimated Expenditure
1. Agriculture & irrigation	18.9	23.3	17.4	92.1
2. Transport & communications	30.4	37.5	27.3	89.8
3. Industries & mines	6.7	8.3	7.0	104.4
4. Social services	11.7	14.4	9.3	79.5
5. Regional development	12.2	15.0	8.6	70.5
6. Others	1.2	1.5	.4	33.3
7. Total development	81.1	100.0	70.0	86.3

Source: Plan and Budget Organization, Tehran

US$1 = 67.5 rials

this total, 23.3 percent was earmarked for agriculture and 37.5 percent for infrastructure (transport and communications). The plan, however, did not go beyond the project lists that had been set out for each sector, and project design was the responsibility of a nonministerial governmental organization, namely the PBO.

As shown in Table 2.2, the actual expenditures amounted to 86.3 percent of the planned expenditures, which contrasts rather severely with the 53.6 percent actually spent in the First Plan. This underscores the need for political stability if a carefully drawn-up development plan is to have any meaning whatsoever.

Because the political upheavals that had characterized the period of the first plan did not occur during that of the second plan, the more stable conditions permitted the completion of certain key projects that were to lay the groundwork for the economic expansion that followed. The construction of large dams—the Amir Kabir Dam on the Karaj River, the Farah Pahlavi Dam on the Sefid Roud River, and the Mohammad Reza Shah Pahlavi Dam on the Dez River—absorbed most of the funds allocated to the agricultural sector; yet because they were multipurpose in nature, the dams contributed to an increase in water-storage capacity of 9.3 billion cubic meters and to a total hydroelectric generating capacity of 692 megawatts. Industry experienced a significant increase in productive capacity, with textiles going from 60 million to 480 million meters of cloth by the end of the plan, cement from 0.1

to 1.2 million metric tons, and sugar from 85,000 to 227,000 metric tons.[2] Transport projects concentrated on expanding the country's highway network and on completing the railway system to Mashhad and Tabriz.

Though not to belittle its considerable achievements, it should be stated that the Second Plan did not bear the marks of a comprehensive plan, much less the imprint of a unified approach. The plan said nothing about the private sector, nor did it even cover the total activities of the public sector. Essentially the plan consisted of an investment program covering that portion of the public funds under the control of the PBO. Oil revenues were divided arbitrarily between the PBO and the Ministry of Finance; consequently, the planning was neither total nor coordinated. Policies and strategies of economic development were conspicuously absent from the Second Plan.

From a methodological point of view, the Second Plan appears to have been very weak. No use was made of any formal mathematical tools at any of the planning levels (macro, sectoral, and project levels). The plan was simply a list of projects, with no application of specific investment criteria. The only guiding hand in determining the size and composition of the plan was the budget constraint.[3] Needless to say, the kind of planning issues that merited consideration were well beyond the ability of the planning machinery, from its administrative structure to its statistical information.

The development of any plan usually implies objectives—ones that can be meaningfully quantified for purposes of action—but the Second Plan did not clearly specify these objectives, let alone the possible conflicts that might exist between them. Thus, the factor of choice, central to development planning, was also absent from the plan. It aimed at "increasing production, developing exports, preparing public necessities within the country, developing agriculture and industries, discovering and exporting mines and subterranean resources, improving and completing means of communication, improving public health, fulfilling any operations designed for the development of the country, raising the educational and living standard of the people and improving living conditions."[4] Given the Second Plan's lack of attention to objectives, it is clear that very little consideration was given to a proper balance between economic growth and social justice.

The plan called for an expenditure of 81.1 billion rials to be allocated to four major economic sectors (agriculture and irrigation, industries and mines, transport and communications, and social services) and to be concentrated rather heavily in social overhead capital. The choices that the planners made revealed their overall tendency to select low-value-added projects with low employment generation. The projects were few in number and highly capital intensive. No attempt was made to compare projects within or between sectors, and no project rankings were undertaken. Rather, the plan was a collection of seemingly unrelated projects that bore no relationship to any kind of policy guidelines.

The results of the Second Plan are very difficult to evaluate, given the lack of clear objectives and quantitative targets. What can be said is that the project estimates were frequently low on the cost side and that the achievements were below expectations.[5] To be sure, administrative inefficiency, specifically in the area of cooperation between the PBO and other government agencies, exacerbated the rather low level of achievements. Yet the failure to coordinate development policy with other economic policies, as should have been done by those who set up the plan framework, also contributed significantly.

Indeed, the lack of a comprehensive approach to planning during this period of the Second Plan was a major contributor to the 1960–1962 recession.[6] An exchange-rate devaluation did not prevent a severe balance-of-payments crisis and a rather severe inflation. An overexpansion of credits to the private sector and a shortage of public funds led to a monetary-based boom that eventually prompted a severe readjustment as funds for development projects dried up and foreign-exchange reserves dwindled to a seven-day supply. Iran's failure to obtain additional funds had forced the government to enter into a standby agreement with the International Monetary Fund (IMF) in 1959 and to accept austerity measures relating to imports, public expenditures, and money-supply expansion.

Nevertheless, the experience of the Second Plan was valuable. It did contribute to the expansion of an infrastructure network essential to raising the overall level of economic activity, whether private or public. Furthermore, it exemplified—by its lack of comprehensiveness—the need for a more coordinated approach to the use of public and private resources in order to avoid a repetition of the economic crisis of 1960–1962, which could be said to have contributed to the political turmoil of 1963. And finally, it provided a learning ground for the PBO and for the public-sector machinery. It thereby contributed to increased efforts toward developing basic statistics and further studies in the fields of planning and economics, and it promoted additional hiring of social-science majors to staff the planning apparatus.

The Third Development Plan: 1963–1967

The Third Development Plan was the first effort in the direction of comprehensive planning. The basic components of the plan were an investment program for the public sector and some forecasts for the private sector. Primary emphasis was placed on the growth target, specified as a 6 percent annual growth rate of gross national product (GNP). Some secondary objectives were also specified, the most important being (1) to enlarge employment possibilities, (2) to achieve a more equal distribution of income, and (3) to maintain relative price stability and equilibrium in the balance of payments.

The Third Development Plan was born out of the recessionary environment following the stabilization program of the early 1960s; therefore the private sector greeted the plan period with a certain lack of confidence. This was to severely affect the forecasts of the Third Plan in a negative fashion. Moreover, totally outside of the plan's framework, the shah in 1963 launched his White Revolution, the six-point program of social and political reforms mentioned in Chapter 1. These measures included land reform, the establishment of the Education, Health, and Development Corps, women's voting rights, and administrative reforms, as well as legislation to introduce profit sharing in industry and to nationalize forest and water resources. Even though nobody doubted the importance of these measures to Iran's longer-run development prospects, it nevertheless remained a fact that the White Revolution needed budgetary support and that this had not been included in the Third Plan. The PBO officials could not but be somewhat irked by the shah's administrative expediency in having launched his program without having integrated it with the plan in terms both of its developmental strategy and priorities and of its financial implications.

All these factors led to several revisions of the plan during its course, as noted in Table 2.3. Moreover, oil receipts grew much faster than the 6.5 percent per annum originally anticipated, and so this channeling of additional resources to the PBO also argued for revised allocations. The original, revised, and final allocations are shown in Table 2.3. The Third Plan was scheduled to run for five-and-a-half years, from September 1962 to March 1968.[7] Its proposed expenditures in the public sector had initially amounted to \$2.5 billion, but by the time the plan was formally approved it was reduced to \$1.9 billion because of anticipated shortfalls in revenue. Private-sector investment forecasts were put at 135 billion rials (US\$2.0 billion).

In contrast to the Second Plan, the Third Plan laid a heavy stress upon industrialization. The development strategy called for continued investments in agriculture and infrastructure in order to lay the foundation for the industrialization drive, but at the same time it emphasized the need to increase industrial production as the cornerstone of Iran's economic development. The plan was for the state to undertake the large-scale investments and to encourage private investment in the light industries. To some extent, this reliance on the private sector to sustain

Table 2.3. Planned and Actual Public Expenditures, Third Plan--1963-1967 (billion rials)

Sector	Original Plan	% of Total	1964 Revision	% of Total	1965 Revision	% of Total	Actual	% of Original
1. Agriculture & irrigation	30.0	21.5	45.0	22.5	49.0	21.3	47.3	158
2. Industries & mines	16.6	11.8	21.9	11.0	27.0	11.7	17.1	103
3. Electricity & fuel	26.1	18.7	27.0	13.5	41.5	18.0	32.0	123
4. Communication & telecommunications	30.0	21.5	50.0	25.0	56.0	24.3	53.8	179
5. Education	13.5	9.7	17.9	9.0	17.4	7.6	17.5	130
6. Health	10.0	7.2	13.9	7.0	13.5	5.9	13.2	132
7. Labor & manpower	6.2	4.4	8.0	4.0	3.6	1.6	2.8	45
8. Urban development	4.5	3.2	8.0	4.0	7.0	3.1	7.2	160
9. Other	2.8	2.0	8.3	4.0	15.0	6.5	13.7	489
10. Total expenditure	139.7	100.0	200.0	100.0	230.0	100.0	204.6	146

Source: Plan and Budget Organization, Tehran

US$1 = 67.5 rials

the industrialization drive was reflected in the relatively low percentage of funds allocated to industries and mines in the investment plan's public sector. Table 2.3 shows that in the original plan this allocation was only 12 percent, as compared to 22 percent for agriculture and 19 percent for electricity and oil.

The table also shows that actual expenditures in the public sector surpassed the plan's initial targets by 46 percent, having climbed from the initial total of 139.7 billion rials to a final total of 204.6 billion rials. The successive revisions were based on unanticipated increases in oil revenues and in the use of foreign loans. The net result was that most sectors expended more resources on investment than had been called for in the original plan, the greatest increases going to infrastructural, agricultural, and urban development. The laggard sectors in the revised plans were in fact the industrial and manpower sectors, the former for the very reasons cited above, and the latter by virtue of the difficulties of investing in this area.

The most notable achievement of the Third Plan was that it expanded the capacity of the productive sectors: agriculture and industry. In addition, the emphasis of public-sector expenditures in the direction of infrastructure not only kept pace with the advances in productive capacity but also allowed for additional expansions in output in the upcoming Fourth Plan by having provided, early on, some excess capacity in such lumpy investment areas as roads, railways, ports, and power generation.

The private sector, despite its having been shaken by the 1960–1962 recession, responded to the initiatives of the public sector with unanticipated vigor. A series of plants that significantly altered the Iranian industrial landscape came on stream at the beginning of the Third Plan: a B. F. Goodrich tire factory, automobile assembly plants (Fiat, Landover, Mercedes Benz, and Layland), and industries producing pharmaceuticals, bricks, pasteurized milk, rubber footwear, leather, detergents, radios, and oil heaters. Although many of these projects were conceived or begun during the period of the Second Plan, they nevertheless came to fruition during that of the Third. The private sector's industrialization was bolstered by a new confidence, a function of the shah's White Revolution and of the state's ability to build the necessary infrastructure. This confidence fed upon itself. The Iran National Paykan assembly plant was opened in cooperation with the Rootes Corporation of the United Kingdom, diesel-engine manufacturers at Tabriz began their operations with British Layland in 1965, another diesel plant was set up later with Benz of West Germany, Rambler opened a large automobile assembly plant in Tehran, and Dentz of West Germany began assembling buses. Among the many that came into production during the last half of the plan were sugar-beet processing plants at Nishapur, Kermanshah,

Khoy, and Esfahan; a glass factory in Qazvin; a nylon thread plant in Tehran; and a steel rolling mill at Ahvaz.

In the public sector there were a few major industrial investments, notably the aluminum smelting plant at Arak, the Shahpur Chemical Company at Bandar Shahpur, and some smaller petrochemical plants in the Abadan area. Yet the public sector's main emphasis remained upon the infrastructure: Existing roads were improved and new ones constructed, the railway line extension to Kerman was begun, and ports facilities were improved dramatically in order to permit the import of those investment goods necessary to support the nascent industrialization. Lastly, an Irano-Soviet steel project calling for an eventual annual output of 1.2 million metric tons was signed in 1965.

Given this background, it would be easy to suggest that the Third Plan was a success. Indeed, the target growth rate of 6 percent per annum was surpassed by 2.8 percent per annum; public-sector investments increased to 204.6 billion rials over the plan period, against the initial forecast of 139.7 billion rials; and private-sector investments reached a surprisingly high 250.0 billion rials. The cost of living index hardly increased during the Third Plan, even though growth was substantial.

Yet the evidence suggests that the good performance was less the result of good planning than of good fortune, and that a series of fortuitous circumstances had coalesced to improve confidence and encourage investment. Even though the economy had matured during the Third Plan, such had not necessarily been the case for the planning process. There were some serious shortcomings, symptomatic of an economic environment in need of planning, but one in which the planning machinery was weak, the planning process was unsophisticated, and there were too few planners with too little data to ensure the degree of comprehensiveness so necessary to a good plan. The planners also set goals that conflicted with one another. For example, the plan explicitly stated that growth was to be combined with a greater attention to social justice, but matters of social justice never received proper attention. The goal of creating employment, for instance, had been ranked well below that of economic growth, and the other secondary goals mentioned earlier never seemed to have been integrated comprehensively within the framework of the plan.[8]

The plan's initial size, estimated at approximately 290 billion rials for both the public and private sectors, had been determined through simple computations of the Harrod-Domar type. Subsequently, in 1965 the public-sector figure was revised upward to 230 billion rials without rationale and without specifying this revision's effects on the private sector. Again, the planning machinery not only failed to consider the reciprocal effects between economic growth and social justice, but it also failed to provide even the basic integration between public-sector programs and private-sector activities. A mere increase in revenues was considered enough to justify an unplanned expansion. Such arbitrariness in modifying a plan would become the nemesis of the regime during the Fifth Plan period.

From a methodological point of view, the planning was severely limited in terms of its comprehensiveness. No formal models or programing methods were used, and no attempts were made to obtain general equilibrium-type (simultaneous) solutions. Rather, the basic method of planning resembled Jan Tinbergen's "stage method," a trial-and-error process that could not be used in its entirety due to a paucity of statistical information.[9] Much of the Third Plan indeed suffered from a dearth of data; consequently, it seemed natural that comprehensiveness should also suffer.

As in the Second Plan, there were four broad sectors: agriculture, industry, transport, and social services. Proper planning procedures at the sectoral level suggest the setting of targets and then the evaluation of trade-offs between investment allocations because of budget constraints. Since no data were available, though, it was difficult to set targets, and none were therefore contemplated. Thus, all of the sectoral allocations had to be determined on the basis of trial-and-error procedures that relied heavily on the subjective judgment of the planners.

Moreover, the administrative machinery did not match the requirements of the planning structure. The Third Plan, as originally envisioned, was to consist both of a plan frame that was to be prepared by the PBO at the broad macro and sectoral levels and of a list of projects that was to be prepared by the executive agencies. Although preparation of the plan frame proceeded according to schedule, the ministries never carried out their responsibility to fill the sectoral investment targets with investment projects. Consequently, the Third Plan was deficient from the outset in terms of concrete projects, and the process of screening the projects in order to fill sectoral investment targets was replaced by a process of generating investment projects. Under such conditions, it was natural that both consistency and optimality in the investment program were conspicuously absent. The allocations nevertheless reflected a definite shift of emphasis from social overhead capital to more productive activities.

To summarize: In terms of its overall objectives, the Third Plan was a success. The 6 percent growth rate of GNP specified in the plan was surpassed by 2.8 percent. In terms of specific, sectoral targets, however, this success was somewhat tarnished; the planned 4.1 percent growth rate of agriculture, the only sectoral growth rate to be included in the plan as a target, reached only 3.0 percent. Many structural transformations took place in the economy, but—as indicated—these were more the result of good fortune than of good planning.

The Third Plan was historically significant, in that during this period the Iranian economy reached the takeoff stage. After a shaky post-Mossaddegh era, the government finally felt secure enough to institute a set of reforms that, even if not successful in the eyes of a perfectionist, were to transform the social and economic landscape. Amid these changes, a new mood of confidence in the private sector led to an industrialization process propelled by state incentives that, even though uncoordinated, saw positive results. The society had begun a transformation. Good planning clearly had not been a predominant causal factor in the process, though, and we are left feeling that the economic results were achieved independently of the plan.

The Fourth Development Plan: 1968–1972

Like its predecessor, the Fourth Plan was an improvement over previous plans in terms of its formulation and implementation. It also showed a relatively greater degree of comprehensiveness, as witnessed by its overall objectives: (1) to increase the rate of economic growth by gradually increasing the relative importance of industry, by raising the productivity of capital, and by using modern techniques of production; (2) to achieve a more equitable distribution of income through employment and welfare policies; (3) to decrease the nation's dependence on foreign countries in meeting its basic requirements, this coupled with a diversification of exports; and (4) to improve administrative services by introducing basic changes in the administrative system and by extending advanced managerial techniques to all ministries and private organizations.[10]

The formulation of the Fourth Plan exhibited on the one hand a great degree of maturity in the planning process and in the planning machinery. The national data base was now large enough to allow for a more sophisticated approach to the calculations of alternatives than had been the case in earlier plans, and the planners themselves reflected the experience that comes with having spent time in the administrative and technical branches of the government's planning institutions. On the other hand, even though the Fourth Development Plan has come to be known as the most successful of Iran's development plans, the question remains as to whether this success resulted from the planning process itself, in its entirety, or was merely a coincidental piece of good fortune.

What is important to note is that although the First Plan had been abandoned in the face of the international political crisis resulting from the nationalization of the oil industry and the Second and Third Plans had been born out of an unsettled political or economic environment, the Fourth Plan faced no such obstacles. Quite the contrary: The years of the Fourth Plan saw no wild fluctuations among the social, political, and economic variables, no exogenous or endogenous shocks to the national entity. The Iranian economy was thus able during this period to build substantially upon the gains from the Third Plan. The economy was finally taking off.

It was now that Iran began to focus, let us say consciously, on a more precise development strategy, and it was also now that industrialization—the central feature of that strategy—began to make rapid progress. The social overhead capital investments of the Second and Third Plans had created an environment in which industrial activity was possible, and the nascent industrialization drive, having begun to gather speed by the end of the Third Plan, now forged ahead. Whereas development planning had formerly been an ad hoc process, it was now systematized in the Fourth Plan so as to define the major medium- and long-term objectives for the Iranian economy: Growth, as the prime goal, would be fueled by the industrialization drive. The financial resources, which would be provided by the oil sector, would allow the required diversification of industries, a diversification included in order to provide the export earnings essential in lieu of oil. The planners quite correctly viewed the oil resources as being limited and the industrialization drive as necessary not only to raise the nation's level of income but also to produce those export goods that one day would substitute for oil exports. The Fourth Plan promoted the notion of industrialization as a necessity in the Iranian development strategy. The shah coalesced these ideas at Persepolis in 1972, when he previewed the Fifth Plan in the presence of the PBO and of senior officials from the ministries.

The data in Table 2.4 show the planned and actual expenditures in the public sector. In contrast to previous plans, the sector of industry and mines received the highest priority, as evidenced by the 20.8 percent allocation and the 22.3 percent actual expenditure. Agriculture received only an 8.4 percent allocation, reflecting the sector's limited possibilities and low absorptive capacity, but infrastructural investments remained at a high-priority level, as did investments in oil, gas, and electricity. Because of the sectoral disaggregation in the Fourth Plan, a strict comparison with Table 2.3 is only possible by combining some sectors in Table 2.4. Combined sectors 1 and 4 in Table 2.4 compare to sector 1 in Table 2.3; sectors 3 and 5 in Table 2.4 to sector 3 in Table 2.3; and sectors 6 and 7 in Table 2.4 to sector 4 in Table 2.3. When this is done, the shift in the direction of industrialization is clearly indicated.

Table 2.4. Planned & Actual Public Expenditures, Fourth Plan--1968-1972 (billion rials)

Sector	Approved Credits (Revised version) Value	Share %	Actual Disbursements Value	Share %	Actual as % Approved Credits
1. Agriculture	46.7	8.4	41.2	8.1	88.2
2. Industry & mines	115.6	20.8	113.1	22.3	97.8
3. Oil & gas	61.7	11.1	57.3	11.3	92.9
4. Water	45.3	8.2	42.0	8.3	92.7
5. Electricity	42.2	7.6	37.7	7.5	89.3
6. Transport & communications	84.3	15.2	71.4	14.1	84.7
7. Telecommunications	46.5	8.4	38.7	7.6	83.2
8. Rural development	10.3	1.9	9.8	1.9	95.1
9. Urban development	9.1	1.6	8.3	1.6	91.2
10. Housing & construction	43.0	7.8	41.6	8.2	96.7
11. Education	19.0	3.4	17.7	3.5	93.2
12. Culture	1.5	0.3	1.4	0.3	93.3
13. Tourism	3.5	0.6	3.3	0.7	94.3
14. Health	15.7	2.8	14.2	2.8	90.4
15. Social welfare	5.7	1.0	5.1	1.0	89.5
16. Statistics & research	1.8	0.3	1.7	0.3	94.4
17. Regional development	2.6	0.5	2.3	0.5	88.5
18. Total	554.5	100.0	506.8	100.0	91.4

Source: Central Bank of Iran, Annual Report, 1972
US$1 = 67.5 rials

The actual expenditures in the Fourth Plan were below the plan's revised targets, accounting for 91.4 percent of the approved credits, but this was still a respectable performance. It reflected the fact that this was essentially a plan with few surprises, one in which the targets were more or less stabilized, as shown by the right-hand column in Table 2.4. Public sector investments were set at about 500 billion rials, and the private sector was expected to invest about 370 billion rials. Gross domestic fixed capital formation grew in fact at 13 percent per year, with the public and private shares in annual investments standing at 58 percent and 42 percent, respectively.

As in the Third Plan period, the most notable achievements of the Fourth Plan were in industrial and infrastructural development. The public sector continued its investments in iron and steel, petrochemicals, machine building, and metal smelting. The Esfahan steel mill accounted for almost half of the credit allocations to the sector of industry and mines in the Fourth Plan. The private sector also expanded its manufacturing activities rapidly, aided by the availability of credit through such specialized banks as the Industrial Mining and Development Bank of Iran and the Industrial Credit Bank. Infrastructural developments were also significant: Electric power production more than doubled from

4.5 billion to 12.0 billion kilowatt-hours, the railway network expanded from 3,600 to 4,400 kilometers, the road network increased by 3,000 kilometers, and port capacity reached 5.0 million metric tons per year by the beginning of the Fifth Plan. In total, these achievements highlight the fact that Iran was in the midst of a successful industrialization drive by the end of the Fourth Plan.

Even though industrial growth was the prime objective, the social sectors were beginning to draw the attention of the planners and the politicians. Therefore, as the data in Table 2.4 show, the credits both allocated for and actually spent on housing, education, health, social welfare, and urban and rural development amounted to just under 20 percent of the total investment expenditures. Moreover, beginning to reflect the increasing concern for a more balanced growth strategy, the planners redefined the social sectors, expanding their number to include those areas where remedial action could and should be undertaken by the state. The introduction of regional development as a sector where financial resources could be absorbed, for example, reflected the increasing concern about such spatial aspects of industrial development as the concentration of the industrialization drive in the major cities, the rural-urban migration, and the pressure on Tehran's infrastructure. Agriculture, by contrast, did not perform as well as had been expected. Employment in that sector therefore decreased substantially during the 1968–1972 period.

Yet the overall growth target of 9 percent per annum was exceeded so handsomely that, on balance, the real GNP increased by 11 percent per year to 1,186.4 billion rials in the final year of the plan. The high growth rates in the sectors of industry and mines, oil and gas, and services, even though offset by the lower-than-expected growth in the agricultural sector, reflected a profound structural change in the economy. The takeoff had succeeded. By 1972–1973, the end of the Fourth Plan, Iran was not only poised to maintain its rapid advance along the path of self-sustaining growth but the modernization and the structural changes were beginning to make what seemed at the time to be a lasting imprint on the society. The gains in per capita income were significant during the Fourth Plan period and, generally speaking, the population's living standards improved dramatically.

As in the case of the Third Plan, the method of formulating the Fourth Plan was essentially one of trial and error. The planning task was undertaken entirely by the economists of the PBO. Breaking it down into a number of stages, they began the process by estimating the total investment requirements on the basis of the overall growth-rate target, and then determined the sectoral investment allocations on the basis of the sectoral production targets. Five broad sectors were considered in the planning: agriculture, industry, oil and gas, water and power, and services. The problems were also the same as in the Third Plan—trial-and-error procedures, lack of statistics, inconsistency, shortage of concrete projects, lack of optimality considerations, and so on. The priorities, as read from the final investment program, favored services—especially social overhead capital—and suggested a shift away from directly productive activities.

To reiterate our previous judgment, it is difficult to conclude that the economic achievements of the 1963–1973 period can be ascribed more to good financing than to good fortune. What can be said is that during this time the planning process matured and the data base improved. It can also be said that during the Fourth Plan period the Iranian economy reached that stage of development where it appeared that an increase in financial resources (local currency plus foreign exchange) would open up new growth vistas. Unfortunately, even as these resources finally materialized in the Fifth Plan period, the growth prospects dimmed and were abruptly snuffed out, at least for a time, by a momentous political upheaval.

The Fifth Development Plan: 1973–1977

The Fifth Development Plan began on March 21, 1973. It was basically a continuation of the Fourth Plan, though the financial allocations soon increased by more than 170 percent. Its emphasis was on industry and infrastructural services.

Even though the initial Fifth Plan was very ambitious, it was abandoned in favor of a more ambitious version as oil prices rose in the last quarter of 1973. The initial version had been based on an estimated oil revenue of 1,417.5 billion rials during the plan's five years (1973–1977), but after the oil-price increase of 1973 the estimated oil revenue for that same period was put at five times the original amount. The shah then decided to revise the Fifth Plan so as to disburse this new wealth. The revised version was prepared hastily and with great optimism over future oil revenues. In addition to doubling or tripling the funds for many sectors, it allocated a vast budget for such projects as nuclear energy development.

The Fifth Development Plan was much more than an investment program. It brought great changes in the social and economic structure of the country and eventually led to a politico-economic explosion. The Fifth Plan period was also a time during which the process of economic planning, under the pressures of the political environment, was virtually reduced to the mere formality of disbursing the financial resources. This time period thus marked a very important interval in Iran's politico-economic history, and we devote the major part of Chapter 4 ("What Went Wrong?") to its analysis.

Here, it remains to be said that by late 1976 the revised Fifth Plan was for all practical purposes abandoned, and preparations were being made for the Sixth Development Plan. A new planning procedure was adopted, giving all executive agencies an input into the plan preparation process; there were doubts about the practicality of this procedure, but it was abandoned before it could be tested. In 1978 the shah decided that the economy no longer needed five-year planning and called, instead, for long-term planning guidelines, together with a one-year development budget. This was presumably the end of planning activities during the shah's reign.

Notes

1. Keith MacLachlan, "The Iranian Economy 1960–1976," in H. Amirsadeghi and R. W. Ferrier, eds., *Twentieth Century Iran* (London: Heineman, 1977), p. 130.
2. George Lenczowski, *Iran Under the Pahlavis* (Stanford, Calif.: Hoover Institution Press, Stanford University, 1978), p. 169.
3. Albert Waterston, *Development Planning: Lessons of Experience* (Baltimore: Johns Hopkins University Press, 1956), p. 61.
4. Government of Iran, Law of the Second Seven-Year Development Plan of Iran, Article 1.
5. Plan and Budget Organization, "Review of the Second Seven-Year Plan," pp. 34, 41–42.
6. Farhad Daftary, "The Balance of Payments Deficit and the Problem of Inflation in Iran, 1955–1962," *Iranian Studies* 5 (Winter 1972).
7. The Iranian calendar year goes from March 21 of the current year to March 20 of the following year.
8. Plan and Budget Organization, "Outline of the Third Plan," pp. 37–39.
9. Jan Tinbergen, *Development Planning* (New York: McGraw-Hill Book Co., 1967), p. 75.
10. Plan and Budget Organization, Fourth National Development Plan, p. 39.

3
The Planning System

Introduction

The process of economic planning in Iran, as initially designed and available on paper, was quite different from the procedure actually used to prepare the development plans and to translate the premises of those plans into practical decisions. The planning process, as laid down in 1949 when the Plan and Budget Organization (PBO) was established, was limited to providing a mechanism to coordinate the government's involvement in public projects, most of which were ongoing. The basic problems with this planning approach were its lack of comprehensiveness and sectoral consistency. During the late 1950s and early 1960s, the planning system went through an evolutionary process to acquire some degree of maturity and sophistication. However, at the later stages of the Fourth Plan and especially at the beginning of the Fifth Plan, various parts of the planning procedure were gradually relaxed, so that by the mid-1970s the entire issue of economic planning had turned into a virtual formality for spending the allocations. This relaxation of the role of economic planning was one of the fundamental problems of the shah's regime.

This chapter explains the procedures used to prepare the development plans as well as the process for implementing them. As a framework for this discussion, we shall begin with an overview of the planning institution and the PBO's functions, it having served as the central element of the planning core.

The Planning Institution

The organizational structure of the public sector has remained basically unchanged since the establishment of the PBO, though the center of power has occasionally shifted from one institution to another.

Figure 3.1 shows the structure of the public sector. Within it, the government sector consists of a number of ministries responsible for carrying out the functions of the government. Each ministry may have

Figure 3.1 Organization of the Public Sector

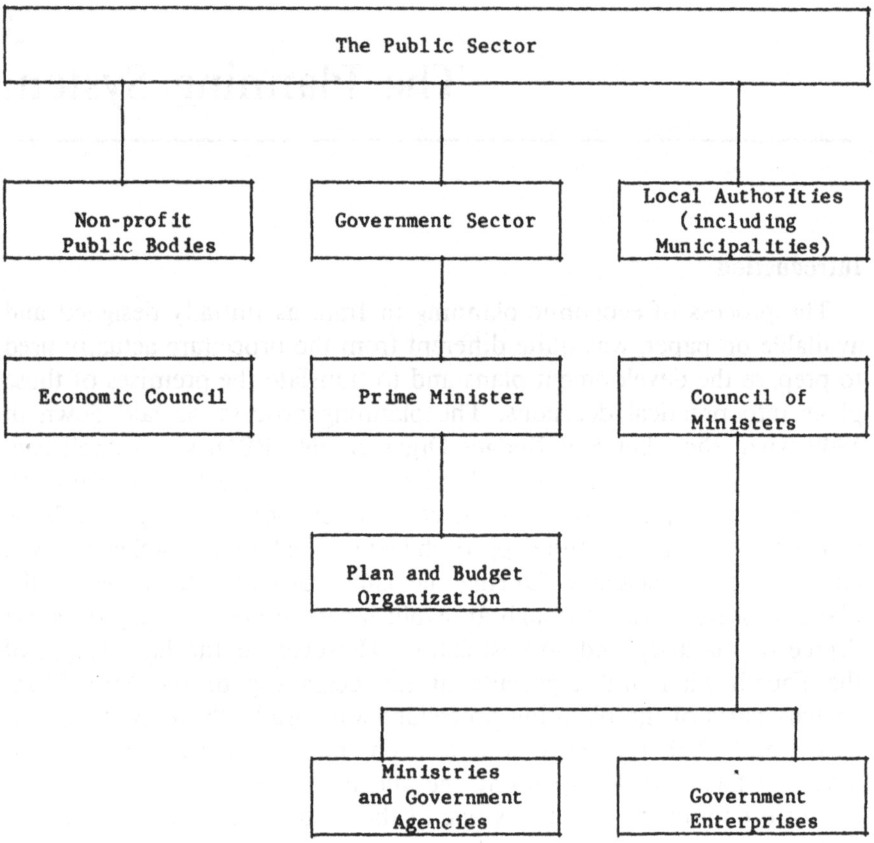

a number of independent organizations affiliated with it: Some of these, which carry out part of the ministry's functions, are called government agencies; others, which operate on commercial lines, are called government enterprises or government corporations. These have been established in accordance with the specific acts of Parliament as corporate bodies with over 50 percent of their capital belonging to the government. Most of these enterprises, which had private-sector shares, were nationalized after the revolution.

All of the activities of the public sector, except for municipalities and some nonprofit public bodies, are financed by the State General Budget. Apart from the aid they receive from the government, the municipalities are in every respect independent and their budgets are not incorporated in the State General Budget. Other agencies and councils exist at the provincial and urban district level, and these enjoy varying degrees of authority and independence at the regional level with regard to the preparation and implementation of their budgets. Examples of these bodies are the boards of trustees for educational regions, public health boards, and provincial councils. According to the law, the prime minister is responsible for the State General Budget, and this function is carried out by the Plan and Budget Organization. Within the government sector, several other institutions are directly or indirectly concerned with planning and budgeting. These are the Council of Ministers, Economic Council, Ministry of Economic Affairs and Finance, and Ministry of Interior.

The Plan and Budget Organization, however, is the central core of the planning institution. The basic functions of this organization are

- to carry out social and economic surveys and studies in order to formulate plans and budgets and to prepare social and economic reports;
- to prepare long-term plans, in conjunction with executive agencies, for submission to the Economic Council;
- to prepare quinquennial development plans;
- to propose to the Economic Council guidelines and policies relating to the State General Budget;
- to prepare and draft the State General Budget;
- to exercise ongoing supervision over the country's statistical procedures and programs;
- to evaluate the productivity and performance of executive agencies and to submit reports thereon to the prime minister;
- to examine the reports and questions to be discussed by the Economic Council;
- to determine the competency of and to classify consulting engineers and contractors;
- to establish the standards, criteria, general principles, and general conditions of contracts relating to development projects;
- to determine and define terms of the foreign loans and credits that have been reserved for projects and programs;
- to control permanently the execution of all approved plans, programs, activities, and projects by the executive agencies;
- to keep the prime minister informed as to the progress of the programs, projects, and activities with respect to the work program proposed, the work actually initiated, and the work completed;
- to prepare and present biannual progress reports in conjunction with development projects and programs and to compile and submit annual economic reports and comprehensive operating reports for each planning period;

- to contribute to the promotion of regional planning, budgeting, and administration in order to achieve balanced interregional and intra-regional development through decentralization within the national context; and
- to establish a national data system.

The Council of Ministers is, officially, the highest policymaking body in the government sector. It consists of twenty ministers and five ministers of state. The prime minister is the chairman of this council.

Decisions regarding development planning and budgeting and implementation thereof are taken by the Economic Council, whose chairman is the prime minister. Its members include a number of ministers responsible for planning, budgeting, and social and economic affairs. The governor of the Central Bank of Iran is also a member of the Economic Council.

The Ministry of Economic Affairs and Finance is responsible, in cooperation with the PBO, for forecasting revenues and other resources and for mobilizing the funds required for the implementation of government programs. It is also responsible for collection of government revenues. All government receipts and payments are consolidated in the Treasury, which is an integral part of the ministry. In other words, all the fiscal operations of the government sector are managed by the ministry. The ministry is also responsible for financial control both during and after the execution stage of the budget and for the preparation of the Budget Settlement Bill.

The Ministry of Interior's concern with planning is conveyed through its affiliated organization, the State Organization for Administration and Employment. The functions of this organization are:

- to formulate and coordinate all activities for improving the management and organization of the governmental sector;
- to propose solutions to problems of government organizations;
- to conduct a program of management studies, research, and services designed to promote management methods and procedures; and
- to give guidance and advice to governmental agencies, toward improving their management and organization.

According to the initial design of the planning institution, PBO was to be the most powerful and authoritative body of the planning network. It was especially noted in the design that PBO was to be directly responsible for the execution of development projects. However, this authority was weakened over time and was significantly reduced in 1972 when the responsibility for the execution of development projects was transferred to other ministries and government institutions.

The Functional Organization of the PBO

The functional organization of the PBO is more or less based on the initial design of the planning process as formulated in 1949. Although reorganizations have taken place to abolish some units or to create or to rename others, the basic structure has not changed (this includes the reorganizations that took place after the revolution).

The PBO, though officially an organization, is administered by a minister. Its relative power and effectiveness fluctuate rather sharply, depending on the minister in charge and on the general politico-economic environment. The major divisions of the PBO, each administered by an undersecretary (deputy minister), are: Planning, Coordination and Supervision, Regionalization, Budgeting, Technical Affairs, Informatics, and Statistical Center of Iran. Each is discussed in turn.

The Planning Division

The Planning Division was intended to be the heart of the PBO, to serve as the country's planning body. However, the importance of its function was barely realized and never materialized. There were major reasons for this failure. First, traditionally the Iranian society does not provide a really suitable environment for implementing economic activities within a planning framework. This does not necessarily mean, of course, that there are no prospects for doing things according to a plan. Rather, it indicates that the institutional design of planning should take this cultural characteristic into account and devise means for coping with difficulties that may arise. The Planning Division's potential was, however, far less than required to accomplish this task.

Second, the PBO was not concerned very much with economic planning, initially. Its basic objective was to oversee and coordinate the activities of a limited number of governmental projects. Nevertheless, with increasing involvement of the government in economic activities, planning received official recognition, and the Planning Division's official role was an outgrowth of this recognition. In practice, though, the division never reached the stage at which it could significantly affect the economic, decision-making process.

Third, the role of economic planning in the so-called mixed economies—such as that of Iran—has always been vague. This vagueness has usually been due to a lack of clarity concerning that portion of economic activity properly undertaken by the government and that portion rightfully relegated to the private sector. In the case of Iran, the tug of war between the interests of the private sector and the essentials of economic planning in the public sector had not only grown severe, but the private sector was winning. Its influence in the government, as well as its ability to manipulate financial laws and regulations, rendered ineffective any serious attempts that the planners could make to improve the allocation of resources. The upshot was that the Planning Division did not know whose interest it was supposed to serve. Thus, the development plan formulated by this division contained no explicit objectives.

Fourth, in the limited range within which the Planning Division could take an active role, it never worked very hard to make an impact. In fact, many of the division's personnel never took the task of economic planning seriously. They believed, based on their past experience, that no matter how hard they worked in trying to determine the priorities, a top-down order could be issued to change everything. They had seen numerous examples of this type of decision making, and so they had actually given up on the major task of economic planning. It is of course difficult to separate the causes from the effects: Was the top-down decision-making process the sole cause for the division's lack of effective planning, or was this top-down process indeed prompted to some extent by the planners' very indifference? There was doubtless an interaction between the two, whereby each sign of deterioration fed back into the system to make the decision-making process more personal and the planners' attitude more passive.

Despite its lack of impact on the economy, the Planning Division had a comprehensive list of official duties that were divided among anywhere from six to ten bureaus at different times. Toward the end of the shah's regime, the Planometrics and General Economy Bureau prepared the development plan's main framework and macroeconomic guidelines, the Productive Sectors and Agricultural Planning bureaus provided sectoral targets, as did the Social Planning Bureau for education, health, and other social affairs. The task of predicting the required manpower was handled by the Manpower Planning Bureau, the International Economics Bureau was responsible for preparing the plan's export-import alternatives, and the Composition Bureau was in charge of putting the whole plan together.

The Coordination and Supervision Division

As far as development activities were concerned, the Coordination and Supervision Division practically comprised the main body of the PBO. It had a very active role in determining how resources were to be allocated among competing objectives.

The division's extensive involvement in the work of the PBO stemmed from the fact that, as initially set up, it had been designed to carry out the major part of that work. The initial objective of establishing PBO was to oversee the progress of a number of public projects. The Coordination and Supervision Division was then involved in the technical and financial supervision of these projects. Because the division was also in charge of the annual and quarterly allocations from the budget for development projects, it thus controlled the key factor for the project directors—the money they could spend. This meant that the project directors, as well as all governmental organizations charged with managing development projects, were more responsive to signals from the Coordination and Supervision Division than to those from the Planning Division. The initial description of the tasks and the design of the work procedures had of course foreseen the requirement for cooperation between the two divisions in allocating the budget. However (as we will explain in the next section), such cooperation was viewed in the early days as being nonessential and in later years as being impractical.

The Coordination and Supervision Division was responsible for the failures of the economic system to the very degree that it was active in making budgetary decisions. The great damage it did to the economy resulted from its gradually having relaxed the procedural standards in order to provide more opportunity for personal decision making.

Its procedural standards had been high in the beginning. To carry out its task of supervising the technical and financial aspects of all development projects, the division had followed a conscientious procedure. Any government agency proposing a new project was responsible for providing the Coordination and Supervision Division with a completed feasibility study, a work plan, and all supporting technical documents. Once these had been received, the division's Project Appraisal Committee (made up of experts invited from the PBO's Planning and Technical Affairs divisions and from the corresponding government agency) would then undertake a thorough analysis of the project's technical, financial, and manpower requirements. The experts would review the engineering design, the drawings, and the detailed calculations to obtain an accurate appraisal of the project's costs and benefits. If the project were approved, the executive agency would submit a technical and financial report on its progress to the Project Appraisal Committee prior to the approval of the annual and quarterly budgets. The progress report, along with field trip reports prepared by the division's engineers, would be used by the Project Appraisal Committee to appropriate the budgetary funds. The entire procedure had seemed a logical approach to the supervision and coordination task, and it was followed until the mid-1960s.

In terms of accomplishment, the 1950s and early 1960s represented the golden age of the Coordination and Supervision Division and the PBO. The division's tasks were specific and explicit, and its personnel's willingness and capabilities in accomplishing them were admirable. Indeed, the division's ability to attract the most skilled manpower of the country was to a large extent related to this high sense of accomplishment.

From the mid-1960s on, however, a gradual change occurred. The appropriations procedure began to be considered too rigid and time-consuming. As a starting point for making the procedure more flexible, the technical-appraisal steps were relaxed. The Coordination and Supervision Division was then supposed to trust to the technical capabilities of the executive agencies and not to interfere with any agency's technical handling of a development project. The division's personnel were thus forced to approve many projects without having had a thorough understanding of their technical characteristics. The next stage of relaxation took place as a result of the interaction among three distinct factors. First, the division's personnel, alienated by the new work procedure, became rather indifferent to the whole task. Second, as the shah himself got involved in economic decision making, it became more and more customary to see preapproved projects ordered from the top. Third, the implementation of such orders required the further relaxation of other steps of project-appraisal procedure, so that eventually almost all of these steps were reduced to bureaucratic formalities.

As a result, the division found itself exerting little control over the budget. Even while its Project Appraisal Committee continued to meet to evaluate development projects, all members of the committee had known beforehand the projects that it had to approve. For those main projects that absorbed the major part of the development budget, the proposing agency would first obtain the royal decree before submitting its proposal to the Coordination and Supervision Division. This practice, in addition to reducing the division's appraisal process to one simply of preparing the paper work, meant that the bulk of the development budget was allocated to projects that were effectively not subject to the division's evaluation or approval. Most of these were large, industrial projects, but in some cases they were luxury undertakings that in no way served the society's primary needs.

The Coordination and Supervision Division was thereby left with only a residual budget to meet the hundreds of requests it received for development projects in housing, education, health, agriculture, and other essential sectors of the economy. The final outcome was a very serious and visible misallocation of resources. The resources for projects that could have led to tangible social benefits had gone to projects that suited the shah's personal taste—his predilection for the symbols of industrial progress.

Historically, the Coordination and Supervision Division was the most involved entity within the PBO. It consisted of twelve bureaus (the number varied from ten to fifteen at different times). Nine of these worked on a sectoral basis: the bureaus of manufacturing and mining, agriculture, environment and resources, water resources, telecommunications, transportation, health, education, and energy. In addition, there were two bureaus that worked with all sectors: The Regional Bureau was responsible for ensuring a sound allocation of the development budget to the country's twenty-three counties, and the Composition Bureau was in charge of compiling the sectoral allocations to determine the budget's total expenditures on development.

The Budgeting Division

The Budgeting Division was a strong organ of the PBO. Its strength had been established at an early stage of its work, when the head of this division automatically became a deputy to the prime minister. Though in later years this precedent was not followed, the division nevertheless retained its overall authority. Despite its power, the division's work was rather simple (at least in the manner in which it was done).

The Budgeting Division was in charge of allocating the government consumption expenditures (current budget) to different public organizations. Since the government consumption expenditure normally grew at a uniform rate from year to year for all government agencies, the allocation decision did not go beyond taking the previous year's figures and adjusting them to fit the new financial availabilities and constraints.

Despite the simple nature of its work, the Budgeting Division faced two distinct (but related) challenges in the 1970s. First, the increased oil revenue changed the smooth money flow of the available financial resources. It became difficult simply to rely on the historical trends of budget allocation. In response, the Budgeting Division did not devise new norms and procedures capable of coping with the change; instead, it chose (or more realistically was forced to choose) to allocate the budget based on orders from the top.

Second, as the number of development projects increased during the late 1960s and early 1970s, their distribution among the government agencies obviously became uneven. It then became necessary for the Budgeting Division to take the development activities of each governmental organization into account in allocating the current budget. This required close cooperation between the Budgeting Division and the Coordination and Supervision Division. The opportunity for such cooperation had been provided in the work procedure's original design through a Budgeting Committee, made up of members from both divisions, but the cooperation did not get very far in practice. Even though for almost all public projects the current and the development budgets played complementary roles, so that it was thus very important that harmony would exist in their allocation, in actual practice projects were often postponed because of insufficiency of the current budget. Another problem was the complaint on behalf of both the Coordination Division and the Budgeting Division that the budget items were mixed up—government agencies were manipulating the wordings of the item description so as to fit it into whichever of the two budgets they felt was more likely to allocate funds. Eventually this situation led to the recommendation that the two divisions be merged into a single division. The implementation, however, had to wait until a few months after the revolution. In March 1979, Budgeting and Coordination and Supervision were practically put together, and in early 1981 they were officially merged.

The Technical Affairs Division

The Technical Affairs Division was initially established to ensure the technical (which mostly meant the engineering) quality of the development projects. This task ranged from detailed studies of the engineering designs to technical evaluations of the completed projects. At the project approval stage, it was the Technical Division that helped the Coordination and Supervision Division evaluate the engineering design as well as the cost of the project. During the execution phase, the Technical Division sent its field engineers to inspect the quality of the construction, mechanical, and electrical work. Finally, at the completion stage, the Technical Division was in charge of issuing the final approval for the quality performance of the project.

To accomplish these tasks, the Technical Division spent a considerable amount of time and effort on preparing the technical standards and the unit prices. The standards were required for evaluating the technical quality of the project at all stages; in addition, they were used by other governmental organizations and even by some private institutions to evaluate the technical quality of their construction work. The unit prices were used for cost appraisal purposes; they were also used by other organizations to appraise their costs of construction and of mechanical and electrical work.

A secondary task for the Technical Division was to help other government agencies choose a contractor or a consulting firm for their projects. It was generally known that the Technical Division maintained general information about the capabilities and capacities of the major contracting/consulting firms. It would compare each firm's amount of engagement with its capacity and would issue a percentage-capacity utilization list for all firms on a regular basis (monthly or quarterly). Government agencies would then use this information to decide which firms they should choose for their current undertakings.

The Technical Division was well known for its satisfactory performance. However, this performance was also jeopardized in the late 1960s and early 1970s when the technical evaluation of a project became a virtual formality. The division's efforts then shifted to its secondary task: helping executive agencies choose their contracting and consulting firms. Of the division's six bureaus, only two, the Contractors' Affairs Bureau and the Consulting Affairs Bureau, remained active. Their task, though voluminous, was simply to maintain two information systems on contractors' and consultants' activities. The remaining bureaus joined the alienated and indifferent majority of PBO employees.

The Informatics Division

The Informatics Division was created to promote the "new technology" of computer utilization in the country. The establishment of this division took place at the same time that computers had become the bureaucratic fashion, viewed as a symbol of advancement and prestige for developing countries. The Informatics Division and its followers (the rapidly growing computer centers of other government agencies) paid a high price to earn this prestige. The average annual expenditure on software and hardware (Informatics Division and other government agencies) was around $45 million during the 1971–1977 period. This aggressive undertaking started in 1971 and was boosted after the increase in oil revenues generated by the quadrupling of oil prices in 1973.

The Informatics Division expanded very rapidly from 1971 to 1975. The number of its personnel reached five hundred, whereas the number of employees in the Planning Division (supposedly the main body of the PBO) did not reach one hundred. The annual budget of the Informatics Division reached about US$16 million by 1978; this figure was far above the combined total of what all the other divisions spent in a year. The idea that the Informatics Division was wasting the financial resources at a rapid pace created a resistance in the other divisions against the use of computer services. Indeed, if one evaluates the performance of the division based on its tangible output—the computer systems that were actually utilized by the planning body, both inside and outside of the PBO—one could view the entire operation as a complete failure. Furthermore, the case of the Informatics Division is a clear example of the mistakes made in choosing the appropriate pattern of development and in allocating the financial resources.

The main factor responsible for the Informatics Division's failure was the lack of understanding about the division's main function. To begin with, the authorities of this division believed that the concept of informatics was a new phenomenon that should be introduced to government personnel in order to provide them the proper tools for increasing their work efficiency. To this end, these authorities devoted a considerable amount of human and financial resources to the arrangement of formal and informal training courses for government employees. In addition, they took a salesmanship approach to persuade government agencies to use computer services; in many cases, the Informatics Division designed and developed computer systems that its staff considered to be useful to some users. The general idea was to supply a service that in time would create its own demand.

As it turned out, however, not only did the supply not create its own demand, but it resulted in a severe resistance on the part of government employees against using computer services. The problem in this regard was with the strategy and, to a larger extent, with the objective. The problem with the strategy was that, despite the educational activities, the main promotional emphasis was not on the concept of informatics but on the provision of hardware and software. Numerous classes and seminars were held to teach various types of programming, but little effort was made to present in a practical manner the ways in which information systems (regardless of whether they were computerized or manual) could increase the efficiency of decision making. In fact, the Informatics Division's personnel did not have the appropriate experience and background to approach the problem in that manner. Most of its personnel were new college graduates who had gone through a nondegree training course to learn the basics of applications and systems programming. They were hardly able to appreciate the practical problems faced by decision makers, and they could not effectively communicate with the potential users of information systems.

More serious than the methodological deficiency was the problem with the objective of promoting computer services at that speed. It was just inappropriate, considering the circumstances that prevailed in the country. Computers and computer services were observable signs of too much Westernization. They imposed a high political cost on the regime and, from an economic point of view, did not yield a benefit comparable to their cost.

The division's second function, which was recognized at a later stage, was to provide the other divisions of the PBO with the computer systems that would facilitate the task of economic planning. To this end, the Informatics Division developed numerous computer systems and data bases that were never used by the planners. The few exceptions were a couple of systems designed to keep updated information on the activities of contracting and consulting firms; these systems were used by the Technical Affairs Division to evaluate the firms and thus to provide government agencies the rationale for selecting certain ones.

The problem with this new function was more with the approach than with the objective. The idea that a section within the PBO could provide information systems for economic planners did not sound illogical, but the approach taken by the division did not provide an effective method to attain this objective. First, the division was too large for this task. If a pure data-processing center were the sole intention, then a group of twenty to thirty people with about one-fifth of the available facilities would be sufficient for the task. The division's unnecessarily large size was not only responsible for the considerable waste of resources, it was also the main reason for other divisions having resisted using computer services. Second, the Informatics Division's personnel were not familiar with the nature of a national planning system and its data requirements. Their view of the information system was limited to administrative systems (this was due to their training). Therefore, they wanted to follow the standard, straightforward approach normally used in the development of administrative systems. If one wants to develop a payroll system, for example, one goes through a set of standard steps (feasibility study, design, development, test, and implementation) and produces an operational system that can be maintained by the user. In the case of national planning systems, however, none of the standard steps can be taken without a good understanding of the planning process. And of course none of these systems reaches the so-called operational stage, because the internal algorithm of the system is not known with certainty and is subject to continuous revision.[1]

Most of the Informatics Division's personnel were not familiar with the special characteristics and requirements of national planning systems. Indeed, the division was viewed as an ivory tower whose employees were completely isolated from the rest of the PBO. Thus, most of them were not aware of the duties of the other divisions or of the general functions of the PBO.

In short, the Informatics Division was different from the other divisions in the sense that it did not have any golden period, having been established only after the PBO had already entered its dark age. It was also different from the rest of the PBO in the sense that the drawbacks to its inefficiency were more visible than in the other divisions. Finally, it differed from them because it symbolized the cost of Westernization, and in this sense it became a source of psycho-political discomfort to the bureaucratic system.

The Statistical Center

The Statistical Center of Iran was established to coordinate the vast data-collection efforts undertaken by the various government agencies. Though it had autonomy in many respects, the center was run as a division of the PBO and was headed by a deputy to the minister in charge of the PBO.

The Statistical Center's range of activities varied from actual data collection to assembling the data collected by other organizations. The actual data collection took place in the form of sampling, surveys, and census taking. Sampling was performed on a rather regular basis in several fields, including agriculture, industrial production, and employment. Surveys included annual household budget surveys for rural and urban areas. The general census was performed every ten years. In addition, the center undertook a large number of ad hoc studies on various statistical matters.

The major problem faced by the center was that of extensive overlapping between the activities of the center and those of other government agencies. The most significant problem in this respect was the overlap between the activities of the center and the data collection efforts of the Central Bank. The bank's data-collection activity covered a wide range, consisting of national income statistics, production and price indices, housing starts, household budget surveys, and so forth. The argument between the Statistical Center and the Central Bank regarding who should do what was never resolved. The Statistical Center seemed to be the more logical place for most of these data-collection activities, but the Central Bank was famous for being the only organ whose data were up-to-date and trustworthy. Many authorities were then unwilling to undo what the Central Bank had already accomplished by transferring these engagements to the Statistical Center.

The Preparation of Development Plans

The process of preparing the development plans differed at various points in time. During the 1950s and early 1960s, development planning was merely an official blending of a number of public projects that had been initiated by various governmental organizations; the preparation of the plan did not involve many macroeconomic considerations and was not based on a notion of coordinated development. During this period, the procedure for preparing development plans was straightforward and clear-cut. The PBO had an explicit and recognized authority to supervise the activities of the executive agencies, and so these agencies were quite responsive to the PBO's information requirements. The collected information regarding the time and budget schedules of public projects was then analyzed and put into the development plans.

During the 1960s the need for a more comprehensive planning procedure was recognized. Though the Planning Division did begin to adopt various notions of macroeconomic stability and sectoral consistency, this adoption did not take place in a systematic manner and did not reach a productive stage; there were no explicit, official changes in the planning procedure. The adoption came in the form of utilizing the views of individuals who happened to be involved at different times. If these individuals were more inclined toward input-output analysis, then that technique was used to arrive at sectoral targets. On the other hand, if these individuals had a tendency to use macroeconomic models, then economic forecasting was the basis of development trends. However, none of these models received formal recognition, and their results were usually ignored when the plan figures were put together.

The institutional preparation of development plans consisted of the following steps (Fig. 3.2):

1. A number of sectoral committees, as they were called, prepared the initial targets and strategies for the various economic sectors. The composition of these committees changed as time went on: up to the early 1970s they were mostly run by the PBO's sectoral bureaus, but in 1977–1978, when the the Sixth Developmental Plan was being prepared, the sectoral committees became more reliant on the executive agencies and, to some extent, on people from the private sector and the research organizations. The purpose of this new development, known as top-down, bottom-up planning, was to arrive at a plan that would be viewed as a consensus between those who prepared the plan and those who were supposed to implement it. In 1977 there were thirty-six sectoral committees, each of which prepared the targets, the strategies, and a preliminary list of the development projects for each sector.

2. The output of the sectoral committees went to the Planning Division of the PBO. This division, with the cooperation of the Budgeting Division and the Coordination and Supervision Division, merged all of the sectoral targets, strategies, and projects into a unified plan. During the process, the Planning Division was supposed to communicate with the sectoral committees to reach an agreement on the basic problems of the sectoral plan, as it related to the general framework of the national plan. The national plan expenditures, along with the predictions of financial, physical, and labor resources, were then submitted to the Coordination Committee.

3. The Coordination Committee consisted of relatively high-level authorities. In addition to the minister in charge of the PBO and his deputies, the ministers of industry, agriculture, and trade were regular

Figure 3.2 Preparation of Development Plans

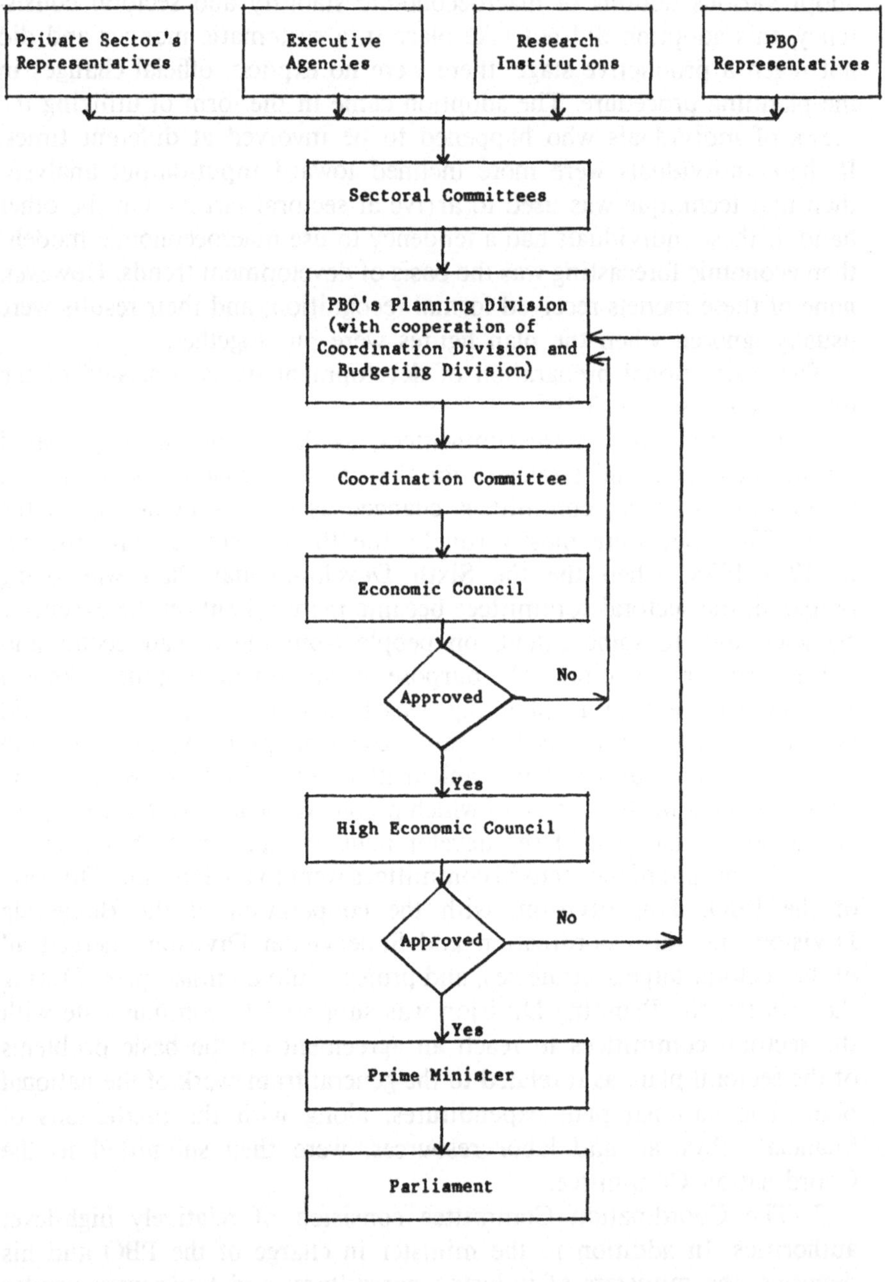

members of this committee. In the process of top-down, bottom-up planning, the committee was in fact the major source of top-down guidelines; it compared the available resources with the requirements of the proposed projects and issued the necessary guidelines to close the gap between the resources required and those available. Up to 1976 (before the top-down, bottom-up principle had been formally adopted), the aforementioned guidelines were utilized by the Planning Division to prepare the plan. After 1976 the procedure was modified to arrive at a consensus between the sectoral committees and the Coordination Committee; therefore, the guidelines would go to the sectoral committees, and each would prepare a new proposed plan for its sector and then send this plan to the Planning Division. The idea was for the planning exercise to continue through this iterative process until some convergence was achieved. This had been the procedure followed in preparing the Sixth Development Plan: When the financial requirements of the projects proposed from the bottom up were about 200 percent more than the available financial resources, top-down guidelines were sent back to the sectoral committees, conveying the limits upon their development expenditures. However, history did not allow enough time for the bottom-up reactions to be observed.

4. The prepared plan (or in some cases the plan alternatives) was then submitted to the Economic Council. This council consisted of the prime minister, nine ministers, and the majority of those officials involved in high-level decision making. It was at this stage that the political acceptability of the plan would officially enter the planning process. The participants were supposed to appraise the social and political dimensions of the plan and modify its targets accordingly.

5. After the plan was modified, it was sent to the High Economic Council. The basic difference between this council and the previous one was attendance by the shah. In the early years, a meeting of this council was viewed as a ceremonial gathering in which the development plan was explained to the shah. In the later years, however, the meeting of the High Economic Council turned into the most crucial step of plan preparation. During this meeting, the shah actually dictated the basic goals and targets of the development plan. This changed the logic of the whole process, and the planning effort was reduced to a futile exercise.

6. After the plan was thus modified according to the guidelines of the High Economic Council, the prime minister sent it to the parliament. This stage, though a pure formality, provided the government with the legal authority to implement the plan. The major targets of the development plan were normally discussed in special parliamentary com-

mittees, which eventually recommended the plan's approval to the General Assembly.

With the foregoing steps completed, the development plan became a legal document that, theoretically, would provide the basis for the annual budgets. In other words, an annual budget was meant simply to be a one-year portion of the development plan (modified for unexpected changes in resource availabilities and production constraints). In practice, however, the development plan was prepared so as to be in agreement with the formalities of the constitution. Once the plan was prepared and had been approved by the parliament, it became irrelevant to current policy issues. This point will be seen more clearly when we discuss the plan's implementation procedure in the next section.

The Implementation of Development Plans

The process of implementing development plans was very well set out in the PBO's "Description of Responsibilities." It began with the submission of a project proposal by an executive agency (Fig. 3.3). When submitting the proposal, the executive agency provided the detailed cost items, the work plan, and supporting technical documents. These were then sent to the corresponding sectoral bureau, which utilized the expertise of the Planning Division, the Budgeting Division, and the Technical Affairs Division, as well as that of its own, to appraise the project. At this stage, the bureau attempted to use all the detailed information to prepare a report describing the cost and benefits of the project, as well as its consistency with the ongoing development plan. The report then went to the Project Approval Committee, which consisted of representatives from the executive agency and of experts from the Planning Division, the Budgeting Division, the Technical Affairs Division, the Regional Division, and the Informatics Division. The presence of all these people in the approval meeting ensured that the project would be technically sound and that its implementation would not create any inconsistency in terms of the current budget or of the development plan as a whole.

Given the project's approval by the aforementioned committee, the next step was the consistency check by the Composition Bureau. This bureau was basically in charge of compiling all of the approved projects and fitting them into a consistent financial framework. Thus, it took the projects proposed by the different sectoral bureaus and prepared an overall annual budget for development expenditures. If there were any inconsistency between the amounts proposed by the different sectors and the total resources available, the Composition Bureau would ask the corresponding sectoral bureau to make the adjustments in its proposed

Figure 3.3 Implementation of Development Plans (Project Approval Process)

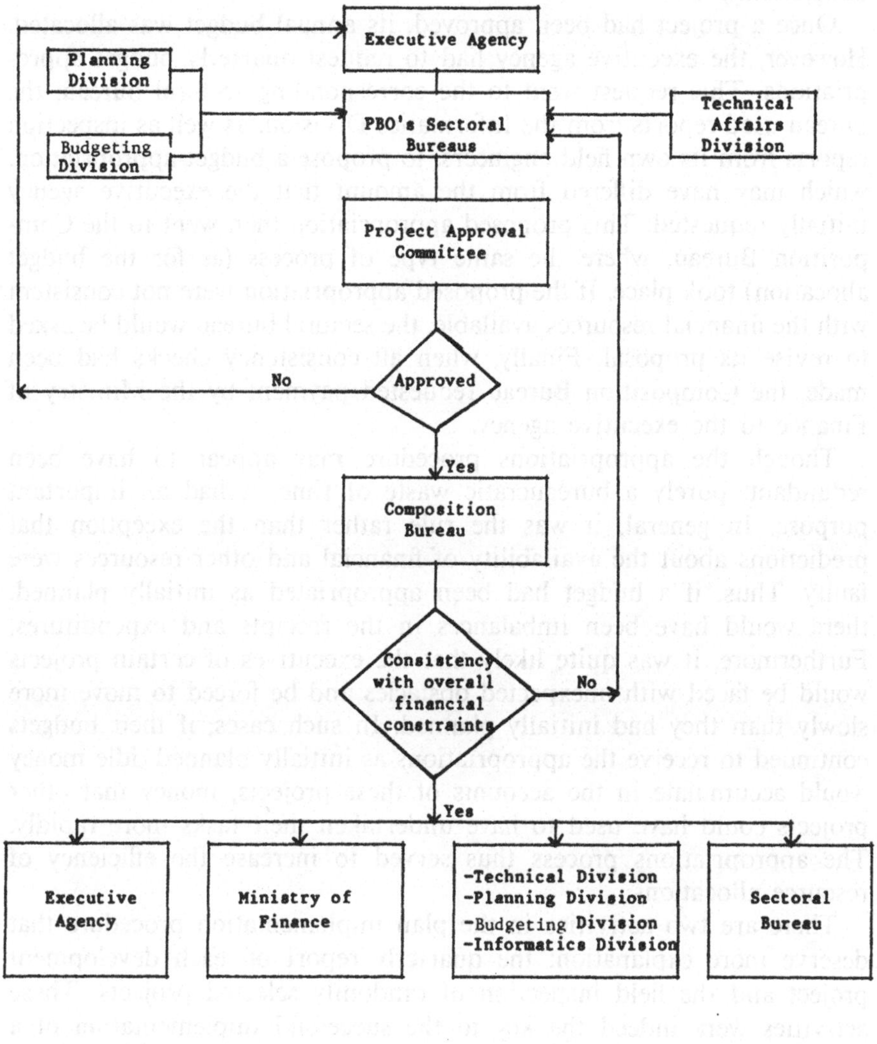

projects. The sectoral bureau would then make these adjustments and send the modified proposal back to the Composition Bureau.

After all the consistency checks had been made, the project's approval was announced to the executive agency, the Ministry of Finance, and all the divisions of the PBO. This announcement activated several information-gathering and decision-making systems. First, the Ministry of Finance included the project's budget in its expenditure plans. Second, the corresponding sectoral bureau scheduled field inspections. Third, the Informatics Division sent quarterly questionnaires to collect the required information regarding the project's physical progress and financial status.

Once a project had been approved, its annual budget was allocated. However, the executive agency had to request quarterly budget appropriations. This request went to the corresponding sectoral bureau; the bureau used reports from the Informatics Division, as well as inspection reports from its own field engineers, to propose a budget appropriation, which may have differed from the amount that the executive agency initially requested. This proposed appropriation then went to the Composition Bureau, where the same type of process (as for the budget allocation) took place. If the proposed appropriation were not consistent with the financial resources available, the sectoral bureau would be asked to revise its proposal. Finally, when all consistency checks had been made, the Composition Bureau requested payment by the Ministry of Finance to the executive agency.

Though the appropriations procedure may appear to have been redundant, purely a bureaucratic waste of time, it had an important purpose. In general, it was the rule rather than the exception that predictions about the availability of financial and other resources were faulty. Thus, if a budget had been appropriated as initially planned, there would have been imbalances in the receipts and expenditures. Furthermore, it was quite likely that the executives of certain projects would be faced with unexpected obstacles and be forced to move more slowly than they had initially planned. In such cases, if their budgets continued to receive the appropriations as initially planned, idle money would accumulate in the accounts of these projects, money that other projects could have used to have undertaken their tasks more rapidly. The appropriations process thus served to increase the efficiency of resource allocations.

There are two activities in the plan implementation procedure that deserve more explanation: the quarterly report on each development project and the field inspection of randomly selected projects. These activities were indeed the key to the successful implementation of a development plan.

The quarterly report on each development plan was filed by the manager of the project with the Informatics Division of the PBO. In this report, the project manager answered a number of questions. The most important of these were (1) the initial budget for the quarter, (2) the actual expenditure in the quarter, (3) the year-to-date budget, (4) the year-to-date expenditure, (5) the percentage of physical progress during the quarter, (6) the year-to-date physical progress, (7) the funds appropriated to the project, (8) the funds available in the account, and (9) the reasons for delay, if any.

The Informatics Division used these data to update the record of each project. It had in its computer system the initial work plan of the project, the timing of the expenditure, and the physical progress. Thus, it was possible to compare these data with the initial plan to determine whether or not the project was suffering any delays. Furthermore, the division could check the consistency between the physical progress and the expenditure of financial resources to make sure that the project manager was not overspending. Finally, the system provided information regarding the availability of funds in the account of each project, so that the appropriations decisions could be made more effectively. In addition, the system provided information about those projects that were facing specific problems, so that such projects could be given special emphasis during the field inspection.

The quarterly report, despite all of its valuable information, faced a special problem that defeated its whole purpose. This problem arose when the project manager was asked to provide a single number (as a percentage) to show the project's physical progress. Since there was no predefined measure that fit all development projects, the project manager gave a subjective answer to this question. The answer could well have been distorted by bias, reflecting the project manager's desire to provide a figure that matched the initial plan and/or the expenditure of resources.

Thus, the critical question raised in the reporting process was: What is meant by physical progress? Unfortunately, the answer to this question was very difficult, if not impossible. Physical progress had a different measure for each type of project and for each location. There was no general formula that one could provide to the project manager. Faced with the vagueness of the answers to the physical progress question, the PBO classified the development projects into such various types as roads, hospitals, elementary schools, and secondary schools; for each type, it then itemized and analyzed the physical stages of project implementation. For some of these items a locational (or hardship) factor was also included. Finally, the same types of development projects implemented in the past were analyzed to determine the weight of each physical activity in the current project's overall physical progress. These analyses were performed for several groups of development projects, but then were stopped in 1978 when the prerevolutionary strikes in the governmental organizations took place. After the revolution, these forms and procedures occasionally attracted the attention of the authorities, but the rapid turnover in higher-level management has not yet permitted the time for such detailed technical analyses of past projects.

Field inspection was another important activity for the efficient implementation of development projects. The PBO's work plan for field inspection called for the random selection of development projects and for the dispatch of experts qualified to examine their physical progress.

Field inspection was one of those rare areas in which the PBO had a bright record (at least for a time). Up to the mid-1960s the PBO placed considerable emphasis on field inspections, and because the number of projects was relatively small, the technical staff was capable of handling this task. In the late 1960s and early 1970s, however, the inspections lost their importance and were not taken to be a serious duty of the PBO. There were two basic reasons for this change. First, the decision making regarding the development projects became more personal. The PBO's involvement in the detailed technical matters of the development projects had come to be viewed as an obstacle to their rapid completion, and so more flexibility was desired in order to facilitate personal decision making—or, looking at it more optimistically, to increase the pace of project implementation. This flexibility was achieved by relaxing various project implementation checks, including the field inspection. The second reason for the decline of these inspections was the shortage of qualified personnel to inspect the large number of projects that came on stream in the 1970s.

Our discussion of the plan implementation procedure may have given the impression that it provided a multi-directional communications network for all the agents involved in carrying out the development projects, and that it thereby led to the plan's effective implementation. It could actually have worked in that manner. In practice, however, things were quite different.

There were two major deficiencies in the plan implementation procedure, both of which were the outcome of the politico-economic developments of the late 1960s and early 1970s. First, as personal decision making became prevalent, several implementation steps were reduced to administrative formalities. The Project Approval Committee still existed, and its members from the executive agency, the Planning Division, the Technical Division, and the other divisions of the PBO, were still invited to appraise the project, but the decision regarding its approval had been made beforehand. Neither the committee nor the sectoral bureau in charge of that project saw any use for a detailed evaluation of the project. The providing of detailed technical documents by the executive agency became immaterial, since it had no impact on the final decision. During the appropriations phase, which led to the actual payment of funds, the Project Approval Committee and the sectoral bureaus knew that their decisions did not make much difference in the appropriation of funds. A field inspection was also made once in a while, as was a technical evaluation of a project's physical progress, but neither made any real input into the allocation of funds.

Second, there were many shortcuts taken in the implementation procedure. A very important, and frequent, case of these shortcuts took place in the Composition Bureau. Theoretically, this bureau was supposed to collect the proposals for allocations and appropriations from the sectoral bureaus and to put them together to arrive at the total allocation or appropriation. If there were an inconsistency, the Composition Bureau was supposed to send the proposals back to the corresponding sectoral bureau for the required adjustment. In practice, however, the Composition Bureau made the decisions itself. It changed the inter- as well as intrasectoral appropriations. In many case, it increased or decreased the appropriation for a project without even informing the corresponding sectoral bureau. This action not only resulted in imbalances and misallocations of resources, but it also alienated the technical experts of the sectoral bureaus, and they became increasingly indifferent to the entire task.

Conclusion

There is no question that the planning procedure and the planning institution in Iran suffered from major shortcomings, including the lack of a mechanism to generate regional balance in development activities. However, the more critical factor for the failure of economic planning in Iran was the gradual loosening of various steps of the project evaluation process. This loosening took place in some instances to speed up the process, but more often to provide an environment suitable to personal decision making. The net result was, however, the same—economic planning turned into a futile formality with no positive impact on the management of the economy.

Notes

1. In administrative systems, the main task at the design stage is to prepare the appropriate input and output forms. The algorithm of the system, i.e., the equations used to compute the new values, is almost always known with certainty, and the analyst obtains these equations when he is doing the feasibility study. For our payroll example, the analyst needs to know how the income tax, insurance, and so forth are calculated. He receives sufficient information in this regard when he studies the work procedures of the bookkeeping department. However, for a planning system that, for example, intends to provide guidelines for the regional allocation of the agricultural budget of the country, the algorithm of the system is not readily available. Most of the internal equations have to

be estimated based on the time-series or cross-sectional data, and they have to be revised as new observations become available. An analyst who is not familiar with the planning process can hardly understand why the planner does not provide him with the calculation procedures the first time they meet (as would be the case with administrative systems).

4
What Went Wrong?

Introduction

By late 1973, Iran was in a particularly advantageous position, as developing countries in the postwar period go. Judged in terms of GNP, the economic performance after 1963[1] was a respectable 10.3 percent current-price rate of growth of GNP until 1967 and a remarkable 16.4 percent from 1968 to 1972. By contrast, the rate of inflation, as measured by the GNP deflator, grew imperceptibly from 1963 to 1967 at a rate of 0.6 percent per annum; 1968 to 1973 witnessed an acceleration to 3.4 percent per annum, a rate judged to be very acceptable, especially by modern standards.[2] Indeed, the coincidence suggests that the socio-economic policies of the mid- to late 1960s and early 1970s had brought to Iran a period of rapid growth with price stability.

The Fourth Development Plan, though a successful economic program from the point of view of growth and stability, had laid down a set of development patterns that were to a large extent responsible for the economic trends that emerged later on. The sectoral imbalances of economic growth, the widening urban-rural gap, the increasing involvement of the government in investment and production of goods and services, the inclining dependence on foreign imports, and the deterioration of balance of payment were all part of these development patterns.

During the Fourth Plan period (1968–1972), the industry and services sectors grew at annual rates of 14 and 14.2 percent, respectively, while the agricultural sector grew at the rate of 3.9 percent. The manufacturing sector became more heavily oriented toward the production of consumer goods and more reliant on imports for sustaining production. The nature of industries being established dictated that the country would be increasingly dependent on the imports of foreign technology, skilled manpower, and capital goods. The normal time lag usually experienced in moving from light to heavy industry was drastically shortened. The whole environment in which industry developed was extremely artificial and not based on efficiency considerations.

The primary development objectives of the period were rapid industrialization and the development of the country's infrastructure; agriculture was, by and large, ignored. The control of food prices in urban areas—made possible by liberal food-import policy and government-sponsored food subsidies—was undoubtedly responsible for the low rate of growth in the agricultural sector. In any event, one of the consequences of the depression in the agricultural sector was the rapid migration to urban areas. Thus, by the final years of the Fourth Development Plan, the economy had turned into a consumption-oriented, largely urban society with an explosive deficit in the balance of payment.

The Tehran Oil Agreements

The Financial Shock

For Iran, the Tehran Oil Agreements of December 1973 must be seen as an external shock to the national entity. It need not have been so, but the policy choices were such that the economic impact of quadrupling oil revenues could only lead to destabilizing internal consequences. The arrogance of the newly found economic power in the international arena was added to these impacts, making the political fallout, both internally and externally, bound to be substantial. It is easy, in retrospect, to reach such conclusions; yet upon rereading some of the shah's pronouncements in 1973 and 1974, one cannot but be struck by his overevaluation of his own political strength at home and especially in the international arena.

In an interview with *Kayhan International* on December 25, 1973, the shah, responding to queries on the high price of oil, said

> We are only pricing the minimum it could be priced in comparison with other sources of energy. . . . Well, some people are going to say this is going to create chaos in the industrialized world; that it is going to be a heavy burden on the poor countries. . . . That is true; but as to the industrialized world they will have to tighten their belts, and they will have to work harder or eventually this help to the other countries of the world will be diminished, and this role taken up—in my opinion—by the new wealth of the oil countries.[3]

The lectures to the West had begun. In the words of the Middle East correspondent for the *Financial Times:*

> It was a performance to match the occasion. On the 23rd December, 1973, while the Ministers representing the Gulf members of OPEC were

> still in formal session, Mohammed Reza Pahlavi, Shah of Iran, called a press conference. His announcement was a staggering new increase in the price of oil. The Shah displayed his usual mannered polish, but his tone had a new confidence—the confidence of a man who knew that his country's financial resources had quadrupled in just over two months.[4]

In point of fact, Iran's government revenue per barrel jumped from US$1.85 to $7.00 in 1973 as a result of the OPEC agreements.[5] By the end of 1974, this figure had climbed to $10.21 per barrel. Put another way, this meant that government oil revenues in 1973/74 rose to $4.6 billion (310.5 billion rials) from the 1972/73 figure of $2.8 billion (189.9 billion rials), an increase of 65 percent, and that the comparable figure for the year 1974/75 was $17.8 billion (1,201.5 billion rials) an increase of 287 percent over the previous year.[6] It is this latter figure that is at the core of the argument that Iran did, in late 1973, suffer an external shock in the form of large financial inflows. As will be shown, it was the poor management of these new resources that progressively led to the alienation of the various social groups, eventually contributing to the tearing of the social fabric and the overthrow of the monarchy. Moreover, it is that very increase in resources that allowed the leader of that monarchy to lecture the industrialized world on its shortcomings and to make statements that would come back to haunt him in later times.

The Confidence Factor

In 1973/74, while the West was off balance, the shah exuded confidence. There were good reasons for this confidence. Of notable importance was the fact that the December 1973 Tehran Oil Agreements represented a clear break with the past, a just victory of the raw-material producers against the industrialized countries, a change in the traditional argument of the deterioration in the terms of trade facing the developing world to the profit of the industrialized world. Here in one swoop, the gains from changes in the terms of trade had been reversed in at least one commodity—petroleum. This was no mean feat. It represented, in the international arena, a major victory for the developing world, and the shah, a close friend of the West (the industrialized world), had helped to engineer this economic *tour de force.* Moreover, he was at the center of the press conference and thus indelibly imprinted in Western minds the association of Mohammad Reza Pahlavi with the Organization of Petroleum Exporting Countries (OPEC) and higher oil prices. In the gasoline queues of 1974 and 1975, western consumers would now vent their anger at the shah and OPEC.

Rather than engage in a "soft sell" on the necessity of higher oil prices, the shah turned critical of Western societies. Brimming with certainty, he spoke about the need to conserve this "noble product."[7] He admonished the West for waste and inefficiency and went so far as to suggest that Western hegemony was at an end and that it was time for the consumers of the industrialized world to tighten their belts. He made provocative statements, such as: "Eventually all those children of well-to-do families who have plenty to eat at every meal, who have their own cars, and who act almost as terrorists and throw bombs here and there, will have to rethink all these privileges of the advanced world."[8]

Confidence in the international arena had been slow in coming. To a great extent, ever since the overthrow of Mohammad Mossaddegh in 1953, the shah had been dependent on the United States for moral, political, economic, and military support. Having replaced the shah on his throne through a Central Intelligence Agency (CIA)-supported military coup in August 1953, the United States had made its presence felt. In order for the shah to achieve confidence, it was necessary for him to loosen his dependence. The reforms of 1963 and the successful growth period of 1963–1973 had allowed such a loosening. In 1971, with the British pullout in the Gulf, the shah became the gendarme of the region, with the blessing of the Kissinger-Nixon strategy of global curtailment of the Soviet Union. Rising oil resources permitted the termination of the U.S. grant-in-aid program in 1972. The dispatching of troops to Oman, in order to help Sultan Qaboos in 1972, reflected a growing independence and an increase in personal confidence.

Thus on the eve of the Tehran Oil Agreements the shah was almost a new man in the international arena, and Iran was rapidly becoming a regional power to be reckoned with. The shah had lessened his economic, political, and military dependence on the West to the extent that he could at least make pronouncements that were listened to. The OPEC price rise of 1973 put the frosting on the cake. Confidence was now a *fait accompli,* as many of the pronouncements of the period reveal.

Internal Repercussions of the Confidence Factor

The importance of the confidence factor in the international arena for this analysis is that the shah began to approach Iran's internal problems with a self-confidence and presumed infallibility that was to lead the country toward the wrong policy choices. What had been painfully acquired in the world of international politics, after many a humiliating experience, was now to be applied to the solution of domestic problems. The shah's vision, which through the programs of the White

Revolution seemingly had launched a successful growth process and which, on the international front, had created a more independent and respected Iran, seemed infallible. The added confidence resulting from the 1973 OPEC success sealed that infallibility in the shah's own mind.

This was to have dire repercussions on the domestic front, as the shah and his government made preparations for deciding how to use the added financial resources resulting from the 287 percent increase in oil revenues. For one thing, it was to lead to a flurry of promises by the shah in the welfare area—promises that would be difficult to fulfill and that the state bureaucracy would be ill-prepared to execute. For another, it was to create a high level of expectations among the population for an immediate improvement in their standard of living, as well as a promise of achieving the "Great Civilization" within their own lifetimes.[9] Moreover, and most importantly, the shah's improved confidence factor was to accentuate the concentration of power, centralize decision making, and eliminate dissent even among his most ardent supporters. In the face of an increasingly complex economy, whose efficiency requirements would be best met by an increasing delegation of authority at all levels, the confidence factor's effect was to reduce such delegation because the shah relied increasingly on his own decision-making powers.

The Stage Is Set

Thus by late 1973 and early 1974, the stage was set for the gross miscalculations that were to follow. The juxtaposition of a historic rise in financial resources—a national windfall gain somewhat akin to the Spanish situation in the sixteenth century—and an overly centralized decision-making process on how to best use those resources was to engage Iran in a two-year spending spree in which the misallocation of resources would endanger the equilibrium in the socioeconomic fabric.

In a sense, the chance of a millennium had been allowed to slip by. Through a faulty decision-making process, aggravated by the confidence factor already discussed, it was not possible for Iran to establish the required policies for the effective use of this 287 percent increase in oil revenues. In this sense, the 287 percent turned out to be a shock to the national entity—had it not occurred, it is clear that the state (the shah) would not have had the resources to permit it to issue promises it could not fulfill. In addition, the state—egged on by the shah—could not have attempted as it did, to do too much in too short a time. Thus it would not have created the inflation that was to have such nefarious effects on the economy. And finally, the state could not have expanded its role in the economy in line with the shah's "Socialistic Visions." That would have prevented the eventual crowding out of the productive private sector, the very element of success in the growth period of 1963 to 1973.

The political and economic threats associated with this financial shock, as well as the management and policy challenges, were not unknown in Iran. Writing in Tehran in 1975, Firouz Vakil said

> Oil revenues may well be a mixed blessing, depending on the size of the annual liquidity injections relative to the availability of complementary factors of production. Indeed, these revenues are, on the one hand, like the blood of the economy carrying badly needed investment resources to particular areas for purposes of expanding productive capacity; and on the other, they are capable of producing an excessive liquidity situation, if capital resources become suddenly out of line with other complementary factors of production (such as skilled labor, technology, organizational skills, natural resources or general infrastructure services). This duality renders the planning task all the more difficult under conditions of financial surplus, since it requires a shift of emphasis in the planning circles from an allocation of resources according to financial constraints to an allocation of resources according to the real scarce factor, or a combination of them.[10]

The Dream of a Great Civilization

The Big-Push Strategy

It was suggested in the previous section that Iran in 1973 and 1974 was subjected to an external financial shock for which the decision-making process was unprepared. Given the confidence factor and the shah's character and experience, the management response was to further centralize decision making, even though the increased complexity of the economy required increasing delegation of authority at all levels. The shah's response, as noted, was in line with the rapid fulfillment of his vision of a Great Civilization. The dream was announced, expectations were raised, and thus the stage was set for the contradictions to work themselves out.

The dream of Great Civilization had established a subjective development goal in the shah's mind. It was then necessary to refine the strategy of development. This was to be a Big Push type industrialization financed by oil revenues. Given that oil reserves were seen to have a twenty-year horizon and that the shah probably knew himself to be fatally ill, the speed with which the Big Push was to be implemented was to be of paramount importance in the shaping of expenditure patterns.

The idea was patterned after the works of R. Nurkse[11] and P. Rosenstein Rodan[12] and evolved from the concept that economic development was constrained by certain "vicious circles."[13] To break these vicious circles, it was argued that the state needed to industrialize on a wide and diversified front so as to ensure a ready market for the output of the new industries. Economies of scale associated with modern technology dictated a plant size requiring a relatively large market, and therefore it was not possible to industrialize piecemeal. In point of fact, these ideas were to be specifically applied to consumer-oriented industries such that the wage earners of the first industry would become the consumers for all industries from the second through the *n*th; thus setting up *n* industries simultaneously ensured an effective demand for the output of these same industries. This was known as the Big Push.

When applied to Iran, an oil-producing country—especially following the oil hike of 1973—the Big Push theory acquired another aspect. It was no longer a vicious-circle-of-poverty theory. Rather it was a concentrated effort on all parts, financed by oil revenues, to pull a country upward by its own bootstraps. In the case of Iran the constraints became infrastructural or human rather than financial. In fact, if too big a push is made financially under such conditions, it may create inflation and excess demand, as output lags behind expenditures. The Big Push then is beyond absorptive capacity (the latter being defined by the scarce factor). In post-oil price hike Iran in 1973 and 1974, the binding constraint was by no means financial. And yet the Big Push was orchestrated by the shah as if it were.

In effect the Big Push concept, as applied to Iran, was not necessarily out of step with the requirements of an efficient development strategy. It was indeed a fact that oil revenues would taper off by the late 1980s, barring major discoveries. There was thus a limited time to transform the financial flows resulting from oil exports into domestic productive capacity. The question therefore was more a problem of size and quality. It was necessary that the *Big Push be in line with absorptive capacity and that the quality of its program not be jeopardized by undue speed and unadapted technology.*

The Twenty-Year Perspective

It was thought at first that the shah, in his drive to reach the threshold of the Great Civilization based on a Big Push industrialization and modernization strategy, would guide the economic ship of state with the utmost care. By the fall of 1973, no doubt anticipating certain OPEC successes, he had instructed the PBO to start work on a twenty-year perspective for Iran.[14] This was to be the blueprint toward which the successive development plans would guide the national entity. It would consist of a blend of normative and positive quantifiable targets, covering the whole range of economic and social sectors, that could reasonably be reached given the anticipated inflows of financial resources from the export of oil and gas. It would also attempt to define the longer-term physical bottlenecks that needed to be sequentially addressed in order to pave the way for a smooth growth path. In its essential concept the idea was sound, as no specific policy constraints were imposed. However, certain targets that had attained a degree of acceptability would have to be examined vis-à-vis their feasibility.

More importantly, however, the request to the PBO signaled that there was indeed an understanding within the political circles as to the importance of recent events. It even leads one to believe that the policymakers (including the shah) were fully aware of the potentially disturbing impact, in the short run, of this newly acquired oil income and that they had decided not to steer away from the existing course until such time as the final twenty-year blueprint had been prepared and tranched into a series of consecutive five-year plans.

In any case, rationality dictated such an approach, and the PBO mobilized two of its divisions—the Planning Division and the Supervision and Coordination Division—to engage in the necessary studies for presentation to the shah by the end of the 1973/74 fiscal year (i.e., by March 1974). It was a large mobilization of manpower, and the results were supposed to have a wide-ranging impact on the future growth strategy.

By late March 1974 the preliminary results of this massive undertaking were ready. They were ostensibly to be presented to the shah for the purposes of a preliminary dialogue before deliberations began on the revision of the Fifth Development Plan (1973–1977). Some of the major findings are cited below for illustration:[15]

1. Based on the assumption of finite recoverable reserves of 85.0 billion barrels of oil, the probable range of total oil and gas revenues over the period 1973–1992 stretched from a low of US$369 billion (24,907.5 billion rials) to a high of $585 billion (39,487.5 billion rials).[16] This in essence warned the policymakers that (1) the financial resources had a limited horizon, (2) their annual distribution as well as the grand total was subject to the vagaries of world supply and demand conditions and therefore highly erratic, and (3) gas income would be a relatively small contributor.

2. Iran could not, on the most optimistic assumptions, become the world's fifth industrial power in this century.[17] This conclusion would lead the shah to accuse the PBO, as he had always done, of being unduly pessimistic. It would lead him to almost completely disregard all the conclusions of the report.

3. Because of agriculture's limited potential, Iran would remain an importer of food; although it could conceivably achieve self-sufficiency in grains, it could not for red meat.

4. The major infrastructure bottlenecks needed to be addressed immediately: transport, ports, power, and water supply. In the power area, the report recommended the use of nuclear plants as a supplement to the complete harnessing of the hydroelectric potential.

5. Because of its natural-resource endowment, Iran should develop heavy industries: steel, petrochemicals, and machine tools.

6. Of crucial importance to the longer-term growth path was the pursuance of an industrialization strategy based on the concept of comparative advantage. It was necessary to promote nonoil exports for the day of reckoning when petroleum exports would begin to drop.

The Results of the March 1974 Discussion[18]

The presentation of certain key results or issues was to take place with the shah in the last week of March 1974. The meeting was to be attended by the senior PBO officials involved, including the minister of state in charge of the PBO, the minister of economics and finance, and the prime minister. It had been decided that the PBO officials would make a quick presentation of the major issues and then wait to obtain the shah's reaction before opening up a dialogue. The hope was that the dialogue would render feasible within the desired horizon some of the normative elements in the twenty-year perspective. For example, it was assumed that the prepared data would make it clear that Iran could not hope to become the world's fifth industrial power in twenty years, and that, by corollary, it would be best to set a lesser objective so as not to engage in faulty decision making. There were, of course, other examples that need not be mentioned here. Suffice it to say that expectations were high that a workable blueprint would eventually emerge from these deliberations.

The meeting took place as scheduled. Yet, instead of the presentations being given by the PBO officials, the government representatives were lectured by the shah on his expectations for a modern Iran. The end result was not the hoped-for dialogue backed up by prior research, but a compendium of directives, in various sectors, devoid of a time horizon. In a sense, the shah dismissed the views of his technocrats and called for a Big Push (in the investment area) interspersed by a few key targets. Some of these were production of 15 million metric tons of steel, electrification of the railway system, the setting up of several nuclear power plants,[19] building oil refineries and petrochemical plants, construction of six-lane superhighways connecting the Gulf ports to the capital, rapid development of the country's ports, and, last but not least, the deployment of an impregnable defense infrastructure. In a nutshell, it was almost as if the government officials had been called in to hear the gospel of the Great Civilization and then sent back to their offices for the urgent task of implementation.

To repeat: there was no dialogue, only a set of directives. The question of feasibility almost did not enter the equation. The report on Iran's long-term prospects was placed on the shelf and, for all practical purposes, never referred to again. In his solitary confidence, the shah had already decided what to do with the 287 percent increase in oil revenues—if not in detail, at least in the broad thrust.

The Oil Resources and Their Allocation

The Meeting in Gajereh

Long-term visions aside, the problem of resource allocation still remained. In early 1974, Iran had almost completed the first year of its Fifth Development Plan, which was scheduled by law to run from March 1973 to March 1978. Obviously, the sudden upsurge in oil revenues had necessitated a revision of the plan. The PBO had therefore been instructed, as early as January 1974, to prepare a major revision to be presented to the shah for final approval sometime in the summer.

The existing Fifth Development Plan was already an ambitious document. It called for a total investment (private and public) of 2,486.7 billion rials, with a targeted real growth rate of 11.4 percent per annum. The public-sector targets are shown in Table 4.1. The program was perilously close to absorptive capacity. How then was the country to use its additional resources? The pressures for an increase in domestic spending were immense, with the shah and his defense establishment in the forefront. Yet it was obvious that a quantum leap in domestic spending might throw Iran off its smooth growth path of the last decade. The first decision, therefore—regardless of wishes, dreams, and the usual coterie of vested interests lurking behind every investment project—was to determine the real inflationary increase in the public-investment level that could be productively absorbed by the Iranian economy.

The PBO set to work on a series of alternatives aimed at achieving a macrobalance. The focus was on the level of public investment that could be productively absorbed by the society in the remaining years of the plan. Unfortunately, within the PBO itself, the Planning Division and the division in charge of projects were at odds on the best course to pursue. The former warned against the danger of inflation if a maximalist expenditure scenario were followed. The latter pushed for

Table 4.1. Fixed Investment by Sector, 1973-1977, Original and Revised Fifth Plan (billion rials)

Sectors	Original	Share %	Revised	Share %	Revised as % Original
Industry & mines	552.2	22.2	845.8	18.0	153.2
Agriculture	180.2	7.2	309.2	6.6	171.5
Transport	188.3	7.6	492.1	10.5	261.3
Housing	402.3	16.2	924.8	19.7	229.9
Oil & gas	461.0	18.5	791.1	16.8	171.6
Others	702.7	28.3	1,334.5	28.4	189.9
Total	2,486.7	100.0	4,697.5	100.0	189.9

Source: Plan and Budget Organization, Iran's Fifth Development Plan 1973-78, Revised: A Summary (Tehran: Plan and Budget Organization, 1975)

US$1 = 67.5 rials

a maximum increase in development expenditures, worrying only about the allocation between sectors.[20] Thus, by the time the prime minister instructed the PBO to present its alternatives to a special expanded session of the Economic Council at Gajereh—a mountain skiing resort near Tehran—the organization was split on its presentation and therefore on its strategy of development for the next five years.

The Planning Division's position paper on the macrobalance implications of increased plan expenditures was based on three scenarios of public investment: (1) a small increase of 31 percent in public investment, from 1,545.8 billion rials in the original plan to 2,031.8 billion rials for the proposed revision; (2) a medium increase of 98 percent to 3,064.5 billion rials; and (3) a large increase of 141 percent to 3,732.8 billion rials.[21] By contrast, the requests from the ministries exceeded even the high scenario by a little more than 945.0 billion rials. It was obvious that the high spending mood would in all probability prevail.

The results of the Gajereh meeting, which took place in July 1974, are important because they set the tone for the spending spree that followed. The prime minister presided over the deliberations. Also present were the ministers of finance, interior, labor, agriculture, industries and mines, housing, the Central Bank governor and the minister of state in charge of the PBO. The presentations were made by the PBO's Planning Division on the problems of the macrobalance and by the PBO's

Supervision and Coordination Division on the sectoral allocations and major projects.

Oddly enough, the two sides of the equation did not match. The Planning Division argued for a low expenditure scenario with at most a 31 percent increase in public investment, because Iran lacked absorptive capacity. Two major bottlenecks—human capital and port capacity—were presented in scenario form as the binding constraints to the different options, as well as to the trade-offs between growth and inflation. The upshot of this presentation was that Iran could in no way engage in a public-investment program over and above the 2,031.8 billion rials figure noted as the low scenario without subjecting itself to inflation, distortions, waste, and inefficiency.

The Supervision and Coordination Division, on the other hand, presented the ministries' views—a maximalist approach in which Iran would not only expend its new financial resources but even opt to borrow. This is indicative of the mood that existed at the time. Ministers and their deputies acted as if money were the binding constraint (basically because it had been so all those years), when in fact human resources and port infrastructure should have guided the allocation of investment resources. The minister in charge of the PBO did not come to Gajereh with a single, united position for his organization;[22] rather he was willing to let the discussions decide the day. To be fair, however, he was the only cabinet official, other than the prime minister himself, who argued in favor of a minimum increase in domestic expenditures. Finance and the Central Bank, the agencies that usually are the first to counsel fiscal caution, were silent. Thus only half of the PBO, with its minister of state, led the resistance to the prevailing sentiment for a spending splurge.

After three days of deliberations at Gajereh, the prime minister made the decision. Over the protestations of many line ministries and other executive agencies,[23] he opted for a 2,848.5 billion rials public-investment figure, well over the recommendations of the PBO's Planning Division and well under the requests of the executive agencies.[24] From the PBO's point of view, it was a more favorable compromise than the extra 816.7 billion rials suggested at first glance. In effect, the prime minister had been convinced by the go-slow approach, and a large portion of the extra 816.7 billion rials was to be composed mainly of imported items, not requiring the use of complementary factors (e.g., purchase of aircraft for Iran Air and for the air force, naval craft for the navy, and so on).

It seemed that the PBO had carried the day.[25] Yet the difficult political problem remained: If the new financial resources were not to be used for domestic investment or consumption, then they had to be placed somewhere. The obvious choice was foreign investment, but where, how, and in what form? (The lowering of oil production may, in retrospect, be judged as the best "might have been" policy, but it was never viewed as a politically feasible decision.)

Foreign investment was a touchy question for domestic and international reasons. The PBO's position was that funds beyond absorptive capacity should be placed abroad. To engage in a maximalist investment strategy could only lead to waste, bottlenecks, disruptions, and, most importantly, a severe inflation, which once underway could only be stopped at a high political price. Yet the expectations of the Iranian people, following the many pronouncements in the past of instant wealth and the impending prospects of a rosy economic future, made the policymakers hesitant to pursue an aggressive foreign-investment policy. It would have been difficult to justify domestically the export of financial resources when there was such a crying need at home. Moreover, the industrialized countries themselves, still reeling from the OPEC oil-price victory, did not look kindly on attempts by Third World countries to buy out some of their major industrial enterprises.[26] Thus, although the PBO seemed to have convinced the cabinet to reduce domestic investments in favor of foreign investments, the political pressures, internal and external, were already mounting for a reversal in direction.

The Meeting in Ramsar

The document that resulted from the Gajereh meeting—the revised Fifth Development Plan: 1973–1977—was presented formally to the shah at a special meeting on August 1–3, 1974, in Ramsar, a Caspian resort town. The figures agreed upon at Gajereh were left relatively unchanged and presumably were cleared beforehand by the shah. The Ramsar presentation was to be an official blessing to the redefined blueprint.

Table 4.2 presents the projected overall finances of the revised Fifth Plan in billions of rials. Of the total anticipated resources of 8,289.2 billion rials (US$122.0 billion), 6,628.5 billion rials (US$98.2 billion) (80.5 percent) was to be derived from the exports of oil and gas. Behind these totals lurked optimistic assumptions on annual oil-price increases, as well as on oil-export growth. Few were predicting that the OPEC price hike of 1973 would lead to a severe recession in the West. At the same time, only 742.6 billion rials (US$11.0 billion), or approximately 9.0 percent of the anticipated total resources and 11.2 percent of anticipated oil revenues, were earmarked for investment abroad. Thus the critical question of foreign investment was dealt with in a perfunctory manner, with a single figure, and very little commentary.[27] To be fair, it was difficult politically to divulge in detail the government's future plans in this area; yet, at the same time, it must be said that the policymakers responded to what they felt were the shah's desires. He

Table 4.2. Revised Fifth Development Plan, Overall Finances 1973-1977 (billion rials)

A. Receipts		B. Payments	
1. Oil & gas	6,628.5	1. Current expenditures	3,388.6
2. Direct taxes	546.8	2. Fixed capital formation	2,848.5
3. Indirect taxes	614.3	3. Repayment of foreign loans	405.0
4. Other receipts	249.8	4. Other payments	904.5
5. Foreign loans	148.5	5. Investment abroad	742.6
6. Sale of bonds	101.3		
Total	8,289.2	Total	8,289.2

Source: Plan and Budget Organization, Iran's Fifth Development Plan 1973-78, Revised: A Summary (Tehran: Plan and Budget Organization, 1975)

US$1 = 67.5 rials

was indeed very reluctant to commit to foreign ventures funds that he felt were needed to lead Iran to the threshold of the Great Civilization.

The shah's failure to address the question of absorptive capacity was to be compounded by the cabinet. No great effort was made to commit Iran to a policy of investing abroad what could not be productively absorbed, even though the PBO's position paper recommended setting up an investment advisory service to manage an eventual portfolio of assets.[28] As Graham has pointed out, "the Shah and Hoveida showed a certain contempt for the cautious views of the economists who could not see beyond problems to a broader vision of an industrialized Iran. The Shah was also dismissive of those who did not share his vision of Iran's future as the world's fifth industrial power by the turn of the century."[29]

Indeed, at Gajereh the PBO had warned the cabinet in quantitative terms of the dangers of engaging in a program exceeding the ability of Iran to absorb financial resources. The manpower and infrastructure constraints had been especially discussed. At Ramsar these questions were again put forward, even if meekly. The shah quickly responded that if manpower was short it would be imported; if ports could not handle the anticipated inflow of goods, then a crash program to improve throughput should be instituted immediately; and if inflation were to pick up, then Iran would deal with this crisis in an innovative fashion. In short, he was not to be influenced by the pessimists. In fact, he would not listen to the realists.

> Those that had doubts in the end stood silent, out of fear, or in belief that the realities of the situation would impose their own logic on the new Plan. The Shah genuinely seems to have believed that the problems underlined by Majidi (head of PBO) could be solved and were subordinate to the lofty objective of accelerating the occasion of a self-sustaining economy, independent of oil. He told the assembled dignitaries at Ramsar: "The Great Civilization" we promised you is not a utopia either. We will reach it much sooner than we thought. We said we will reach the gates in 12 years; but in some fields, we have already crossed its frontiers.[30]

At Ramsar, then, the constraints were swept aside, and the assembly agreed officially on a slightly expanded version of the Gajereh spending program. Unofficially the message to the government by the shah was a green light for a "hyper boom." The most important economic questions of the plan revision—the allocation of financial resources between domestic and foreign use or the alignment of the domestic spending program with the country's absorptive capacity—were not dealt with adequately, and thus came back to haunt the regime politically in the form of economic discontent. The shah, who had said "it would be an unforgivable sin to waste this unique opportunity,"[31] was to allow history to slip between his fingers.

The Expanding Role of the State

The new plan, although moderate in contrast to the requests of the ministries, contained promises that could not possibly be kept. In one motion it radically expanded the role of the state in the economy. In every sector, oil money was to be spent on bigger projects and more wide-ranging social programs. The demands of the program on the Iranian bureaucracy required an almost overnight expansion as well as a concurrent simplification of procedures.

Table 4.3 shows the macroplan targets of the revised Fifth Plan, as well as the comparable figures for the Third and Fourth Plans. Besides representing a quantum jump in income, as shown by the 25.9 percent average annual growth rate of GNP, the data clearly show the increasing importance of the public sector. The ratio of public-sector expenditures (consumption plus investment) to GNP increased from 25.1 percent in 1967/68 at the end of the Third Plan to 34.2 percent in 1972/73 at the end of the Fourth Plan. From mid-1974 this ratio was to be increased again to 42.9 percent by the end of the revised Fifth Plan. Thus, in line with increasing oil revenues, the role of the state expanded dramatically in the Fourth Plan period, and as of 1974 it was predicted to expand again. As a corollary, this meant that the burden of satisfying the rising level of expectations would increasingly lie on the shoulders

Table 4.3. GNP Projections Based on the Revised Fifth Plan (billion rials)

Items	Third Plan 1967/1968[a]	Fourth Plan 1972/1973[a]	Fifth Plan 1977/1978[a]	Per Cent Annual Growth Rates 4th Plan	Per Cent Annual Growth Rates 5th Plan
Consumption expenditures	540	898	2,168	10.7	19.3
Private Sector	(442)	(645)	(1,322)	(7.9)	(15.4)
Public Sector	(98)	(253)	(846)	(20.8)	(27.3)
Gross domestic fixed capital formation	151	287	1,053	13.7	29.7
Private Sector	(77)	(141)	(319)	(12.9)	(17.7)
Public Sector	(74)	(146)	(734)	(14.6)	(38.1)
Net exports of goods & services	-5	-20	465		
GNP (market prices)	686	1,165	3,686	11.2	25.9
Population (millions)	26.5	31.5	35.9	3.5	2.6
Per capita GNP (rials)	25,886	36,984	102,674	7.7	22.3

Source: Jahangir Amuzegar, Iran: An Economic Profile (Washington, D.C.: The Middle East Institute, 1977), p. 176

US$1 = 67.5 rials

[a] The figures for the Third and Fourth plans are actual. The Fifth Plan data are the projected values found in the document and therefore reflect the thinking of mid-1974.

of the Iranian bureaucracy. And, of course, in the formulation of the revised plan, the question of whether that bureaucracy was up to the task of implementing the growth programs had never been asked.

In fact, the revised Fifth Plan turned out to be well beyond the absorptive capacity of the administrative apparatus of the state. Yet the state (or government) was to be caught in the unenviable position of being forced on the one hand to expand its role in the economy and on the other, of being made to fulfill the promises it had made, albeit at the urging of the shah. Eventually, the bureaucracy itself would be called to task by the shah for failing to carry out a program that he himself had promised to the people. In the euphoric period following the Tehran agreements, it was simply assumed that what the state lacked to implement the shah's vision of a Great Civilization was money, and now that the money was there, the projects only needed to be inscribed in the plan and in the budget.[32]

Nowhere is the failure of the system more evident than in the acquiescence at Ramsar of the top echelons of the bureaucracy to the shah's programs. The shah failed to appreciate the perils of trying to do too much in too short a time, but the shah's government did not refuse to carry out a program it knew it could not implement. In this sense, the cabinet failed to evaluate the true importance of the decisions taken at Gajereh and Ramsar. It was as if economic problems were secondary, and inflation a bad dream with no political consequences. In reality, the issues discussed at Gajereh, and glossed over at Ramsar, were of such importance to the future of Iran and Iranians that the cabinet should have been prepared to take a political stand. On paper it did achieve a moderation in the spending plans, by arguing inflation. Yet, as events unrolled, it was to give way to domestic spending pressures, as the 1974/75 budget will show.[33] Rather than resign, it tried to carry on business as usual. This myopia, history would not forgive.

The 1974/75 Budget: Planned Inflation

The Plan and the Budget

"It is the earnest hope of all Iranians, guided by their great leader His Imperial Majesty the Shahanshah Aryamehr and inspired by his wise commands, that this Plan will prove to be the spearhead of one of the country's most brilliant and significant transformations, and that its implementation will bring great prosperity to the nation and its people, and guide Iran more rapidly to the period of the Great Civilization."[34] Thus began the text and the hopes of the revised Fifth Plan. Yet, to become an action program, the plan had to be translated into a series of annual budgets. With one year elapsed (1972/73), there remained only four annual tranches; when combined, these at least theoretically would add up to the revised plan.

The first official indication that the revised plan document would only be of legal and academic interest came in the 1974/75 budget process. Already inflated, the revised plan had made no mention of the time pattern of expenditures. That had been left to the budget process, and it was widely anticipated that public expenditures would take a few years to catch up with the quantum jump in public revenues. It had been the hope of PBO's Planning Division that the remaining budgets of the Fifth Plan would follow a regular increase in annual expenditures, rather than take a quantum jump in 1974/75 to be followed then by regular increases. The petroleum revenue was the quantum jump, because it would throw Iran off the smooth growth path it had been on during the last decade. In the PBO's view this was the time to exercise caution and fiscal moderation, to generate investments in foreign ventures, and to accumulate financial resources for the day when they could be repatriated for productive use.

The 1974/75 budget dashed all these hopes and reconfirmed the spending biases, not only by its contents but also by the institutional way in which it was processed. By mid-August 1974, its completion had in effect become an imperative task, since the government had wanted to finish the plan before tackling the budget. This seemed only logical.

Normally the budget document consisted of an Annual Economic Report, for which prime responsibility was assigned to the Planning Division of the PBO in cooperation with the Bank Markazi and the Economics Division of the Ministry of Finance, and the budget data itself for the government and the public enterprises. With the responsibilities under one roof, that of the PBO, the possibilities of a coordinated and harmonious document did exist. In 1974/75, however, the budget turned out to be a carte blanche for spending.

The final figures were to be hammered out in three days of special meetings with the prime minister. Thus, Hoveyda came to the PBO and in close contact with the Budget Division of the PBO proceeded to invite in the executive agencies for discussion. Neither he nor the minister of state in charge of the PBO requested the attendance of the Planning Division staff of the PBO. It was as if they did not want to introduce the lone voices of dissension on excessive spending to a task that, in everybody's view, needed to be accomplished quickly.

In any case the results were quickly known, since within three days the process was over, signifying that agreement had been reached between the PBO and all executive agencies. It seems clear that the chief policymakers wanted to avoid any of the polemics that surrounded the

Table 4.4. The Budget Transition Based on Actual Expenditures of Revenues (billion rials)

Items	1973/1974	1974/1975	Percent Change
Revenues	459.0	1,390.5	203
1. Oil & gas	310.5	1,201.5	287
2. Other	148.5	189.0	27
Expenditures	479.3	1,140.8	138
1. Current	317.3	729.0	130
2. Capital	162.0	344.3	113
3. Advance payments	--	67.5	--
Deficit/surplus	-20.3	249.7	

Source: Bank Markazi Iran, Annual Report, 1974/1975 (Tehran, Bank Markazi Iran, 1975)

US$1 = 67.5 rials

plan and to arrive at a politically acceptable document as soon as possible. The net result was, of course, an overinflated budget, designed with total disregard for the plan, and a strong blueprint for underwriting inflation. It was as if the prime minister, the PBO, and other government agencies had sat down to plan the accentuation of inflationary pressures by widening the gap between supply and demand.

Planned Inflation

It seems hard to believe that the policymakers did not know what they were doing. Rather, one must conclude that under the political conditions in mid-1974, their only choice, other than resignation, was to underwrite an excessive spending program and a large inflation. Thus began the two-year economic boom in Iran, covering roughly the 1974–1976 period, characterized not only by an incredibly large waste of resources but also—more dangerously—by a disruption of the economic growth path.

That inflation should not have been planned, but in fact was, is reflected in the data of Table 4.4, which show the actual revenues and expenditures for the crucial years of the transition. The oil and gas revenue increase of 287 percent, which we earlier characterized as an oil shock to the national entity, is clearly shown by the data. As noted in Table 4.4, it was translated into a 130 percent increase in current expenditures and a 113 percent increase in capital expenditures, as well as generating a budget surplus of approximately 249.7 billion rials.

Most students of fiscal matters would immediately point out that an almost 140 percent annual increase in government expenditures could only be a blueprint for inflation. The question then is why did the policymakers, the top echelon bureaucrats, accept this as a viable budget, and why did they underwrite inflation at a time (mid-August 1974) when the Bank Markazi's annual report, released in July, already complained of the building up of inflationary pressures in a boom atmosphere.

The answer must lie in the fact that they did not, could not, or would not conceive of the potential social disequilibrium to be generated by strong inflationary pressures. Needless to say, the 1974/75 program budget was probably more ambitious than its realizations; only a glance at the data should have been enough to reveal the seriousness of the situation. Yet it was glossed over. It was almost as if the document itself was more important than the contents, since the law required the documents but did not legislate the contents.

In addition, the answer must also lie in the reality that the shah, the defense establishment, and the line ministries wanted to increase spending in line with their particular plans and visions, and that therefore the chief economic policymakers—the prime minister, the minister of state in charge of the PBO, the governor of the Central Bank, and the minister of economics and finance—had either to take a political stand or give way. By giving way, they underwrote an economic path toward the generation of malcontent and eventual revolution. That they must have thought, in giving way, that the problems could be dealt with (or "they'll never be able to spend it all, anyway" or "we'll cross that bridge when we come to it") suggests that the problem was dealt with in a naive fashion. The historic event of December 1973 (the oil-price hike) was not translated into historic policies to deal with the special circumstances. It was indeed naive to underestimate the nefarious effects of virulent inflation. In view of their special responsibilities by virtue of their positions, it is not enough to argue that the top policymakers, like everybody else, were carried forward by the euphoric torrent of the times. And it is untrue to suggest that they had not been forewarned, since at Gajereh, and even at Ramsar, some spending moderation was exercised. In Tehran, a month later, the whole argument was abandoned and the plan laid on the shelf, in favor of a spending spree, a frantic search of how to spend what there was.

The Economy in High Gear: 1974–1976

While these deliberations were going on, the economy was heating up. By mid-July 1974, the Central Bank wrote in its annual report,

"Shortages in building materials, the low rate of agricultural growth (as compared to other sectors) and scarcity of imported materials, combined with infrastructure bottlenecks created limitations in the supply of commodities and broadened the gap between aggregate supply and aggregate demand."[35] Already, as the revised plan and budget were being drawn up, even before the finalization of spending policies, as a result of the liquidity injections the national entity experienced a widening gap between supply and demand. This situation had been totally predictable and in fact had been presented in scenario form in the PBO Planning Division's original position paper.

Table 4.5 shows the variations in the uses of the national product and income over the 1973–1976 period in constant 1959/1960 prices. Table 4.6 indicates the same data but in current prices. In short, aggregate demand was seen to be increasing much more rapidly than aggregate supply, even though imports had quadrupled. Inflation was the inevitable result of these developments.

Amuzegar has given six reasons for the post-1973 inflation:

> First, there was a sudden burst of current expenditures in both the public and private sectors—particularly non-development outlays. . . . Second, total credit by the banking system to the private sector increased private liquidity by an average of 42 percent a year. Third, a number of different bottlenecks (e.g., port capacity, transport facilities, warehousing, etc.) raised insurmountable barriers against supplementary supplies from abroad. . . . Fourth, domestic agricultural production, although notably increasing, could not meet unexpectedly rising demand (particularly for meat, dairy, fruits and some vegetables). Fifth, accelerated private and public investments in increasingly sophisticated industries accentuated the burgeoning shortages of skilled manpower. And, finally, the raw materials boom in world markets in 1973–74, and the ensuing virulent worldwide inflation, added cost push pressures on top of rising aggregate demand.[36]

The culprit was, at least for the first five explanations, the large liquidity injections emanating from the oil-price rise. The government and the shah would, of course, react as if the causes were of the cost-push type (the sixth reason, imported inflation). In any case, compared with average price increases of 3 percent to 4 percent as measured by the various indices during the period 1962/63–1972/73, the widening gap between aggregate demand and aggregate supply began to contribute to significant price increases beginning as early as 1973/74. Both the wholesale and consumer price indices climbed to the double-digit levels in 1973/74, accelerated in 1974/75, and by the second quarter of 1975/76 reached an average annual rate of increase of 18 percent and 24 percent, respectively.[37] The 1974/75 Bank Markazi report stipulated that from March to August 1975 the consumer price index rose at a 28

Table 4.5. Uses of Iran's National Product and Income (billion rials at 1959/1960 prices)

Items	1973/1974	1974/1975	1975/1976
Consumption expenditures	834.8	981.2	1,129.5
Private sector	(600.6)	(662.8)	(758.1)
Public sector	(234.2)	(318.4)	(371.4)
Gross domestic fixed capital formation	240.5	297.6	486.4
Private sector	(109.0)	(109.1)	(197.8)
Public sector	(131.5)	(188.5)	(288.6)
Net external balance	-56.7	-119.2	-313.6
Terms of trade adjustment	168.2	331.6	399.4
Gross National Income	1,186.8	1,491.2	1,701.7

Source: Jahangir Amuzegar, Iran: An Economic Profile (Washington, D.C.: The Middle East Institute, 1977), p. 23

US$1 = 67.5 rials

Table 4.6. Uses of Iran's National Product and Income (billion rials at Current Prices)

Item	1973/1974	1974/1975	1975/1976
Consumption expenditures	1,227.5	1,820.0	2,277.0
Private sector	(902.1)	(1,238.8)	(1,508.0)
Public sector	(325.4)	(581.2)	(769.0)
Gross domestic fixed capital formation	363.3	563.1	1,100.2
Private sector	(160.4)	(199.5)	(453.2)
Public sector	(202.9)	(363.6)	(647.0)
Net exports of goods & services	260.9	792.9	298.7
GNP (market prices)	1,851.7	3,176.0	3,675.9

Source: Jahangir Amuzegar, Iran: An Economic Profile (Washington, D.C.: The Middle East Institute, 1977), p. 28

US$1 = 67.5 rials

percent annual rate.[38] Unofficial figures suggest that the real inflation rate was even higher.

When is an economy out of control? And why? These are the questions that should have been asked throughout the second half of 1974 and the first half of 1975. The evidence was clear. As was stated in 1975:

> The overspending of financial resources, in the face of non-financial bottlenecks, represents a loss in real resources with inter-temporal implications. To begin with, it sets in motion a set of inflationary pressures in the near term that may be difficult to halt without drastic restrictive measures. This is corroborated by the cumulative aspects of inflation, as the infinitely taxed group in the society attempts to recover their loss of purchasing power. It must not be forgotten that inflation has redistributive effects, that, if severe enough, can act to break the social fabric. Secondly, the amount of real resources lost—real in the sense that they represent exported barrels of oil—are resources that could have been used in the future to expand productive capacity at such a time when the relationship between annual financial inflow and annual absorptive capacity would permit it. When used in the present these resources are simply dissipated in the form of higher prices.[39]

By 1975 the economy was indeed out of control, and Iran as a nation was losing on two counts. First, inflation was disrupting the socioeconomic equilibrium of years past; second, the nation was losing real resources (barrels of exported oil) as the cost of development projects soared. "Less and less was being achieved at greater and greater cost."[40]

The Drive to Survive

The Response: Sequential Policy Mistakes

With the economy in high gear, with the widening gap between supply and demand, with a classic case of demand-pull inflation on its hands, the government began to respond to inflation as if the underlying causes were cost related.[41] Somehow the shah and his cabinet refused to acknowledge that only a restriction in public-sector expenditures would halt inflation and the consequent waste. As a result, the cost of development projects soared, current expenditures earmarked to absorb 45 percent of the revised plan outlays increased to 63 percent as investment projects became more and more difficult to implement, demurrage charges piled up in the ports, land prices shot up, money supply increased at an annual rate of 61 percent, and the import bill turned out to be 125 percent above the previous year's. To have cut public-sector expenditures, even in the face of this disastrous evidence, would have been tantamount to admitting that the benefits of the Great Civilization were much farther away than originally thought. It was more comfortable, at this stage, to assume that inflation could be contained through other measures.

As it turned out, each one of the temporary palliatives that was used only contributed to alienating the major social groups in the society—workers, peasants, industrialists, bazaaris, bankers, and, last but not least, the bureaucrats and the Islamic Shiite clergy. Not only was the state making promises it could not keep, it was at the same time interfering in the rights of various social groups to make a living and to try to keep abreast of the rising costs associated with earning that living. At least that became the general perception from below.

The state contributed to the inflationary process by refusing to allocate a realistic financial package for domestic spending. Now, by refusing to recognize the true nature of the inflation, it engaged in corrective policies that could only serve to alienate the various participants in the economic process, highlight the glaring inequities in the society, encourage corruption and the black market, and finally cast an evil hue on the whole process of economic development through modernization and Westernization.

Bottlenecks

Throughout the early years of the oil boom—that is, 1974 and 1975—the government reacted to physical bottlenecks as if their resolution required more effort. Expansion of supply was the key word rather than restriction in demand. Nowhere were the problems more serious than in the area of transport and manpower, and nowhere had the problems been more carefully presented. Indeed in the PBO Planning Division's position paper on the revised Fifth Plan alternatives, it had been suggested that the initial major constraints would appear in those areas, with the emphasis placed on port capacity and skilled manpower. In fact, these had been considered as the binding constraints on growth. Yet even with this awareness the government preferred to follow the shah's optimistic dictates, originally stated at Ramsar, that innovative emergency resolutions of bottlenecks were required rather than a cutback on targets.

The problem of port capacity provides an illustrative case in point. At the beginning of the Fifth Plan, port capacity was 3.8 million metric tons, and the plan envisaged a 9.8-million-ton capacity by 1978. The plan revision increased requirements to 29 million tons by the end of the same year.[42] Needless to say, the time lag in delivering this expanded capacity was not even taken into account when the spending plans were made. It was simply assumed that the inclusion of a sufficient budget for port expansion would suffice.

The import upsurge in 1974/75 and 1975/76 was the natural consequence of the 1974/75 budget. The situation in the southern ports was well illustrated by Robert Graham:

> At Khoramshahr, the principal port, over 200 ships were waiting to unload their cargoes by mid-1975; ships were having to wait 160 days and more before entering harbour. At one point more than one million tons of goods were being kept in ships' holds awaiting the opportunity to unload . . . 12,000 tons were being unloaded per day but only 9,000 were being removed per day. At the most congested point in September/October 1975, there were over 1 million tons of goods piled upon the jetties and around the port.[43]

To solve the congestion, the government needed to expand port capacity, warehousing, and transport facilities. Emergency programs were instituted. To illustrate, consider the purchase of two thousand trucks and six hundred trailers (there was a shortage of trucks) by the government, purchases that caused no immediate relief because the trucks needed drivers and there was a shortage of Iranian drivers. When the drivers could not be found, they too were imported. Yet the program was ill-conceived and harried, with the end result being a lot of unused trucks rotting in the sun and a lot of disappointed Korean and Pakistani drivers.[44]

Attempts to remove serious physical bottlenecks through emergency high-cost programs always led to the imposition of other constraints. It seemed that the state had forgotten the sectoral interrelationships in the economy. The net result in this case was a further waste of resources, not to mention the additional costs to be tacked on to the final prices of imported goods. This in turn resulted not in consumer satisfaction, but to disaffection and alienation.

In another area—that of manpower—the PBO Planning Division's position paper had stated categorically the manpower shortages to be expected in the three alternative scenarios. The revised Fifth Plan explicitly recognized that there would be a shortfall of 720,000 people, of which 80 percent would be skilled and semiskilled industrial and construction workers.[45] The reaction at Ramsar had been that to correct this imbalance between financial resources and human resources, the government would proceed to import foreign labor rather than cut back on its development expenditures.

The result was a massive inflow of expatriates of all types. The skilled managers, technicians, and engineers came from the Western countries; the doctors from India and Pakistan; the maids and household help from the Philippines, Bangladesh, and Sri Lanka. Finally, to work the increasingly depopulated agricultural lands, there were the Afghanis. Quite apart from the social repercussions of such a massive inflow of expatriates, there were to be economic repercussions of importance to the course of events.

To begin with, the expatriate salaries were well above those of Iranians with commensurate skills. In the PBO alone, an average computer programmer provided by a foreign consulting firm was paid about $3,500 per month in 1975/76 (not including housing, which was provided by the company), and the firm, in turn, was paid $10,000 a person-month for providing these services. The scale at which expatriates paraded around the country and garnered for themselves the best housing, the best food, the best schools for their children, and the best of everything was bound to cause resentment. The Iranian middle classes were resentful because they could not share in the same pattern of life although their skills were no less in most cases. The resentment of the lower classes stemmed from the immigrants' values, which clashed with traditional Iranian values and from their behavior—they were (as at Bell Helicopter in Esfahan) often loud, boisterous, alcohol consuming, and disco-dancing oriented. Nontraditional establishments—restaurants, bars, dance halls, and discos—often sprang up in traditional and Islamic environments to meet the new demand; this fostered and heightened nascent resentments on the part of the local population. Alienation with the modernization program and the development leap was, then, just a step away.

More concretely, the heavy payments to expatriate personnel were a large load on the government budget and a major contributor to the inflationary process. Middle-class Western expatriates displaced upper- and middle-class Iranians in the best housing. This was especially evident in Tehran, where by mid-1975 there were already thirty-five thousand foreigners. Landlords preferred to rent to expatriates because they paid more and because their departure was assured. Iranian laws gave too many rights to the tenant, and the landlords reacted accordingly. Thus rates went up in the richer part of town, dragging up with them the rents in the poorer sections. In this situation, how could Iranians feel that they were benefiting directly from the sudden oil wealth, when the best of everything, by virtue of purchasing power, went to the expatriate community? It was a classic situation for breeding alienation and resentments of the foreign element.

Even though this type of demand pull on rents and housing costs was important, the general level of government expenditures contributed significantly to a sudden and continuous rise in the price of land. At first this was most evident in the cities—Tehran, Tabriz, Esfahan—but it quickly spread to the countryside. Land values increased on a day-to-day basis, and land speculators, including the real estate agencies, flourished. But on the other side of the coin, the high cost of land doubled the costs of development projects, thus requiring even-larger financial injections by the state and—to complete the circle—an ever-greater supply of money with which to buy land. On the production side, rising land prices discouraged industrial investment as well as agricultural production. With land prices so high, and given the geographic peculiarities of Iran where cities grew around water points that in turn irrigated agricultural activities, the urban land-price boom was bound to affect the price of agricultural land. It no longer was profitable to produce wheat at government-controlled prices on land that, if sold, would bring in ten times the income in interest. So land was taken out of the production cycle and placed in the speculation cycle, agricultural workers migrated to construction activities, and the food shortfall was compensated by imports. This was an expensive way to develop and from the social point of view, highly dislocating.

With rising rents, resulting from the land boom, and the rural-urban migration, workers began to require higher wages. Rent had become the major element in the cost of living, and people of all classes had difficulties in meeting their rent payments. In 1974/75 wages rose by 30 percent in the urban areas, but even this was not enough to compensate for rising rents. Based on government salary scales, returning Iranian students could hardly cover their rents if they decided to join the public sector; with the generous scholarship programs of past years, many had to do so.

To solve the resulting housing shortage, the government reacted with an even-greater effort. Industrial projects now had to have housing components for the workers, thereby tripling development project costs. The already strained market for building materials was thereby further aggravated. The armed forces competed with urban housing (public and private) for cement, bricks, steel, and so forth. The frenetic pace only led to frenetic increases in costs, with little effect on supply. Delays on the supply side then aggravated inflationary pressures.

The circle seemed endless. The situation had become untenable by mid-1975/1976. The whole question of lessening inflation while engaging in a Big-Push development strategy had been erroneously concentrated on emergency programs to solve bottlenecks. Since each bottleneck was replaced by another, the "more effort" approach only aggravated the situation by requiring more expenditures in an already cash-laden and goods-poor economy. Rather than retrench on the fiscal front, the government—at the urging of the shah—pushed forward, oblivious to the social repercussions and the resulting discontent.

Price-Control Policies

> The warning signals that Iran was over-spending had come much earlier (than 1976); but the response had been muted. In July 1975 for instance the Finance Ministry authorized foreign borrowing by Government agencies. Only seven months previously this had been thought unnecessary before 1978. At the same time the instructions were sent to all Ministries to observe the utmost care and economy; to be followed by an order to submit monthly accounts to the PBO for scrutiny.[46]

Although the signs were clear that the widening gap between supply and demand was beginning to tear the social fabric, the government and the shah, now more aware of the obvious disequilibriums, persisted in their spending plans.

Because "more effort," more emergency-high-cost programs did not break supply bottlenecks and lessen inflation, the next policy move was to institute price controls. Again, rather than face the facts—that the economic situation required a cutback in public expenditures and a decrease in aggregate demand—the shah opted for a program that would only lead to further discontent and encourage the black market. In early August 1975 the shah announced a price-control policy aimed at restoring the prices of over twenty thousand commodities to their pre-oil boom levels. Empowering the minister of commerce—otherwise known as the Bulldozer of Hoveyda's cabinet—to arrest the costly sellers, the shah attacked publicly profiteers who were ostensibly responsible for the inflation. Industrialists, merchants, retailers, and bazaaris were the main targets.

To institute price controls and to implement its antiprofiteering campaign, the Commerce Ministry published official price lists and then hired university students to go out into the marketplace for verification. The campaign, seemingly successful, in the first two weeks led to the arrest of some eight to ten thousand persons, including some of Iran's most prominent industrialists.[47] It was not a program to restore confidence. Prices were often set arbitrarily by ill-informed inspectors, and more often than not the young university students with public power in their hands offended elderly merchants and business people, not to mention the more successful patrons of private enterprise. The minister of commerce, himself an economist by training, boasted that Iran's inflation rate would be zero, if not negative, by the end of the year.

This optimistic projection was, of course, unrealizable. Practically the only benefit of the price-control program was that the official inflation indices went down, as all government agencies were ordered to use the published lists. Practically, however, the price-control program was a failure, as it encouraged a drop in production activity and an increase in the black market. Shortages became more evident as importers now refused to import at controlled prices. But of greater significance than the obvious failure of this pompous price-control attempt was the dampening effect on the private sector's confidence and, therefore, its willingness to invest in Iran.

Pushed around, arrested, and humiliated, many industrialists reacted by stopping production, exporting their capital, or moving abroad. Merchants and bazaaris hoarded their goods rather than offer them at less than desirable prices. The pillar of economic success in the 1963–1973 period—the entrepreneurial and merchant class operating in a capitalist framework with outstanding results—was being alienated and ostracized. Profits were acquiring a bad name, private investment fell off, and the consequent decrease in the supply of goods did nothing to alleviate the demand-pull inflation. Rather the deals went under the table, and the number of deals decreased as capital flew outside the country.[48] Meanwhile, the inflation continued unabated.

Price controls for agricultural goods, instituted earlier through a program of subsidized sales to the urban areas, acted as a disincentive to production of the basic foodstuffs such as wheat, meat, sugar, and barley. Government food imports added to supplies stretched thin by the pressures of demand in the urban areas. Migration to the urban areas, due to disincentives on the farm, tended to decrease agricultural supplies while increasing demand. To counteract the rising discontent of the lower-income urban groups, the government had embarked on a high-cost subsidy program. This program not only represented a misallocation of resources but also failed to satisfy demand at those controlled subsidized prices. The results were often shortages and queues for bread, meat, and sugar. Periodically the consumer would be faced with penury. The new urban poor, who had left their land because they could no longer earn a living at these controlled prices, now faced different disruptions in the cities. The government, having opted for a subsidy policy with domestic production disincentives, now found itself trapped between the high cost (and inflationary aspect) of these subsidies and the potential political unrest that would result from their removal. The end result was discontent on the part of agricultural producers for not receiving a fair price, migratory urban workers for the high cost of housing and penury in basic foodstuffs, and consumers in general for the lack of available goods.

The Imperial Commission

The year 1976 proved to be the undoing of the boom. Throughout the period from late 1973 to early 1976, the shah and his government had persevered in their course to achieve unachievable targets; they had persisted in maintaining a widening gap between supply and demand. Their policies to combat inflation had not only been ineffective, but, on top of the dislocations created by a rapid increase in the general price level, had specifically contributed to the alienation of various groups—industrialists, merchants, workers, peasants, consumers, the middle class, the urban poor.

The boom was not dampened by a conscious policy choice to reduce aggregate demand by cutting back on public-sector expenditures; rather it came about as a result of the vagaries of the international oil market. The pressures for reduced spending came from outside rather than inside, from a shortfall in anticipated oil revenues rather than from a realization that domestic dislocations had reached an explosive stage. The shah in a *Newsweek* interview on March 1, 1976, was persistent in stating that the boom was not over and in being astounded at Western skepticism. "Why? Because we will have a 17 percent growth rate this year? Is this bad? Last year [1975] we had a 42 percent growth rate, but a 20 to 22 percent inflation rate. This year we will have zero inflation. Is this what bothers the critics?"[49] He was still brimming with confidence, the confidence that had marked his pronouncements ever since his December 25, 1973, interview on the oil-price hike.

That confidence had left him unswerving in the pursuit of his domestic targets, regardless of social costs. It had also led to an overestimation of oil revenues in the revised Fifth Plan, an overestimation highly related to the optimistic and confident mood following the 1973 Tehran Oil Agreements. Oil revenues for the 1973–1978 period had been anticipated to be 6,628.5 billion rials. The data in Tables 4.4 and 4.7 show a realized total of approximately 5,334.5 billion rials or a shortfall of 19.5 percent or so. The confidence of the shah and his cabinet at Ramsar had precluded a careful analysis of the impact of rising oil prices on the Western economies. No one had bothered to forecast a possible recession, which did indeed materialize in the most virulent form since the end of World War II, and consequently no one had bothered to anticipate what the vagaries of the oil market could do to the carefully laden development plans of an oil exporter. Oil had been assumed to be a necessity in the revised Fifth Plan, and the 6,628.5 billion rials figure in that plan was based on steadily increasing output and price assumptions.

As it turned out, oil sales fell in 1975 by about 12 percent. Prices agreed on at successive OPEC meetings increased, but at rates less than those anticipated in the plan, as follows: Vienna, September 1975, 10 percent; Bali, May 1976, price freeze; Doha, September 1976, 10 percent for Iran and others, 5 percent for the United Arab Emirates (UAE) and

Table 4.7. Actual Budget Receipts and Expenditures (billion rials)

Item	1975/1976	1976/1977	1977/1978
1. General budget			
(a) Taxes	259.2	296.3	397.6
(b) Oil & gas	1,193.4	1,314.9	1,314.2
(c) Domestic loans	---	---	143.1
(d) Foreign loans	5.4	77.0	95.2
(e) Other	273.4	109.4	143.8
Subtotal	1,731.4	1,797.6	2,093.9
State enterprises	483.3	1,042.9	1,107.7
2. Total state receipts	2,214.7	2,840.5	3,201.6
3. Total expenditures	2,214.7	3,019.3	3,319.0
4. Gross deficit	---	(178.8)	(117.4)

Source: Plan and Budget Organization, Annual Budget (various issues 1975 to 1977)

US$1 = 67.5 rials

Saudi Arabia; Stockholm, July 1977, 5 percent for Saudi Arabia and the UAE, others price freeze; and Caracas, December 1977, price freeze for 1978.

With increases in expenditures rapidly outpacing increases in receipts, the fiscal year 1976/77 showed an abrupt turnaround in the politics of plenty (of money). As shown in Table 4.7, Iran was returning to the international market for borrowing to meet budgetary shortfalls. As it was, the budget, with a small deficit of 20.3 billion rials in 1973/74 and a large surplus of 249.7 billion rials in 1974/75, now showed a gross deficit of 178.8 billion rials. Given the promises and the lectures of the policymakers, the 1976/77 budget figures were a shock to both domestic and international investors. How could it be that Iran was again a borrower? But there it was, as noted in the balance-of-payments data shown in Table 4.8. Imports of goods in 1973/74 stood at $4.9 billion, and in 1975/76 they were at $16.0 billion. Moreover, the rate of increase in imports was much larger than the rate of increase in foreign-exchange receipts. It had taken only two years to absorb the annual capacity to import.

With the prospects in the international oil market in terms of foreign-exchange receipts for Iran dimmed, the shah tried to maintain his

Table 4.8. Foreign-Exchange Receipts and Payments: Iran 1975/1976-1979/1980 (million U.S. dollars)

Item	1975/1976	1976/1977	1977/1978	1978/1979	1979/1980
Current account (net)	2,914	4,157	1,094	-501	6,318
Current receipts	21,972	24,404	25,590	22,737	22,648
1. Oil & gas	19,074	20,671	20,905	18,115	19,395
2. Other goods	447	472	524	417	431
3. Services	2,451	3,261	4,161	4,205	2,822
Current payments	-19,058	-20,247	-24,496	-23,238	-16,330
1. Goods	-16,046	-16,060	-16,553	-13,551	-11,340
2. Services	-3,012	-4,187	-7,943	-9,687	-4,990
Capital account (net)	-3,607	-1,766	1,505	316	-98
Capital receipts	961	1,709	3,617	2,273	1,224
1. Government loans	300	560	1,755	619	3
2. Other	661	1,149	1,862	1,654	1,221
Capital payments	-4,568	-3,475	-2,112	-1,957	-1,322
1. Loan repayments: government	-729	-711	-680	-604	-937
2. Foreign investments: government	-2,941	-1,786	-1,092	-417	-99
3. Other	-898	-978	-340	-936	-286
Errors & omissions	-391	-103	-585	-394	-464
Basic balance	-1,084	2,288	2,014	-579	5,756

Source: Bank Markazi Iran, Bulletin (Winter Quarter 1980), pp. 258-261

development targets throughout much of 1976, but then finally gave way to the grim realities. In an interview given to *Kayhan International*'s Amir Taheri in October 1976, the shah abruptly reversed course. Instead of carte blanche expenditure, the government was told to economize in all areas, finish the projects now underway, and leave the rest of the Fifth Plan objectives for the Sixth Plan.

Having belatedly recognized the dangers of profligate spending, the shah, while finally tackling the demand-pull aspect of inflation, set up a special Imperial Commission to investigate delays, wastage, and corruption in the administration of development projects. Day after day televised meetings of the Imperial Commission began to review the excess of the boom years and to reveal the poor management of some of the ministers. Even though there were certainly many instances of corruption and wanton waste, it was clear from the beginning that the bureaucracy was not up to the task of managing the impossible. Oil revenues had been well above the country's absorptive capacity, and no amount of exceptional management skills could have prevented the resulting fiasco. Only a decision at the top to be realistic in expectations of Iran's absorptive capacity could have resolved the problem without ensuing waste. Yet the decision to go full speed ahead was imposed on the government by the shah—albeit, his ministers did not protest too much—and now the representatives of the bureaucracy were being placed on show trial for having tried to do the impossible and failed.

The policy decision to set up this Imperial Commission, to try to lay the blame of faulty policies on those who only obeyed orders, could only cast doubt on the one who gave orders. The public trials of high government officials in a televised forum for all to see could only create resentments on the part of the bureaucratic class or stir up watchers' resentments against the shah and his government. In a sense, the shah had placed himself on trial, and through the media ensured that the message would go out clearly and far.

Throughout 1977 the Imperial Commission reported on the inefficiencies of the Hoveyda cabinet. When Jamshid Amuzegar was sworn in as the new prime minister in August 1977, the Imperial Commission was continuing its work. Not only were Hoveyda's ministers subjected to courtlike investigations, but also Amuzegar's newly appointed ones. The shah was determined to place the blame for waste and inflation on an inefficient and corrupt bureaucracy. This was a decision that would only serve to publicize his own weaknesses and to further alienate from his throne a potentially supportive group, the government employees of all levels.

The Slow Down

Slow down was what the Iranian economy needed after 1975. However, this had to wait until 1977 when the whole economic environment had become impatient for some real changes. Many projects were then cancelled, delayed, or shelved temporarily. The PBO's preliminary Sixth Plan calculations showed, on more modest and realistic assumptions, that the completion of the Fifth Plan projects would leave very little in terms of financial resources for new projects in the 1978–1983 period. The new plan had already been mortgaged by prior decisions; that is, even with a 30 percent increase in oil revenues over the revised Fifth Plan figure of 6,628.5 billion rials to 8,617.1 billion rials, the financial resources would not be sufficient to undertake very many new projects. Fifth Plan euphoria had tied the hands of policymakers for many years to come.

During the first half of 1977 nothing was more of a reminder to the restive population of economic promises failing to materialize than the power blackouts. The economic expansion of 1974–1976 had run up against an energy shortage that enforced on Tehran and other urban centers a forced program of blackouts. The foreign contractors working on the Reza Shah Kabir Dam were faulted for not delivering the required power to the national grid as promised, yet the blame in people's minds remained squarely placed on the government. As a result, following the shah's abrupt change in tone from expansion to contraction in late 1976, his need for a scapegoat caused the shah to dismiss the Hoveyda cabinet in August 1977, hoping that a new government could begin afresh with more coherent policies.

The power failures were only the most visible signs of an economic strategy gone bankrupt. It remained to be seen whether the shah could disassociate himself from the economic policies that had led to inflation, shortages, promises gone sour, and general discontent. To do this, he would have had to pick a prime minister and a cabinet of veteran political personalities with deep-rooted connections to both the traditional and modern strains of the society. Instead, in mid-1977 he appointed as prime minister Jamshid Amuzegar, a man who had been in the various ministerial cabinets for the last nineteen years and was thereby closely associated with past policies, especially those of the last four years. Amuzegar in turn picked a cabinet of hard-nosed young technocrats, anxious to disassociate themselves from the past policies and keen to show during the televised sessions of the Imperial Commission the progress being made against waste.

The Amuzegar government was given a relatively freer hand with economic decision making than its predecessor.

> He [Amuzegar] immediately launched a deflationary program, which brought a sudden growth in unemployment, especially among the unskilled and semi-skilled, and this, coming after rising expectations, helped create a classic pre-revolutionary situation. The combination of inflation, shortages and large and evident income distribution inequities probably contributed more to a growing discontent than did the standard factor cited in the West of too rapid modernization.[50]

To say the least, the roller coaster of economic promises went up too fast as oil revenues quadrupled and the boom picked up; then when the resources ran out and the magnitude of the waste was assessed, it was made to come down too fast, leaving many broken promises in its wake.

The abrupt turnaround in economic policy, from inflationary to deflationary, did not create many adherents to the regime. The man in the street did not understand why he had been promised a rosy future and now was unemployed. It was not enough to blame past governments of which the present prime minister was an integral part. If anything, the change around was too abrupt. The urge to economize pervaded all ministries and therefore tended to render decision making more cautious. Projects were retarded, contracts discussed ad nauseam, and for the government employees themselves, there were some reductions in overtime payouts.

The Amuzegar deflationary program came too late and too abruptly. By the time the government had begun to feel its way around, the January 1978 riots of Qom began a process of political upheaval that was to culminate in the overthrow of the monarchy one year later. The inflation/deflation debate had become academic in the face of political survival. One can only say that, as the importance of political issues ascended and those of economic issues descended, it must have seemed ever so tragic to realize how many faulty policy decisions had driven the ship of state to its present state—decisions that with some greater courage and a more serious awareness of their important consequences could have prevented this steady erosion of confidence.

Conclusion

Ambitious outlooks and aspirations prevailed in all the oil-producing countries following the December 1973 Tehran Oil Agreements. They all subsequently suffered, in retrospect, an *embarras de richesses;* they all operated under a "lyrical illusion," "an exhilarating state of near euphoria where state planners and the rank and file alike were disingenuously confident that oil money would solve all problems."[51] Let us say for simplicity's sake that policymakers were more engineers than economists, and therefore less aware that the maximum growth rate will be bound by factors other than money when the latter is plentiful.

As the foregoing has attempted to show, Iran was no exception in this "lyrical illusion." Rather, by virtue of its special circumstances, it turned out to be an extreme case; that is, a case where the differences between the promised vistas and the realities were so great that the social fabric tore and revolution ensued. In this failure of rapid modernization, the alienated social groups coalesced to overthrow the proponents of the Great Civilization, because it did not seem so great any more, at least in its actual experience up to the end of 1978.

That the 287 percent increase in oil revenues was a financial shock to Iran as a national unit has been clearly documented. That it need not have been so also seems clear. What separates Iran from the rest of the oil producers is that the policymakers—the shah, the prime minister, and his major ministers who together formed the High Economic Council—made the wrong policy decisions at the wrong time and thereby progressively alienated every social group in the society. At this historic juncture they did not give due weight to the historic decisions they were making. One might even say that they did not feel the true importance of these decisions, which were taken in an almost cavalier fashion, abstracted from their potential repercussions. The dissenting voices were always brushed aside, as if the pessimism and the caution they introduced would spoil the dream.[52]

The overconfident shah of the post-1973 period launched the overspending spree with his dream of a Great Civilization. In doing so, he set in motion an inflation that was to topple his regime. The inflation alone would not have succeeded, but the shah and his cabinet devised policies upon policies that could not but aggravate the situation. The reluctance to use a progressive retrenchment in government expenditures as the most effective way to control the demand-pull inflation—that is, the reluctance to abandon the dream—led them to enact high-cost emergency programs, price controls, antiprofiteering campaigns, subsidy and welfare schemes falling short of promises, and large labor-import programs, all with disastrous repercussions. By behaving as if the inflation were of a cost-push nature, they thought they could continue with the boom and thus lick inflation. So erroneous were these policies that it must be asked how it was ever thought that success would ensue and how the ministerial cabinet that presided over the implementation of these measures did not realize—or refused to realize—that there was *à la limite* the possibility of resignation rather than carrying on in the direction many must have known to be fraught with dangers.

To abruptly inflate the economy carries its own dangers; having done so, to abruptly deflate it is to throw gasoline on the political fire. And then to accompany deflation and the consequent unemployment with a public exposure of the errors and waste of the past to a nervous and discontented population via the celebrated Imperial Commission is tantamount to political suicide, to putting oneself on trial. Only an overconfident ruler—overconfident in his own decision-making ability and in his power—could have taken such risks. This was the final parting of the ways between the shah and his subjects. The bureaucracy, ostracized by the Imperial Commission and blamed publicly for being unable to do the impossible, was to pull down the regime by going on strike in late 1978, thereby adding its substantial weight to the long list of the discontented.

Notes

1. This was the year that was to herald the shah's program of modernization and reform, otherwise known as the White Revolution.

2. Firouz Vakil, "Iran's Basic Macroeconomic Problems: A Twenty Year Horizon," *Economic Development and Cultural Change,* July 1977, p. 713.

3. *Kayhan International,* December 25, 1973.

4. Robert Graham, *Iran: The Illusion of Power* (London: Croom Helm; New York: St. Martin's Press, 1978), p. 15.

5. Vakil, "Iran's Basic Macroeconomic Problems," pp. 713–715.

6. Bank Markazi Iran, *Annual Report, 1974/1975* (Tehran: Bank Markazi Iran, 1975), p. 14.

7. *Kayhan International,* December 25, 1973.

8. *Iran,* p. 15.

9. ". . . Great Civilization—a national state of national well-being with industrialization achieved and a full regeneration of Iran's ancient heritage." Ibid., p. 17.

10. Firouz Vakil, *Determining Iran's Financial Surplus, 1352–1371: Some Management Concepts,* Tehran Papers no. 2 (Tehran: The Institute for International Political and Economic Studies, June 1975), p. 6.

11. R. Nurkse, *Problems of Capital Formation in Underdeveloped Countries* (New York: Oxford University Press, 1953).

12. See P. R. Rodan, *Capital Formation and Economic Development* (Cambridge: Massachusetts Institute of Technology Press, 1964).

13. Of note is the idea that a country is poor because it is poor: i.e., poor means low savings, low savings mean low investments, hence low growth, and thus continuing poverty.

14. "A Twenty Year Macroeconomic Perspective for Iran, 1972–1992," *Planametrics and General Economy Bureau* (Tehran: Plan & Budget Organization, 1974).

15. These conclusions are presented in a random fashion to point out that many major issues had been totaled and quantified at least in a preliminary manner. They represented the synthesis of a great deal of effort, thinking, and research on the part of various government agencies, and especially the PBO.

16. "A Twenty Year Macroeconomic Perspective for Iran, 1972–1992."

17. Nikki R. Keddie, *Roots of Revolution: An Interpretive History of Modern Iran* (New Haven: Yale University Press, 1981), p. 170.

18. These discussions were attended by one of the authors (Firouz Vakil) in his capacity as a PBO official.

19. Each plant was to generate approximately 1,200 megawatts and to go on line during the Sixth and Seventh Development Plans.

20. The project lists and their associated costs were submitted to the PBO by the executive agencies or line ministries. The Supervision and Coordination Division merely reflected these requirements with some modifications and presented them as the sectoral elements of the plan.

21. Firouz Vakil participated in the drafting of the PBO Planning Division's position paper. The same data are also shown in Graham, *Iran,* p. 77.

22. Firouz Vakil feels that the head of the PBO did not feel politically strong enough to tackle the shah by himself and thus took the role of presenting both sides so that after the deliberations the prime minister would choose the optimal scenario. The process in fact worked out this way, but a united PBO might have carried greater weight in the events that followed Gajereh.

23. For example, the Telecommunications Company targeted for itself the goal of 2 million telephones by March 1978, whereas up to 1974 only 500,000 telephones had been connected in Iran since the beginning of usage. Although financially feasible, the target was well over what could have been done physically, given the other constraints in the society—human, management, legal, infrastructure, and so on. It was this type of target setting that guided the sectoral revisions in the proposed plan.

24. One of the authors, in a conversation with the minister of housing at the time, understood from his remarks that if he did not seek out funds, then other agencies would. Therefore, to maintain balance was irrelevant in this "administrative competition" for funds. Inflation and waste were secondary considerations.

25. Graham, *Iran,* pp. 78–79.

26. Attempts by Iran to purchase shares in Grumman Aircraft were blocked on security grounds by the U.S. government. This example serves to highlight the reluctance of Organization for Economic Cooperation and Development (OECD) countries to accept OPEC investments in their major industrial ventures. Iran's Krupp investment turned out to be an exception.

27. Plan and Budget Organization, *Iran's Fifth Development Plan 1973–78, Revised: A Summary* (Tehran: Plan and Budget Organization, January 1975), pp. 1–25.

28. For a discussion of this issue, see Vakil, *Determining Iran's Financial Surplus 1352–1371,* pp. 2–45.

29. Graham, *Iran,* p. 79.

30. Ibid., p. 80.
31. *Kayhan International,* August 4, 1974.
32. As viewed by each executive agency, the scarce factor was indeed money. But when added together the agencies' programs amounted to a race for scarce building materials and manpower.
33. The 1974/75 budget was to totally disregard the antispending arguments presented at Gajereh and ostensibly incorporated in the revised Fifth Plan.
34. Plan and Budget Organization, *Iran's Fifth Development Plan 1973–78, Revised.*
35. Bank Markazi Iran, *Annual Report, 1974/75,* p. 62; stated again in Graham, *Iran,* p. 83.
36. Jahangir Amuzegar, *Iran: An Economic Profile* (Washington, D.C.: The Middle East Institute, 1977), p. 233.
37. Ibid., p. 253.
38. Bank Markazi Iran, *Annual Report, 1974/1975,* p. 74.
39. Vakil, "Iran's Basic Macroeconomic Problems," p. 719.
40. Graham, *Iran,* p. 87.
41. Robert Looney, *Economic Origins of the Iranian Revolution* (New York: Pergamon Press, 1982), p. 166.
42. Plan and Budget Organization, *Iran's Fifth Development Plan 1973–78, Revised,* p. 297.
43. Graham, *Iran,* p. 93.
44. Ibid., p. 88.
45. Plan and Budget Organization, *Iran's Fifth Development Plan,* pp. 71–73.
46. Graham, *Iran,* p. 93.
47. *Kayhan International,* August 8, 1975.
48. The lack of confidence imparted to the private business community by the price-control policy was exacerbated by the shah's announcement in August 1975 of a compulsory scheme to sell 49 percent of the share of manufacturing establishments to their workers and the public. About 1 million workers and 2.7 million peasants were supposed to benefit. The program was slow to be instituted, and the benefits were close to nil. It further strained businesspeople's confidence and contributed to additional slack in private investment. At the same time, paper shares were not perceived as a tangible improvement by the recipients. It was premature to expect them to behave as small Western stockholders.
49. *Newsweek,* March 1, 1976.
50. Keddie, *Roots of Revolution,* p. 177.
51. Jahangir Amuzegar, "Oil Wealth: A Very Mixed Blessing," *Foreign Affairs* (Spring 1982), p. 287.
52. Prime Minister Amir Hoveyda was fond of saying that "whatever the economists recommend, I will always do the opposite."

5
Demise of the Shah and Establishment of the Islamic Regime

Introduction

The fall of the shah was related to a host of political, social, and economic factors. The intention in this book is not to construct a single-faceted theory to explain the process that led to his demise. Rather, it is to describe the manner in which economic forces interacted with other factors to create and amplify a multiclass discontent that proved fatal to the regime.

In his recent book, *Economic Origins of the Iranian Revolution,* Robert Looney suggested that a number of latent tensions inevitably resulted from the development process itself so that the authorities had no advance notice of the mass alienation developing in the country.[1] In *The Rise and Fall of the Shah*, on the other hand, A. Saikal put forth the idea that the shah pursued two objectives that were inherently contradictory: to preserve a strong monarchy while transforming Iran into a modern state, based upon the model of Western capitalism. According to Saikal, these twin objectives required policies that necessarily conflicted, creating a fundamental dilemma.[2]

R. K. Ramazani stated that the way in which the vast oil reserves were used magnified every weakness in the Iranian economy. According to him, the grandiose plans for developing the economy and atomic energy, the massive imports of food and consumer goods, the rapidly rising rate of inflation, the spreading corruption, the shortage of electricity, the infrastructural bottlenecks, the decline of agricultural productivity, and the maldistribution of wealth all contributed to the demise of the shah.[3]

S. Akhavi suggested in *Religion and Politics in Contemporary Iran* that the secularization policies pursued by the shah and his father seriously undermined the clergy's power and interests, leading to widespread resentment toward the dynasty among the ulema. Eventually this provoked active opposition when the increasing bureaucratization of power was perceived as threatening the independence that they and their religious institutions had traditionally possessed in Iran.[4] Taheri pointed to other factors in the Tehran daily newspaper *Kayhan International* saying that the public uprising against the shah was due to an accumulation of discontent with tight control, overcentralization, lack of sufficient open debate, and a general feeling that corruption, inefficiency, and arrogance had stricken the bureaucracy.[5] And James Bill, in "Iran and the Crisis of 78," described the Iranian revolution as a multiclass phenomenon in which the people of Iran rose en masse against a hated and decrepit system.[6]

In light of our discussion in previous chapters of this book, we may put the above views in the following perspective: (1) the development patterns and strategies that were chosen and implemented by the shah's regime moved the economic system out of its sectoral, regional, and social balances; (2) the management system of the country was rigidly top-down, with the shah making the major economic decisions himself and with no provision or tolerance for the feedback of corrective signals; and (3) the injection of vast oil revenues into the economy intensified the incapabilities of the system and led to explosive trends.

These conclusions should not, of course, be taken to imply that economic forces were the only (or the most important) factors behind the collapse of the regime. They merely suggest that the economic system itself had developed an internal mechanism that intensified the further deterioration of the politico-economic situation. As Friedman and Schwartz observed in *A Monetary History of the United States*: "Economic collapse often has the character of cumulative process. Let it go beyond a certain point and it will tend for a time to gain strength from its own development and its effects spread and return to intensify the process of collapse."[7]

Strikes and Chaos

Strikes within government agencies constituted a critical factor in the toppling of the shah's regime, and academia played the most important role in instigating and leading them. Universities were in fact the original source of the strikes. University students and instructors had used the strike tool to express themselves even in the early 1970s, when the shah's regime had firm control over the political system, so they were quite familiar not only with the effectiveness of this tool but also with the risks involved in organizing a strike. In 1977 they realized that the regime was troubled with certain human-rights questions being asked by the international community; having seen some softness in the regime's treatment of the opposition, they concluded that the risk involved in organizing strikes was now much less than it had been a few years earlier, when the regime had harshly broken up every strike attempt. Therefore, the university students and a majority of their instructors made an enormous effort to persuade the government employees to go on strike, and they furthermore encouraged people of all classes to join the demonstration against the regime. University campuses became known as the place where everybody could go to find out what was happening in the country. Most universities, and Tehran University in particular, served as the focal points from which antiregime demonstrations originated.

Government employees, though having played a passive role for several years, were prepared by the end of 1977 to take an active role in public affairs. Their role, however, was not to help the government, but to stand against a regime they viewed as a corrupt dictatorship. Each government agency soon had its own strike committee and strike schedule. The most visible of all the strikes was the one by the employees of the Ministry of Power. Their strike schedule called for a shutdown in electrical power for a number of hours in the day and for a one-hour blackout in the evening. The evening blackout was imposed during the time that State Radio and Television broadcast the news; its stations had already been charged by the opposition with distorting the news, and people had been invited to boycott them. The importance of the evening blackout was that it signaled to the entire nation that the shah had lost his grip on the bureaucratic system. The electrical shutdown was also a significant factor in paralyzing the economy.

Strikes by the employees of public and private banks intensified the country's already troubled financial system. People had been persuaded by the opposition to withdraw their money from the banks, and those who wanted to cooperate with the opposition had already done so. The strikes and disorders within the banking system now added another dimension to the problem: People feared that they might not have access to their accounts on the days they needed their money and, indeed, that keeping any money in the bank appeared to involve a high risk. As a result, the banking system became increasingly helpless, and this led to further disorders in the economy.

The strike by the employees of the National Oil Company weakened the shah's regime in two distinct ways. First, the sharp decline in oil exports not only jeopardized the main source of foreign exchange but also extended the crisis beyond the borders of the Iranian economy, for the shah's internal troubles were now the subject of discussion in the international financial community. Second, the strike caused a shortage of consumer fuels. The long lines in front of the gas stations and the high price of fuels on the black market not only increased the public's frustration but also amplified the feeling that the entire system was out of order.

Employees of the Plan and Budget Organization (PBO), who had not played any coordinating role in economic affairs for several years, had become the coordinators of strikes within all government agencies by mid-1978. The Employees' Association of the PBO hosted a series of antiregime lectures in the main PBO building and invited the employees of other government organizations to attend. In addition, many formal and informal meetings were held with employee representatives from other government agencies to discuss and coordinate the antiregime activities. The PBO's involvement in this respect had become so extensive by the fall of 1978 that Ayatollah Rouhollah Khomeini appointed Ali Akbar Moinfar as the national strike coordinator, an appointment that encouraged the PBO employees to intensify their efforts even further to unite government employees in their resistance against the shah. Late in 1978 the military government pinpointed the PBO as a center of unrest and attempted to break up its employees' so-called antiregime conspiracy, but this attempt, like many others the military government made, did not take a harsh form to alter the situation, and the PBO employees became even more confident of their ability to organize the resistance.

In sum, the government agency strikes that proved fatal to the regime were organized and well coordinated, and they were probably the first events in recent years to have given the government employees a sense of accomplishment. Khomeini effectively took control of the government while he was still in Paris. The agenda for government employees' activities arrived in the form of Khomeini's tapes or announcements on a regular basis, and the National Strike Committee (along with its coherent network) made sure that his orders were distributed widely and effectively.

The Breakdown of the System

Ayatollah Khomeini and his followers have ardently attempted to interpret the fall of the shah as being the result of a purely Islamic revolution. This has persuaded some analysts to search for the reasons for his fall in the context of Islamic and/or revolutionary movements. Despite all these efforts, however, it is clear that the cause of the shah's demise was neither a revolution nor an Islamic movement.

The Marxist theory of revolution refers to the consequences of the so-called class struggle in a society. From among the numerous views about the manner in which this class struggle takes place, Iran seems to fall into the category of neocolonialism, which is characterized by two features: (1) an imperialist exploitation exercised by economic—as opposed to political or military—domination, and (2) a comprador bourgeoisie acting as the ruling class through which imperialism operates.[8] (The comprador bourgeoisie consists of those who ultimately dominate the operations of the commercial, industrial, financial, agricultural, and bureaucratic sectors of the economy.)

According to this theory, the bureaucratic bourgeoisie exploits the masses by misuse of political positions and administrative corruption. As the economic role of the state expands, so the scope of the bureaucratic bourgeoisie expands. Part of the income acquired by this sector of society is spent on building luxury mansions and on purchasing luxury consumer goods; another part is invested in commerce, industry, and agriculture; and the rest is deposited in foreign and domestic banks, thus establishing an indirect partnership with other sectors of the bourgeoisie. The comprador bourgeoisie needs to be supported by the regime and, consequently, is forced to offer stocks to people in higher positions of the government. No state investment program exists that is not directly tied to the interests of the private sector. The end result of such capital investment is the concentration of wealth in the hands of the bourgeoisie and the improvement of the living standards of this special class.

Thus far, the explanation of trends and situations seems to fit the case of Iran fairly well. However, the final outcome predicted by this theory does not match the pattern of events in Iran. The theory of class struggle suggests that the bureaucratic bourgeoisie will continue to support the interest of other sectors of the comprador bourgeoisie, that there is a class unity between the bureaucratic and other sectors of the bourgeoisie, and it is their common interests, direct and indirect, that bring them together. This unity constitutes a front against the people, and the confrontation between this class and the working class will develop into a class struggle that will eventually lead to the defeat and elimination of the former group. This is, in fact, the point of deviation between the implications of the class struggle theory and the actual events that led to the fall of the shah.

As explained in the previous section, the so-called bourgeoisie—especially the bureaucratic group—were among those who initially led the movement against the shah. The economic incentives for such actions on the part of these groups were not very strong. As James Bill has explained, for the middle class there is an inherent tension between rule by absolute monarchy and control of its own destiny. The professional middle class of Iran had reached at least 13 percent of the total employed population,[9] and, as more and more Iranians acquired modern higher education (either at home or abroad), the class continued to swell in size. For a long time middle-class citizens tried to participate in the ruling of the country; however, they were alienated and their demands fell on deaf ears. Their opposition to the regime started several years before the demise of the shah and ranged from passive roles played in the administration of a system they despised and the denunciation of the government they thought was unresponsive to their needs to overt lectures and even armed struggles.

The second question that should be addressed is how "Islamic" the movement against the shah was. Two distinct aspects of this question can be examined. First, was there an Islamic economic system for which people arose? (This is, in fact, the economic interpretation of an Islamic movement.) Second, what was the role and position of the religious groups that were involved in the movement against the shah?

With regard to the people's expectations and desires to establish an Islamic economic system, prior to the fall of the shah there was no clear definition of the Islamic economic system. (Presently, there is a considerable amount of discussion regarding a definition for such a system.) In fact, people did not expect religious leaders to be involved in the administration of the country. Even Ayatollah Khomeini himself stated in September 1978 that the religious leaders would not administer the state or participate in the official government.

However, one cannot deny Khomeini's leadership in the role that the religious figures had in the movement against the shah. It has been noted that the basic reason for the acceptance of Khomeini's leadership by all opposition groups was their fear that if a complete solidarity were not preserved, the movement would have the same fate as that of 1953. The religious network also provided a ready-made informal organization in which opposition groups could unite their efforts against the regime.[10]

Nevertheless, after the fall of the shah there was a confrontation between liberalism and extremism. From this confrontation, a specific wing of the Islamic community[11] emerged as the winner of the political struggle for rule of the country. Therefore, the concept of Islamic government is more an outgrowth of the political consequences of the events that occurred after, rather than during, the fall of the shah.

The Establishment of the New Regime

After the fall of the shah, despite the intricate picture of Iran's situation convened by the media, it was not very difficult to reoperate the economy. Workers—especially government employees—were satisfied that the main problem, the dictatorship, had been eliminated. They were therefore enthusiastically ready to put all their forces back to work. The only requirement seemed to be a "let it go" signal, which the Bazargan cabinet was more than willing to give.

The initial settlement of the regime was actually quite smooth. The high-level authorities of the previous regime, as well as the owners and managers of some private-sector enterprises, had been removed, but workers and government employees had already become accustomed to living without them. Very soon, then, the basic wheels of the system started rolling again. The public sector became actively involved in social and economic affairs. Many government employees volunteered to go to villages and distant rural areas to complete tasks that could help the development of these areas. The private sector began to initiate business at an accelerating rate. In many factories, workers announced their willingness to bear additional work loads and to make any other sacrifices that could improve the efficiency of production and reduce the dependency of the country on foreign trade.

Surprisingly enough, the smooth functioning of the economy did not last more than a few weeks. Afterward, numerous conflicting trends started to emerge. The first significant conflict occurred within the Bazargan cabinet. The members of the cabinet were very soon divided into two groups: one with a more liberal attitude toward the management of the economy and the other with a tendency toward religious fundamentalism. In retrospect, the differences between the two groups seem insignificant as compared to the trends and tendencies that later developed. Nevertheless, at the time their differences affected their attitudes to the point that members of the two groups were hardly willing to communicate.

The head of PBO, Ali Akbar Moinfar, was a member (in fact the leader) of the fundamentalist wing. Later on (after the takeover by the Islamic Republic party) he became known as a liberal, but at the time of the Bazargan government he seemed to act as a fundamentalist. In any event, his approach to re-running the economy was restrictive. He did not intentionally choose this approach to stop the economy in its course of new operation, but being unfamiliar with economic concepts, he misunderstood the purpose of economic policies. An example of this misunderstanding, which significantly affected the performance of the economy, was his serious resistance to an increase in government expenditures at the time the economy urgently needed it. He was not trying to avoid inflation or to cope with unavailable resources. Rather, he believed that government money was the Moslems' Treasury and had to be spent in an Islamic way. Not having practical guidelines for spending the money in an Islamic way, the Plan and Budget Organization ended up imposing significant financial constraints on an economy that had started rolling just a few weeks earlier.

The second trend that blocked the operation of the economy was the conflict that emerged between the Bazargan cabinet and the Islamic fundamentalists (or those who appeared as Islamic fundamentalists), who were by far more extremist than Moinfar or other members of the Bazargan cabinet. They viewed the reoperation of the economy as the settlement of the system on its previous infrastructure, which they intended to change. The basic reasons behind this intention were given as anticapitalism, antiliberalism, anti-Westernism and pro-Sovietism. The impact of this new development on the economy was twofold. First, the Bazargan cabinet, which gradually became a symbol of a liberal, pro-Western government, tried to deny the procapitalism charge by nationalizing some of the large industrial companies and some insurance and banking institutions. Although the accomplishment was far less than what the fundamentalists wanted, a new trend was established. Limitations to private ownership were introduced, such as nationalization of medium-sized industries and companies and confiscation of "extra" housing units and noncultivated lands. As a result, the private sector hesitated to move ahead; instead it waited to find out more about the direction of infrastructural changes.

The second impact resulted from the intervention of Islamic fundamentalists in economic affairs. These interventions came in various forms—Bazargan referred to them as "government outside of government" or "too much intervention by individuals with no official responsibility."[12]

According to the figures published by the Central Bank of Iran, real GNP fell by 6 percent in 1978/79, 3.5 percent in 1979/80, and by more than 10 percent in 1980/81. The reasons for the decline in national production included labor problems, economic sanctions, the Iran-Iraq war, and so on, by and large the outcome of the conflicts between the political groups already discussed.

The decline in national production has affected all sectors of the economy. However, the industrial sector has suffered the most serious impact. It is estimated that the total production in this sector has been declining at a rate of 20 to 30 percent a year since the 1979 revolution.[13] The high rate of inflation remained a serious economic problem from 1979 through 1982. The official figures indicate the rate of price increase on food items ranged from 25 to 35 percent from 1979 to 1982. However, given the continuing shortages of basic food items and the imposition of rationing for most of these commodities, a strong black market has emerged in which the rate of price increase has been several times greater than the official indices. Unofficially, the rate of inflation on food items is reported to have been between 30 to 60 percent during those same four years.

Oil exports fell from the prerevolution level of more than 5 million barrels a day to around 3.4 million barrels a day after the revolution. The sharp decline in the volume of oil export did not reduce oil revenues in the same proportion, because the international price of oil had risen by more than 50 percent. The policy to cut down the oil export, favored by almost all political groups and decision makers, was a sound one. The lower level of oil export was sufficient to meet the foreign-exchange requirements of the country and, at the same time, to avoid the exhaustion of oil reserves at a rapid pace that had been set forth by the shah's regime.

In late 1980, oil exports fell to less than 1 million barrels a day. The sharp decline was due to the damages of the war with Iraq and, more significantly, to difficulties in marketing the oil because of the risk involved in loading the oil at Kharg Island. These difficulties forced the oil export even further down, to around 500,000 barrels a day. The situation was much improved by late 1982, when Iran could find new customers for its oil by discounting its price to between $27 to $29 a barrel (while the official OPEC price was $34 per barrel). In late 1982, the level of production was increased to around 3.2 million barrels a day, from which about 2.7 million barrels a day were exported.

The collapse of the OPEC meeting in January 1983 and the subsequent expectation of a price war among oil-exporting countries changed Iran's attitude toward cooperation with OPEC. In the London meeting held in March 1983, Iran did not play as hostile a role as it had played in previous meetings; since that time Iran has been considered to be one of the well-behaved members of OPEC.

Imports were decreased in the first and second years of the new regime. The reduction in imports was partly due to the stringent controls designed to keep out "undesirable" and "luxury" goods and partly due to the slowdown in industrial production (lower level of imports of capital and intermediate goods). During 1981 and 1982, imports started to rise again. The slowdown in industrial production was now feeding back into the system in terms of lower levels of production of consumer goods. The shortage of consumer goods and the rapid increase in imports were also related to the consequences of the Iran-Iraq war. The import partner-countries were Japan, West Germany, Spain, France, Italy, and Netherlands, with Japan and West Germany providing more than 40 percent of total imports.

Government expenditures fell rather sharply in the first year after the revolution and then picked up in 1980/81. The deficit in the government budget, which had begun in the final years of the shah's regime, persisted through 1980 and 1981 and drastically increased in 1981/82. The budget deficit and budget commitments came as a complete surprise to the authorities of the Islamic regime. For years they had thought that their country had enormous financial resources (which the shah and his associates were wasting) and that the economy could be managed by a small proportion of those resources. Now they were surprised to learn how many commitments the government had and how difficult it was to limit public expenditures. In any event, government deficits have been mostly financed through the banking system; this, of course, has contributed to the high rate of inflation.

The Search for an Islamic Economic System

Ever since Ayatollah Khomeini's regime took over the government, many of his supporters and associates have shown extreme enthusiasm in implementing an economic system characterized by Islamic laws. This is especially desirable if the regime wants to unite its action with its slogans of a non-Western, non-Eastern politico-economic system.

The search for an Islamic economic system is not a new endeavor. Many international scholars have spent considerable efforts in determining the practical guidelines of economic affairs within an Islamic framework of life. Unfortunately, the results have thus far been controversial, with little agreement about how an Islamic economy should be managed.

As explained by M. Abdul-Rauf,[14] one of the relevant values that delineates the economic framework prescribed in Islam is complete commitment to God, the creator and provider of all ecological resources. Wealth is a favor from God, which should be sensibly treated, not abused, destroyed, wasted, or left idle. Although people are created equal, and no one may claim inherent merit over another, they are created with different talents and are bound to attain different degrees of success. It is "the man's duty to accept his fortune, not to despair or be resentful, although he should struggle as hard as he can for his best interest."[15]

Thus far the description may sound like a free-market system. However, the individual's possessiveness and concern for satisfying personal needs have to harmonize with obligations to society. Abdul-Rauf went on to say ". . . a Muslim is not to let his neighbor smell his cooking without letting him share it, nor should he let his children play outside with new toys unless he has presented his neighbor's children with similar toys."[16]

The Islamic welfare economy is not based upon increasing the aggregate welfare of the community through encouragement of the individual to maximize his or her own interest and to be indifferent to the interests of others. Instead, it is based upon the "bond of universal brotherhood in which the individual, in seeking to benefit himself, avoids malevolence to another."[17] Every Moslem is obligated to the duty of giving alms when they are collected by the religious leaders to be used to help the needy. Furthermore, usury and earning without effort are prohibited, and "labor" and "work" are identical.

This new description resembles that of the socialist system. Combining this description with the aforementioned implications of free-market economy, we may be inclined to believe that an Islamic economic system should be one type of the so-called mixed economies in which elements of a free-market system and socialism would interact to bring about a system more equitable than capitalism and more efficient than socialism. It is, however, not possible to arrive at an answer so easily. According to Islamic beliefs, "Resources are given in abundance and scarcity is caused by human limitations. The economic problem, in the Islamic culture milieu, is not scarcity of commodities nor lack of efficient organization of the means and sources of production and distribution. Rather the problem lies with man and human greed."[18]

In this way, Islamic economics, or at least some of the system's advocates, rejects "the classical and marxist economics both of which are based on the premises of scarcity of resources."[19] Whether or not the contemporary economics is rejected by Islam, the fact remains that the present state of the art of planning and development is far from being capable of (or suitable for) providing policy guidelines *based* on "dealing with the problem of human greed."

On the practical side, the Islamic Republic of Iran asserts that its constitution is based on the Islamic system and represents the "Government of God." This constitution was prepared by an Assembly of Experts in the fall of 1979 and then ratified in a referendum held on December 2–3, 1979.[20] The constitution devotes several sections to the economic affairs of the country. It points out that economic measures such as wealth and income are not, by themselves, important in an Islamic system:

> In strengthening the economic structures, the basis is the people's need for growth and perfection, not anything else in the economic order such as concentration of wealth and profiteering. In materialistic schools the economy is its own goal and, for this reason, in cycles of growth, the economy is a factor of destruction, corruption, and decay. However, in Islam, the economy is a means intended to be a part of the work of improvement—and the means cannot become the end.

> From this viewpoint, the Islamic economic program is to provide a suitable field for creativity of human diversity and, in this respect, provide opportunities to create work for all persons and to satisfy the need to perpetuate the movement to perfection according to Islamic rule.[21]

Principle 44 of the constitution states that the economic system of the Islamic Republic consists of three sectors: governmental, cooperative, and private, with systematic and sound planning. The wording of the constitution seems to emphasize the public sector as the main body of the economic system: The government sector consists of "all major industries, foreign trade, major mines, banking, insurance, power production, dams and major water-carrying networks, radio and television, postal, telegraph and telephone system, air, sea, land and railroad transportation and others similar to the above, which in the form of public ownership are at the disposal of the government." Thus far, the description of public sector seems by and large to advocate a socialist system. This is especially true if we add in the welfare aspects of the economy, according to which the government is responsible for providing free education (through high school and higher education within acceptable limits); for securing basic needs such as housing, nourishment, clothing, hygiene, and medical care; and for "establishing a suitable environment for all to start a family." In addition, the government is to organize the economic structure so that individuals can exert their professional effort and, at the same time, have the "opportunity and enough energy for intellectual, political and social self-improvement and an active participation in the leadership of the country as well as to improve skills and demonstrate creativity."

The description of the cooperative sector remains vague. It "establishes and assigns the cooperative companies and organizations which have been created in cities and villages in accordance with Islamic regulations." The only additional explanation in this respect is that government should provide this sector with interest-free loans and "other legitimate means" to prevent the concentration of wealth in the possession of specific individuals or groups.

The description of the private sector sounds like a residual part of the economy. It consists of "those portions of agriculture, animal husbandry, industry, trade and services which supplement the activities of the government and cooperative sectors." The limitations to the private-sector activities are, further, that "no one may, because he is the owner of a particular type of business, deprive others of the opportunity to do the same job." However, the main description comes in Principle 47: "Personal property obtained through legitimate means is honored. The details for this will be determined by law." This creates (as we will discuss later in this chapter) the main dilemma for economic planners and policymakers alike. If personal property is honored, how can government prevent the accumulation of wealth? Where and in which sectors can a private investor use capital? How can government limit the expansion of a private enterprise? The Islamic constitution leaves these questions (and many others) to be answered by the legislators. The legislators, on the other hand, have thus far not been able to arrive at a mechanism through which government can operate the economy while simultaneously honoring private ownership of the means of production and limiting "profiteering."

In regard to long-term strategies, the constitution dictates emphasis on "increased agricultural, animal and industrial production in order to secure public needs and bring the country to a self-sufficient state and rid it of dependency." Furthermore, Principle 48 of the constitution emphasizes more harmonious regional development, stating:

> There should be no discrimination with regard to benefits to be gained from the use of natural resources, the utilization of public funds on the provincial level, and the distribution of economic activities among the provinces and various regions of the country. This is so that every region will have within its reach capital and opportunity to fulfill its needs and develop its skills.

New Efforts on Economic Planning

Economic planning became a controversial issue after the revolution. First, during the first year after the revolution, the government seemed to be too busy settling down and coping with the problems of the transitional stage. The annual budget for that year was prepared on a piecemeal basis. Within the Plan and Budget Organization, there was serious confusion with regard to the real mission of the PBO: Many people were not clear as to whether the Islamic system would need a planning machinery.

Second, the question of private ownership and its status within the framework of an Islamic economic system presented the most imperative obstacle to economic planning. This problem persisted until 1982; at that point the planners literally decided to ignore it, in order to move forward toward development of some planning mechanism. However, from 1979 to 1982 it was the most controversial issue in the discussions on economic planning. Within the PBO, as within the whole country, there were two groups: One wished to interpret Islamic economics as a means of abolishing private ownership of factors of production, the other emphasized the respect that Islam has for private property. It was hoped that the constitution would solve the problem. The constitution was prepared by the end of 1979, but it left the same question for the parliament to answer. The details of private ownership were then supposed to be determined by law. The parliament acted on some legislation (the so-called Class C bill that would limit the ownership of land under special circumstances), but it could not provide an overall answer to how the limitations to private ownership should be implemented.

Third, all the attempts to design a planning system were directly affected by the political confrontations that took place in 1980 and 1981. The conflicts between the Islamic Republican Party and other political groups were also present in the Plan and Budget Organization. Every few months a new group was formed to design the planning system. By the time that this group could get a feel for the real problems, a change in the political environment would lead to the removal of that group and emergence of a new one. The new group would now be considered to be more Islamic, but after a while not Islamic enough. In this way, different groups and individuals were eliminated and alienated as the Islamic Republic Party pursued its monopolistic attitude.

Fourth, the design of the planning system was impaired by the lack or insufficiency of planning skills and expertise. Employees of the PBO had hardly done any real planning in the past, so they did not know much about designing a planning system. The problem became more serious as the alienation and the passive attitude were spread among the employees of the PBO. This was, of course, related to the more global events in the country. From the very early days of the Islamic regime, the religious leaders chose to silence the intellectual community by attacking its dignity and credibility. The Islamic regime, like the previous regime, had realized that it was very difficult to bring about the political and social conditions that satisfy the intellectuals. The solution was to keep them silent. However, rather than the shah's "buying them out" policy, the Islamic republic chose a "shutting them up" strategy. The net accomplishment was the same. The intellectual community and its followers, the members of the bureaucratic system, became indifferent with respect to the problems of the government and passive in terms of cooperation with the regime. The Islamic regime did not seem to have any concern for this lack of cooperation. Many of the newcomers were too ignorant to realize how much they did not know. However, since 1983 the Islamic regime seems to have realized its problem in this respect and has relaxed some of the extreme social and political conditions (through the so-called eight commands of Ayatollah Khomeini announced in January 1983). Several religious leaders have invited the educated people who left the country to return to Iran.[22]

Despite all the foregoing problems, in January 1982 the Plan and Budget Organization submitted a document entitled "The Planning System" to the Economic Council. The system was approved by the council and was then (at least theoretically) put into practice. This document represented a turning point in the politico-economic affairs of the country. Its importance lay not in its presentation of the planning system per se, but in the change of approach and attitude. In the previous five years the insistence of Khomeini's regime on labeling everything "Islamic" had spread quite widely. One could hardly find a single paragraph in administrative communications that did not use the term *Islamic* to describe or justify something. Surprisingly, however, "The Planning System" not only did not carry the term *Islamic* as a delineator, but avoided using this term in its entire text. The subjects of Islamic economics and Islamic economic system were left out and did not play any role in determining the planning system. Instead, the planning system was viewed as "a machinery which produces the development plan." The system was designed so that "there is a flow of information from bottom to top and from top to down."

The 1982 planning system encompasses the required procedures to undertake the following tasks: (1) preparation of a long-term (20-year) plan that determines the overall course of economic development; (2) preparation of a medium-term (5 year) plan within the framework of the long-term plan; (3) preparation of sectoral plans within the framework of the medium-term plan; (4) determination of national projects within the framework of the sectoral plans; and (5) preparation of regional plans and determination of regional projects within the framework of the medium-term plan and the sectoral plans.

The planning system is based on a centralized decision-making process with regard to the allocation of resources and a decentralized decision-making process with respect to the implementation of the plan. The central authorities are to appraise the availability of resources and, with the help of regional authorities, determine the sectoral and regional allocation of these resources. However, allocation of the regional budget to various development projects remains at the discretion of the regional authorities, given that they are to take account of sectoral guidelines. The system explicitly recognizes that a realistic plan for any region can only be prepared by those who work (as planner or in other related professions) in that region. Furthermore, it is hoped that the preparation of a regional plan by the residents of that region will persuade a more effective public participation in the planning affairs.

The organization of planning is shown in Figure 5.1. The chart (which is translated from the same chart in "The Planning System") is the only page of "The Planning System" that has a flavor of the Islamic regime. The flavor is, of course, indicated by the first box (the leader). At the present time, this refers to Ayatollah Khomeini. However, interestingly enough, the document starts the description of the planning process at the second box (parliament) and does not mention a single word about the role of the leader. Further, Figure 5.2 (which is again the translated version of a chart included in the document) shows that the leader does not play any actual role in the planning process.

In any event, according to the new planning system, each development plan is prepared through the following steps:

1. Parliament and the Council of Ministers are responsible for determining the socioeconomic targets and overall development strategies. To help them choose the appropriate targets, a group of PBO experts studies various plan alternatives and submits the results to a committee consisting of PBO experts, representatives of parliament, analysts from universities, and other organizations that may be involved. After this committee approves the proposed plan, it is submitted to the Economic Council. If the plan is approved by the council, it is then sent to the Council of Ministers. Finally, one or several alternatives are chosen and submitted to Parliament for final approval.

2. The flow of information with regard to economic needs and possibilities works from bottom to top: It starts at the village level and then goes through the town and city levels to reach the county level. The information is analyzed and the framework of the regional plan, as well as a listing of major projects, is prepared. In doing this, the county authorities take account of sectoral and regional guidelines that have already been conveyed from the Central authorities. The proposed regional plan is then sent to the PBO and the corresponding ministries. The planning council of each ministry analyzes and modifies the regional plans to arrive at an acceptable sectoral plan. The sectoral plan (with a regional distribution) is submitted to the Plan and Budget Organization. At any stage in the above process, the basic information can be sent to the Statistical Center of Iran where it is maintained for public use.

3. The Plan and Budget Organization analyzes the sectoral regional plans and consolidates them into a unified plan consistent with the development targets and guidelines issued by the Council of Ministers and Parliament. This unified plan should contain the sectoral distribution of resources, the growth rate of each sector, imports and exports, government receipts and expenditures, and so on.

4. The development plan is then sent to the Council of Ministers and Parliament for the final approval. The communication among the

Figure 5.1 Organization of Planning in the Islamic Republic. Translated from chart in "The Planning System" (Tehran: Plan and Budget Organization, 1982).

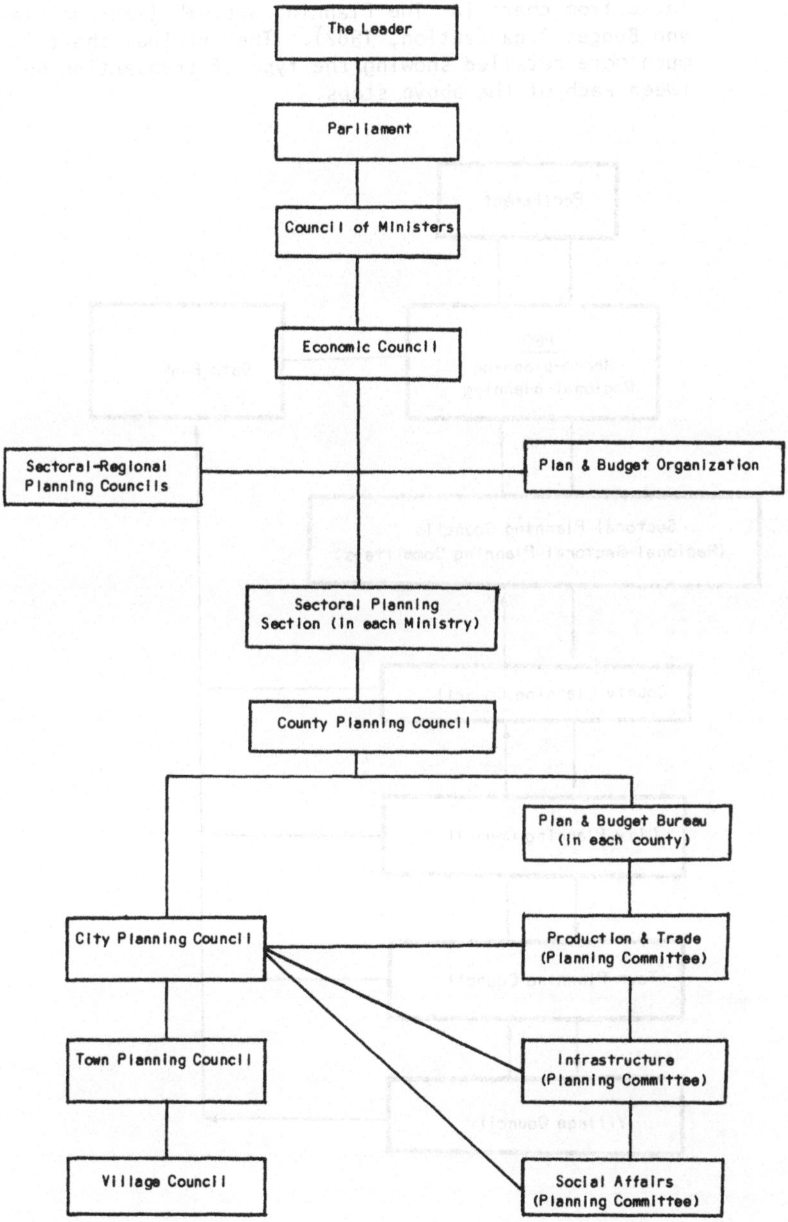

Figure 5.2 Institution of Planning in the Islamic Republic. Translated from chart in "The Planning System" (Tehran: Plan and Budget Organization, 1982). The original chart is much more detailed showing the type of transaction between each of the above steps.

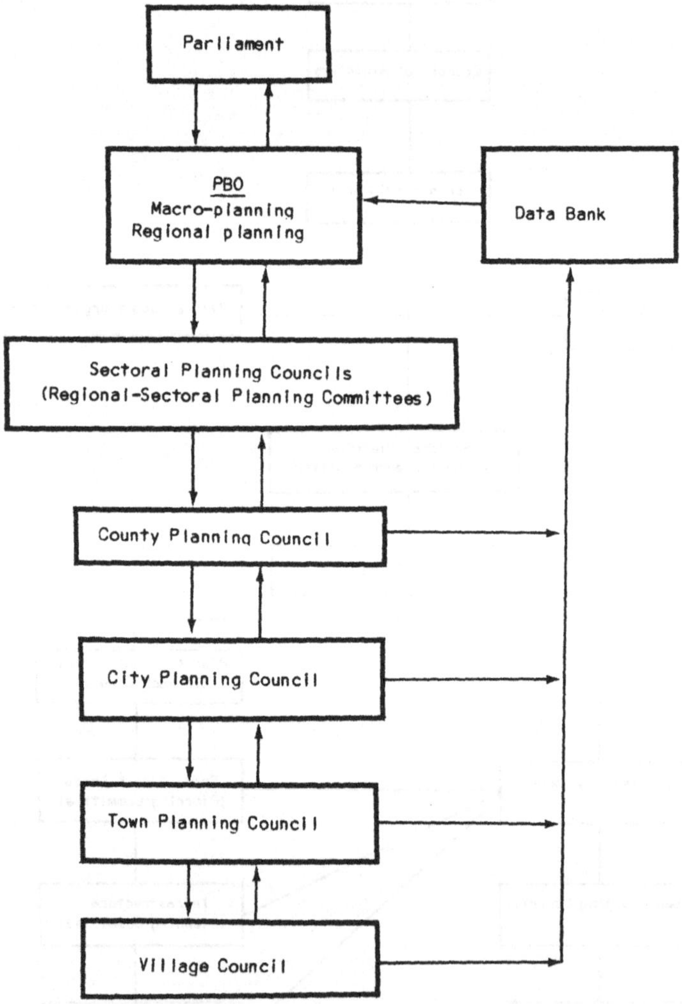

PBO, the Council of Ministers, and Parliament continues, and the plan is modified until it is acceptable to the parliament.

5. Parliament and the Council of Ministers then communicate the approved plan to the PBO.

6. The PBO notifies the regional and sectoral planning bureaus of PBO of the plan's global trends, such as sectoral growth rates and sectoral allocation of resources.

7. The regional planning section, with the cooperation of sectoral planning bureaus, then proposes the regional distribution of each sector's development budget.

8. The Regional Planning Council utilizes the proposal along with other information with regard to the natural-resource potentials and needs of regions to formulate a detailed plan consisting of development projects in each sector and region. It then announces this plan to the Planning Council of each *ostan* (county).

9. The County Planning Council uses a similar procedure to divide the budget among cities. The City Planning Council then distributes the development budget among towns; they, in turn, divide their share among small towns and villages.

"The Planning System" explicitly recognizes that planning techniques and procedures are never perfect and that they should be improved continuously. To this end, the document suggests the establishment of a bureau to study these techniques and procedures on a regular basis and to propose the required changes and modifications to improve the efficiency of the planning system.

Although the implementation of the planning system has not yet been completed, the prospects for a successful planning exercise are relatively bright. The initial design for the system seems to follow the ideas proposed by PBO personnel in the past. Indeed, the present planning system resembles, in many respects, the top-down, bottom-up procedures that had been proposed just before the fall of the shah. However, it remains to be seen whether this time the planning effort will accomplish its mission or whether, as in the past trials, it will face political obstacles and barriers.

Conclusion

The issues of planning and a planning system have been surrounded by a considerable amount of confusion and controversy since the revolution of February 1979. These have been of two distinct types: those arising from the disorders of the past revolutionary period and those related to such fundamental questions as the structure of an Islamic economic system and especially the status of private ownership of factors of production. Added to these difficulties are the country's political rivalry and the impact that has on planning efforts.

Although it is too soon to make any judgment with regard to the effectiveness of economic planning under the present regime, it seems that some fundamental problems have been resolved. The issue of Islamic economics has been dropped for the present time, and a mixed economic system has been adopted. The initial design of the planning system is sound and feasible. The establishment of the institutions required to implement this plan will, of course, be a real challenge to the Islamic regime, but it still seems achievable. However, the crucial determinant of the planning system's success is the political support it must have. At the present time the support is evident, but will it still be available when the implementation of the planning system begins to limit the personal power of policymakers? Only time will supply the answer!

Notes

1. Robert Looney, *Economic Origins of the Iranian Revolution* (New York: Pergamon Press, 1982).
2. A. Saikal, *The Rise and Fall of the Shah* (Princeton: Princeton University Press, 1980).
3. R. K. Ramazani, "Who Lost America? The Case of Iran," *Middle East Journal* 36, no. 1 (1982).
4. S. Akhavi, *Religion and Politics in Contemporary Iran: Clergy-State Relations in the Pahlavi Period* (New York: State University of New York Press, 1980).
5. Amir Taheri, "Public Discontents," *Kayhan International,* July 13, 1978.
6. J. A. Bill, "Iran and the Crisis of 78," *Foreign Affairs* 57, no. 2 (1978).
7. M. R. Friedman and A. Schwartz, *A Monetary History of the United States* (New York: The National Bureau of Economic Research, 1963), p. 78.
8. Discussed in B. Jazani, *The Socio-Economic Analysis of a Dependent Capitalist State* (Tehran: Organization of the Iranian Fedaei Guerillas, 1973).
9. Bill, "Iran and the Crisis of 1978," p. 323.
10. J. A. Bill, "Power and Religion in Revolutionary Iran," *The Middle East Journal* 36, no. 1 (1982), p. 22.
11. It should be noted that the Islamic community is not identical with the group presently ruling the Islamic Republic. There has been a vast screening of religious figures, at all levels, to exclude those with moderate views regarding the political system.
12. In fact, Bazargan (who probably did not know that Khomeini was going to be the ultimate authority in almost every affair of the country) complained on several occasions about Khomeini's intervention in government affairs.
13. Plan and Budget Organization, *Annual Report on the Performance of the Economy: 1981–1982* (Tehran: Plan and Budget Organization, 1982).

14. M. Abdul-Rauf, *The Islamic Doctrine of Economics and Contemporary Economic Thought* (Washington: American Enterprise Institute, 1979).

15. Ibid., p. 5.

16. Ibid., p. 23.

17. M. Abdul-Rauf, *The Islamic Doctrine of Economics and Contemporary Economic Thought,* p. 2.

18. Ibid., p. 12.

19. A. H. Bani-Sadr, *Divinely Integrated Economics* (Tehran: 1977).

20. For an English translation of this document, see R. K. Ramazani, "The Constitution of the Islamic Republic of Iran," *Middle East Journal* 34, no. 2 (1980), pp. 182–196.

21. Islamic Republic of Iran, *The Constitution of Islamic Republic,* section 1, "Economy, a Means Not an End." The remaining quotations in this section are from the constitution (author's copy in Farsi).

22. It is true that more than two million people (this is the official figure and does not include illegal exits) have left the country. It is also true that among these people, there have been a large number of educated individuals. However, the problem of the Islamic regime is its inability to gain the cooperation of those who are in the country, not the high number of people leaving the country.

6
The Future of Planning in Iran

Considering the widely expanded role of the public sector in the Iranian economy and the short- and medium-term irreversibility of this role, it is hard to believe that the economy can be managed without a capable planning system no matter who takes power in the country. That is, the need for a well-designed planning system has been and will be independent of the political struggles and takeovers. It is, in fact, expected that the planning body will remain, at least theoretically, an important part of the bureaucratic system during the remaining years of this decade. However, the feasibility and efficiency of the planning system is very much related to the prevalent political environment. Thus, the future prospects for economic planning should be explored by studying the alternative political trends and the impact that each trend would have on planning efforts and accomplishments.

Our discussion of the political trends (in relation to planning) will concentrate on two questions: Should the Islamic regime remain in power, what will be the likely attitudes toward economic planning? What viable alternatives to the Islamic regime exist and what will be the planning prospects under each of these alternatives?

The Future of Planning Under the Islamic Regime

Any close observer of the Islamic regime would notice that the management system of the present regime entails a significant fallacy of composition. The analysis of future prospects is affected by the manner in which the analyst chooses to explain this phenomenon. The fallacy emerges from a paradox between the micro- and macroaspects of the country's management system. At the microlevel—i.e., the level of individual decisions and decision makers—one observes that authorities of the regime are unusually incompetent and that their decisions are made in a strikingly naive manner. Consequently, one is led to believe that the regime will collapse or will explode the country and itself in a matter of months. On the other hand, when one studies the macrolevel—the overall trends of political, social, and economic events—one sees that the system has been moving along a relatively well-designed path. This is probably the main reason for difference of opinions about the strength and stability of the Khomeini regime.

Those who have lived in Iran in the recent past and who have observed the organization of the regime at a microlevel view the Khomeini regime as an incapable autocracy that is resorting to all possible means to stay in power for a few more days. They consequently believe that the present regime is destined to fall after Khomeini's death. On the other hand, analysts who have observed the events from outside the country are more impressed by the overall trends. They thus have the opinion that the Khomeini regime is sufficiently strong and stable to survive the present troubles and that, in a relatively short period of time, the regime will have the momentum and solidarity to survive after Khomeini. It is certainly too soon to make any judgment as to which group is right; however, studying the overall pattern is useful for developing some ideas about future possibilities.

At present, the question of private ownership of means of production has not been thoroughly answered. Many interpretations of the Islamic system view private ownership as "respectful." Authorities of the Islamic regime are still in two wings, one supporting and the other opposing the further limitation of private ownership. Nevertheless, one point is clear. The discouragement of private business, along with the expansion of the rationing system, has eliminated many elements of the free-market network and has pushed the economy toward a situation that cannot be handled except through a centrally planned system. This is the basic reason (or justification) why pro-Soviet leftists support the Khomeini regime. To them, Khomeini's notion of oppressed people's government is equivalent to the Marxist concept of dictatorship of the proletariat. Thus, they do not see any major difference between Khomeini's ideology and their own. Furthermore, they believe (although they are not willing to express it publicly) that religion is a superstructural phenomenon that will fade away over time, while the society's infrastructure, which they believe is being built according to socialist norms, will remain effective in determining the future social, political, and economic events. Accordingly, these leftist groups and their Soviet supporters are hopeful that the continuation of present trends will eventually lead to the establishment of a socialist regime.

The assumption that the economic system is moving toward socialism is, of course, subject to considerable uncertainty. Many authorities within the Islamic regime are now resisting quite seriously any laws or regulations

Figure 6.1 Liberalist Attitudes of Major Political Groups. JAMA is the Iranian Moslem Association; Mojahedin refers to the People's Mojahedin Organization.

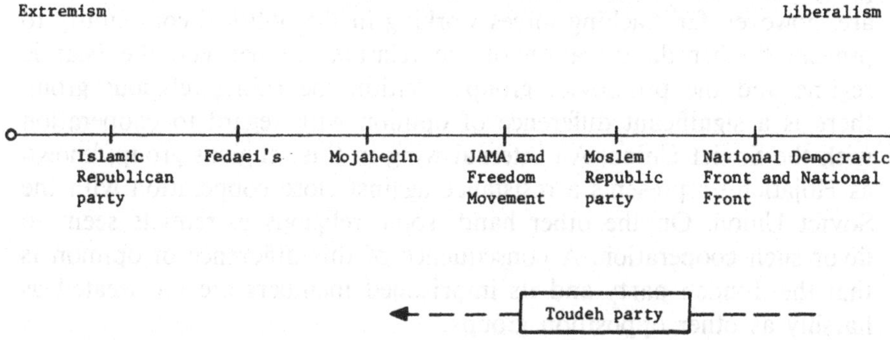

that discourage the activities of the private sector. A paramount example of this resistance is, of course, the case of the Class C bill on land ownership. This bill, as initially prepared by some radical members of the parliament, imposed a ceiling on the ownership of land by each individual to three or two "ordinary" pieces of land, depending on whether the owner worked on the land. By the time the bill passed in Parliament, it contained numerous exemptions so that many wealthy landowners could keep their land simply by doing some paperwork to deal with formalities. Then the Guardian Council pronounced the bill to be non-Islamic and thus invalid.

A very important event in relation to the struggles within the Islamic regime over the question of private ownership was the outlawing of the pro-Soviet Toudeh party. To appreciate the significance of this event with regard to the politico-economic trends, we must look back to the process of eliminating political groups that the Islamic regime has pursued in a systematic manner.

Figure 6.1 shows the approximate position of significant political parties in a spectrum of liberalism and extremism. The elimination started with the most liberal parties, the National Democratic Front and the National Front. The position of the Toudeh party was inconstant. In the early days after the fall of the shah, the Toudeh party supported Bazargan. However, when the Bazargan cabinet began to weaken, the Toudeh party harshly attacked Bazargan and his associates. It was clear that the Toudeh party opposed liberals, but it always chose its strategy to suit the prevailing conditions of the nation. Finally, the elimination process reached a last stage. The two finalists were the Islamic Republic party and the pro-Soviet leftists (Toudeh party and Fedaeis).

There have been some serious confrontations between the ruling religious groups and the pro-Soviet Toudeh party. In January 1983 more than twenty Toudeh leaders were arrested and imprisoned on charges that they were spying for the Eastern bloc. In May 1983 the Toudeh party was outlawed, and hundreds of its members were arrested. There are, however, far-reaching forces working in the political community to prevent further deterioration of the relationship between the Islamic regime and the pro-Soviet groups: Within the ruling religious group there is a significant difference of opinion with regard to cooperation with the Soviet Union. An internal wing in this religious group, known as Hojatieh,[1] represents a resistance against close cooperation with the Soviet Union. On the other hand, some religious extremists seem to favor such cooperation. A consequence of this difference of opinion is that the Toudeh party and its imprisoned members are not treated as harshly as other opposition groups.

Although further inclination of the Islamic regime toward the Soviet Union would promote the role of economic planning, the future position of the Islamic regime with regard to economic planning seems to be clear. As explained in the preceding chapter, the role of planning within the framework of a mixed economy has been largely recognized, and the political struggles within the ruling group are not likely to alter this recognition.

Economic Positions of the Opposition Groups

The presence of opposition groups and their economic stands will normally impact the economic system in two distinct manners. First, the present regime may actually adopt some of these stands in order to soften the opposition or to decrease the attractiveness of the opposition groups' positions to the people. Second, the opposition groups may actually take over the government in the future and implement their economic positions. The appraisal of the future prospects for economic planning in Iran would then require an understanding of the economic positions of the major opposition groups.

The number of opposition groups is presently so large that we cannot even briefly cover their views in this short section. However, what makes the task somewhat easier is that we are only concerned with the economic positions of these groups and do not need to discuss the details of their political activities.

The present opposition groups can be classified into the following categories: (1) leftist groups, (2) liberals pursuing a democratic republican regime, (3) promonarchy groups, and (4) Islamic groups. The groups in the first three categories of this rather vague list have clear economic positions but, at the present time, do not have much prospect for being viable alternatives to the Khomeini regime. On the other hand, the groups in the fourth category have a less clearly defined stand with regard to the economic system they purport to implement but are much stronger in terms of their political power and organization. Thus, for our purpose—discussing the economic position of the opposition in relation to future prospects for economic planning in Iran—it is more essential to discuss the direct and indirect implications that can be made with regard to the economic stand of the fourth group.

Among the Islamic groups, the People's Mojahedin Organization (PMOI) is by far the strongest opposition group, which also makes it the most viable alternative to the Islamic Republic of Ayatollah Khomeini. This organization was founded by Ali-Asghar Badi-zadegan, Mohammad Hanif-nezhad, and Saeed Mohsen in 1965. The initial goal for the formation of the organization was to find a proper answer to the following question: "When the struggle against imperialism of so many peoples around the world has ended in victory, or at least come close to the final triumph, how is it that our country, with all its striving and struggle, is still caught in the thrall of imperialism and reaction?"[2] This was, of course, a question related to the defeat of the opposition movement in 1963.

The founders of PMOI arrived at the following conclusions in their assessment of the struggles in the past:

- The principal factor in the defeats they had incurred in struggles was patently not the lack of readiness on the part of masses of people; it was the absence of conducive subjective conditions—primarily, the lack of qualified leadership.
- As the conditions for the struggle became more and more complex, the leadership did not demonstrate the ability to adapt to the complexity of the situation. Thus, the methods and modes of struggle had not been compatible with the social situation. In this respect, the founders of PMOI determined that armed struggle was the necessary mode for this stage of the revolution.
- The struggle fundamentally lacked appropriate revolutionary organization.
- The struggle—particularly the leadership—had not been professional.
- The struggle had not been approached as a "science with its own body of knowledge and methods."
- The struggle had not had an ideological orientation.

In response to the deficiencies of previous struggles, Badi-zadegan, Hanif-nezhad, and Mohsen formed PMOI. Later on it went through various ups and downs both from the point of view of ideology development and of armed struggle.[3]

The study of these ups and downs would certainly provide a historical perspective of the organization. However, for our discussion we will limit ourselves to reviewing the present ideology and strategy of PMOI. The ideology of PMOI is:

> Islam, based on the Towhidi (Divinely integrated) world view, as the guide to leading the society to the complete obliteration of exploitation and the establishment of the Towhidi system, for this ideology, in any historical situation, rests on the most deprived (in Qoranic terms: the "abased") social classes and the most progressive forces which, under the present conditions of Iranian society, the workers and their allies, the peasants, are the proper representatives thereof. . . . The PMOI, believing in the total elimination of exploitation of man by man on all levels and in every dimension through the obliteration of class distinctions, will carry on its struggle until the Towhidi classless society is brought into being.[4]

During the early months of the Islamic regime, PMOI presented a supportive and generally active role in political affairs. The members and supporters (or sympathizers) of the organization, though believing in Ayatollah Mahmoud Taleghani as their true religious leader, defended the Islamic regime of Ayatollah Khomeini. However, this friendship did not last long. There were several fundamental reasons for the fracture of this amity. First, the emerging Islamic Republic party (IRP), which had successfully and rather easily eliminated other political groups, viewed PMOI as the main political rival. PMOI offered the same Islamic sentiment (which appeared to be an attractive feature and prerequisite for political acceptability at the time) as the IRP did. In addition, the PMOI had been established for more than a decade and had a history of armed struggle against the shah's regime. The initial attacks by IRP on PMOI took the form of increasing crackdowns on PMOI's sale of literature and its meetings; these crackdowns were often carried on by a group called Hezbollahi (God's party). At the beginning, IRP did not admit that this latter group was part of the IRP operation. However, later on, as IRP took over the government, Hezbollahi brothers were recognized as an important wing of IRP with a significant role in saving the revolution.

Second, the vast base of PMOI's political activities and its increasing popularity among the younger generation had become an important concern to the Islamic regime. PMOI had penetrated almost all universities, colleges, and high schools. Its educational classes (in both ideology and military training) were widely attended, and its relatively large number of publications were extensively circulated. The number of PMOI supporters and sympathizers in the private and public organizations increased rapidly. In short, the characteristics of PMOI's activities and prospects were so promising as to create great concern to any other regime in power.

The first overt conflict between PMOI and the Khomeini regime occurred in the summer of 1979, when PMOI questioned the legitimacy of the new constitution. Its objection to the process of preparing the constitution went so far as to have its members boycott the referendum set up in December 1979 for the approval of the new constitution by the people.

In the subsequent presidential election, the PMOI candidate, Massood Rajavi, was eliminated by the Khomeini regime. Thus the conflict between the regime and PMOI became increasingly visible. This emerging trend coincided with the widening gap between Bani-Sadr's group and the Islamic Republican party. PMOI gradually joined Bani-Sadr's supporters and became the strongest base for Bani-Sadr's popularity within the younger generation.

In June 1981, as Bani-Sadr was being removed from the presidency, a series of violent clashes took place between PMOI supporters and the Khomeini regime. That was a new turning point in the conflict. Since that time, both sides have turned to militant acts in order to deal with the conflict. On June 28, 1981, PMOI launched a major frontal assault on the ruling Islamic Republic party. An explosion in the Tehran headquarters of the IRP killed seventy-two persons, including Ayatollah Beheshti, leader of the IRP. In response, the regime decided to eliminate PMOI. Thousands of PMOI members and supporters were executed.

After Bani-Sadr's ouster and his escape to France, PMOI and Bani-Sadr announced the formation of the National Council of Resistance. The council then announced its program for the establishment of the Democratic Islamic Republic of Iran after the fall of the Khomeini regime. A discussion of this program should provide some general understanding of how a possible takeover by PMOI would change the political and economic system of Iran. According to this program, after the fall of the Khomeini regime a provisional government would take charge of the "transition of sovereignty to the people of Iran." In this provisional government, the leader of PMOI would serve as the prime minister and Bani-Sadr would act as the president of the country. Within a six-month period, the National Legislative and Constituent Assembly would be formed, and the provisional government would resign. The assembly would then have a maximum of two years to compile a constitution and to determine the new republic's system. During this period, the assembly would also assume the duties of preparation of legislation needed for running the current affairs of the country, appointment of a government that would undertake the administration of the country's affairs following the resignation of the provisional government, and supervision of the administration of the country's affairs.

After the two-year period, the new constitution would be composed and all authorities, institutions, and powers of the transitional period would become null and void. The outline of the provisional government's program is as follows:[5]

- Achievement of popular sovereignty through a legitimate and national resistance (to recognize the rights of the people in decision making and self-determination).
- Following the historic objectives of the provisional government and the real path of unity. That is, linking the Iranian nation's past struggle against diverse forms of despotism, colonialism, and exploitation to its promising and constructive future.
- Salvation of genuine, progressive, national, and patriotic values.
- Emphasis on the national, democratic, antiimperialist contents of the revolution.
- Formal recognition of the content and features of the revolution aimed at radically changing the despotic, colonial, and exploitative culture and relations in order to, in the view of devout Moslems, lead to real unity and Towhid (divine integration).
- Establishment of a guarantee for the victory of the revolution and against retrogression by total annihilation of repression and exploitation and reliance on the impoverished Iranian workers and peasants.
- Conducting the nation's affairs through a council system that would gradually be expanded into all spheres and administrative organizations of the country.
- Refutation of the unilateral capitalist concept and interpretation of growth. The program views growth as the interaction of economics with freedom, culture, and human deed.
- Unity of program and action.

Thus far, the program does not provide much information about the economic objectives of the provisional government. However, in chapter 3 of the program, where articles of the program are described, there are a few hints about the economic objectives. In explaining the meaning of independence, the program describes its policy as: "Terminating all subsequent imperialist relationships . . . to prevent economic dependency; exercising national sovereignty over all natural resources and national wealth; withdrawing from a monoculture economy and a budget which relies only on oil as a source of revenue . . . ; nationalizing foreign trade . . . ; giving priority to agriculture; and revitalizing national industries. . . .[6] At the same time the program emphasizes that "Independence and hostility against imperialism do not mean enmity towards industrial countries in their historical, economic, technical, artistic and cultural totality."[7] Also of interest is the following: "The provisional government accepts domestic investments, as well as private and personal property, provided that they do not develop boundless dimensions, dependent and comprador tendencies; and do not paralyze the socioeconomic growth of society. . . . Unchecked liberalism by giving ground to compradorism leads to a new politico-economic dependency."[8]

This is, in fact, where the provisional government's program falls into the same trap as the Khomeini regime's economic system. After private ownership of factors of production is allowed, it becomes quite difficult to implement policies that keep this ownership within restricted dimensions. As discussed in the previous sections, this dichotomy is generally observed in Islamic views of the economic system. They are usually bound to respect the private ownership of capital and at the same time are motivated to contend against "the exploitation of man by man." This philosophy then leads to contradictory policies, adding to the instabilities of the economic system.

Still on the economic side, the program includes a long list of promises for workers and peasants. Both in the agricultural sector and in the industrial sector, workers will be relieved of all government deductions such as taxes and insurance payments. In addition, they will enjoy housing, transportation, and sanitation facilities (presumably subsidized by the government), and their children will be provided with nurseries, kindergarten, and free university and college education.

This is yet another weakness of the program. First, given that such goals are feasible, one would wonder how the provisional government would implement them in its short life (six months). These goals seem to be of much longer-term nature, and their extent and method of implementation seem to require careful studies and planning. It then seems more logical to leave the choice of these goals to the National Legislative and Constituent Assembly or even to the Legislative Parliament, to be formed after two years. Second, as was the case with Khomeini's associates before they took over, the National Council of Resistance seems to overestimate the resource availability of the country. Given the financial resources that Iran can have in the short and medium term, realization of such promises are quite unlikely.

In summary, the People's Mojahedin Organization, which seems to be the most powerful opposition to the Khomeini regime, is better prepared and has a more solid framework of thought with regard to the economic system than Khomeini's supporters had when they took over the government in 1979. Nonetheless, even if and when PMOI succeeds in forming its own government, it still will have a long way to go in terms of defining what economic system it purports to implement. Furthermore, the management of an economy heavily reliant on the oil revenue will be much more difficult, given the presently gloomy prospects of the international oil market, and in terms of resources will be much more restrictive than the program seems to imply. Finally, any step toward reducing the country's dependence on oil revenues or providing more equal distribution of income would require a very sophisticated and comprehensive planning system, a phenomenon that seems to have been, by and large, ignored by PMOI.

Considering the circumstances in the past, one would expect that if PMOI ever takes over, it will have a chaotic period at the beginning in which various views about private ownership and economic planning will impair the effective management of the economy. Although this period might be shorter than the one experienced by the Islamic Republic, the eventual outcome is likely to be the same. Again, a mixed-economy framework would be chosen for short- and medium-term purposes, and the role of economic planning would be recognized as a necessary tool for the management of the economy.

Available Tools for Economic Planning

The technical capabilities of the planning institution for the preparation and implementation of development plans are actually very weak. The planning machinery has never had a chance to work effectively and thereby to develop the required potentials. However, within the limited range in which the idea of planning has been put into practice, a few useful tools have emerged. A brief discussion of these tools should provide some insight into the factors facilitating the future practices of economic planning in Iran. Furthermore, the discussion of these tools and the problems faced in their development may shed some light on the potential uses of these techniques by other developing countries.

In this section we discuss two distinct but related issues. First, we explain the experiences of the Iranian planners with regard to planning models in the areas of macroplanning, regional planning, and optimal planning. Second, we discuss the evolution and development of information systems that, in fact, constitute the statistical basis of national planning.

Role of Macroeconomic Planning Models

The first step toward preparation of the national development plan is to construct a macroeconomic framework through which planners can ascertain the overall picture of the economy under alternative assumptions with respect to policy environment and desirable targets. This is normally done with the help of the so-called macroeconometric models. For the case of Iran, one such model has been constructed by Firouz Vakil for the Plan and Budget Organization.[9] This is basically an expanded version of the Keynesian model whose formulation and estimation results are given in the Appendix. In an abstract form the model consists of the twenty equations set out in the section on the macroeconomic model in the Appendix, where the justifications for the relationships are given. The model is formulated so that the "twice dualistic" nature of the economy can be incorporated into the expenditure functions. There is, on the one hand, the conventional dualism that distinguishes between the traditional and the modern sectors of the economy. This duality is incorporated into the model by the separation of rural and urban production and consumption. The second type of duality, oil and nonoil production, is introduced by the separation of oil and nonoil production and their impacts on the economy.

Furthermore, it should be pointed out that the macroeconometric model of Iran is constructed so that it can be utilized to perform simulation and policy analysis. Simulation is done by estimating the values of exogenous variables over the desired horizon, plugging them into the model, and obtaining the values for key macrovariables. The simulation exercise can be repeated under alternative conditions with respect to exogenous variables and policy instruments to provide a structural analysis of the economy. Alternatively, the model can be utilized in such a framework as to arrive at the policy package that will maximize the aggregate welfare of the society. A simple approximation to this process is to choose certain target variables from the set of endogenous variables, set their required level for the end of a particular planning horizon, and then determine what policy package can most efficiently steer the economy toward those targets.

Although this macroeconometric model requires some modifications and updating before it can be used for future planning purposes, it sets out the framework and the fundamental relationships of the Iranian economy. It can serve as a useful instrument for medium- and long-term forecasting as well as a tool for answering some "what if" questions.

Role of the Regional Planning Models

There is by now no doubt that any real attempt at economic planning in Iran should incorporate a comprehensive measure of regional imbalances and should make a serious effort to reduce these imbalances. The model developed by Farhad Noorbakhsh for the Plan and Budget Organization is an extremely useful tool for this purpose.[10] Noorbakhsh's model is an extension of the Wroclaw taxonomic method. It uses a set of development indicators to measure the development gaps among Iran's twenty-three *ostans* (counties). It then sets out a methodology for choosing the sectoral targets for each ostan so that the regional gaps are eliminated in the long run.

A very abstract sketch of the model is given in Figure 6.2; the mathematical formulation of the model is presented in the Appendix. At the first stage, the model utilizes fifty-five development indicators to measure the extent of development in each ostan. These indicators are classified into the following groups:

A. Economic Indicators
   - (A-1) Industrial
   - (A-2) Agricultural
   - (A-3) Employment

B. Social Indicators
   - (B-1) Urbanization and migration
   - (B-2) Living facilities
   - (B-3) Education
   - (B-4) Health

C. Political and Organizational Indicators
   - (C-1) Communication
   - (C-2) Management capabilities
   - (C-3) Participation in political affairs

The complete list of these indicators is given in the Appendix at the end of the book.

In order to compare and compose these indicators, which are expressed in various units, the model standardizes each one. This is done by calculating the mean and the standard deviation of each indicator over all ostans. Having the standardized values of fifty-five development indicators for twenty-three ostans, the model proceeds to calculate the simple and composite distances among the twenty-three ostans. The simple distance is measured in terms of one indicator; the composite distance is measured in terms of two or more indicators. In order to

Figure 6.2 The General Structure of the Regional Planning Model

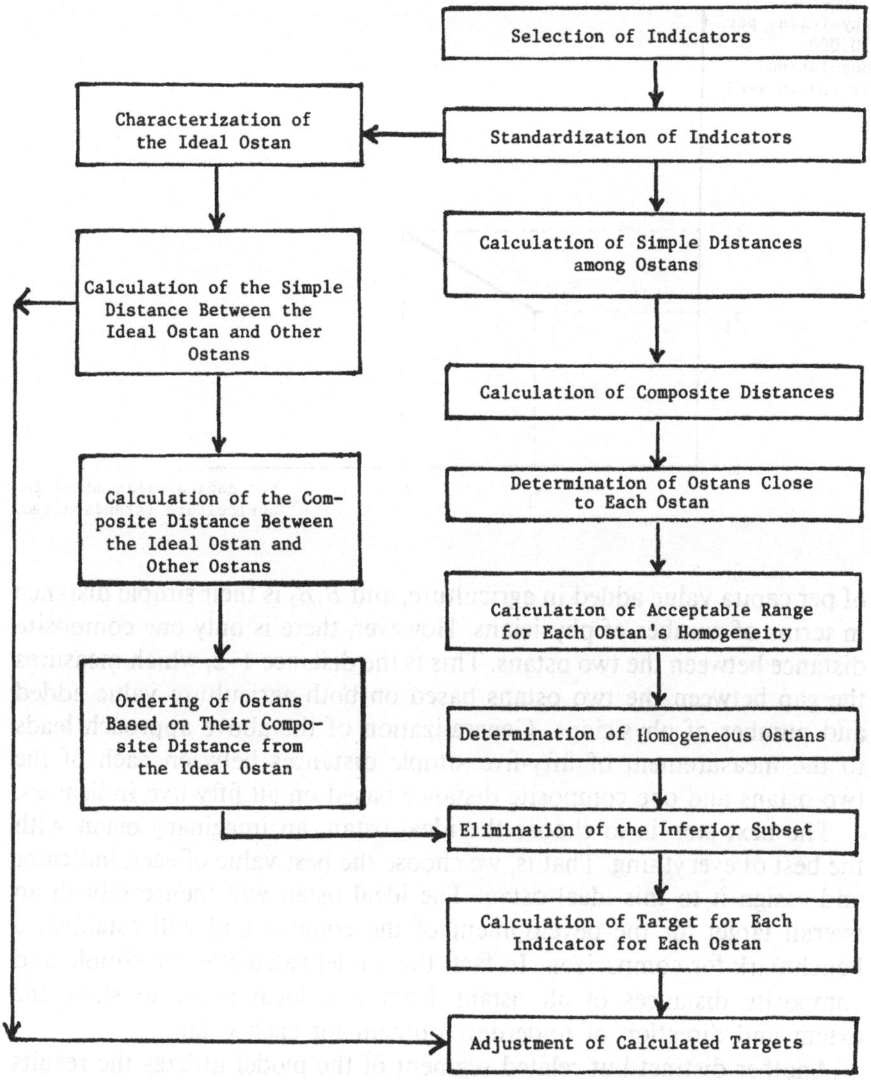

see this more clearly, let us take two indicators: the number of physicians per ten thousand population and the per capita value added in agriculture. Let us further assume that we are concerned with the measurement of the distance between ostans 1 and 2. In Figure 6.3, the distances OA_1 and OB_1 show the coordinates for the first ostan and OA_2 and OB_2 show the same thing for ostan 2. There are two simple distances between the two ostans. A_1A_2 is the distance between the two ostans in terms

Figure 6.3 Simple and Composite Distances Between Regions 1 and 2

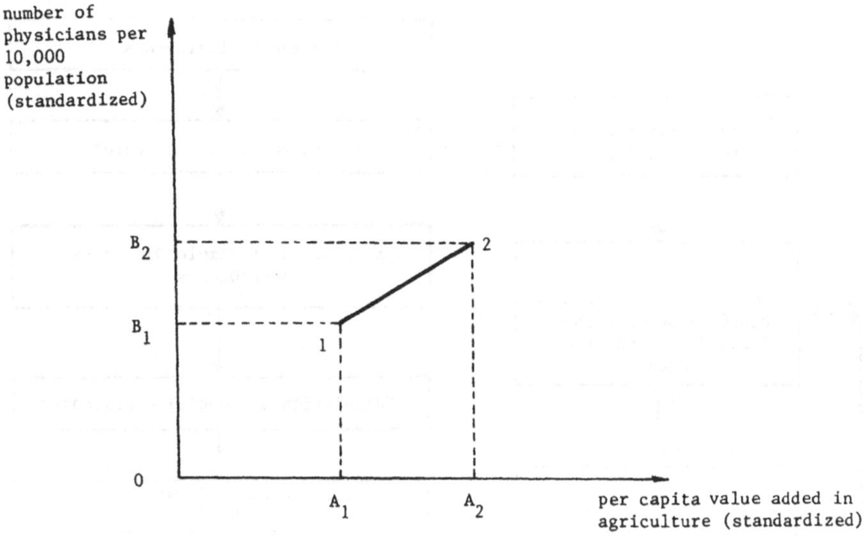

of per capita value added in agriculture, and B_1B_2 is their simple distance in terms of number of physicians. However, there is only one composite distance between the two ostans. This is the distance 1–2, which measures the gap between the two ostans based on both agriculture value added and number of physicians. Generalization of the above approach leads to the measurement of fifty-five simple distances between each of the two ostans and one composite distance based on all fifty-five indicators.

The next step is to choose the ideal ostan, an imaginary ostan with the best of everything. That is, we choose the best value of each indicator and assign it to this ideal ostan. The ideal ostan will then establish an overall target for the development of the country and will establish a benchmark for comparison. In fact, the model calculates the simple and composite distances of all ostans from this ideal ostan to show the extent and direction of underdevelopment for each ostan.

Another distinct but related segment of the model utilizes the results of the previous segment to calculate the targets for regional development. This segment of the model first groups ostans by their development patterns and then calculates the target for each indicator and for each ostan so that the regional gaps are eliminated in the long run.

In order to group the ostans, the model takes the simple distances of ostan 1 from all other ostans (for each indicator) and calculates the average and standard deviation of these distances for ostan 1 and each indicator. It then establishes an acceptable range and determines which other ostans are located in the same range. These ostans are said to be homogeneous with ostan 1, from the point of view of a specific indicator and the composite indicator. The same process is repeated for all ostans and a general grouping is performed.

In order to calculate the development targets, the model takes the group of ostans that are homogeneous with ostan 1. It then eliminates those ostans that are, from the development point of view, below ostan 1. The model then calculates the average value of the indicator for ostans above ostan 1 and announces the resultant value as the target for ostan 1. The idea is then to elevate ostan 1 to the average of ostans in the same group but above ostan 1. The same process is, of course repeated for all ostans and all indicators.

Finally, the model takes into account the fact that resource constraints may not allow for the achievement of all calculated targets. The targets should then be adjusted downward to match the resource availability. The model makes this adjustment so that the burden of the resource constraint is imposed on more advanced ostans and the underdeveloped ostans receive more attention. To this end, the model utilizes the simple distances between the ideal ostan and other ostans to determine the extent of relative underdevelopment of each ostan. Then the initial targets will be adjusted to be inversely proportional to the measures of underdevelopment.

A byproduct of this model is the ordering of Iran's twenty-three ostans according to their development pattern, which is reproduced in Table 6.1. The column entitled measure shows the composite distance of each ostan from the ideal ostan. As can be seen from the data in Table 6.1, the first ostan is Ostan Markazi, which is far more developed than all other ostans.

Role of Optimal Planning Models

Optimal planning models are usually used to arrive at the long-term development strategies of the economy. In general, this exercise is required to preserve the efficiency of long-run policymaking. However, in the case of Iran, the need for optimal planning is more critical because Iran's major wealth is its oil reserves, which will not last for more than a few decades. It is then very important to analyze the oil-extraction policy of the country in relation to the long-term interests of the nation.

The model developed by Razavi for the Plan and Budget Organization[11] provides an optimal planning framework within which the oil-extraction strategy is related to the economy's requirements of foreign exchange, on the one hand, and to the national welfare, on the other. The construction of the model rests on the underlying principle of public ownership of the country's oil resources by both the present and the future generations. The government, as a representative of the people,

Table 6.1. Ranking of the 23 Ostans by Level of Development

Rank Order		Measure of Underdevelopment
1	Ostan Markazi	0.367
2	Ostan Esfahan	0.654
3	Ostan Khuzestan	0.687
4	Ostan Yazd	0.689
5	Ostan Gilan	0.710
6	Ostan Fars	0.721
7	Ostan Semnan	0.733
8	Ostan Mazandaran	0.742
9	Ostan Kerman	0.747
10	Ostan Khorasan	0.772
11	Ostan Kermanshahan	0.773
12	Ostan Azarbayjan Sharghi	0.789
13	Ostan Azarbayjan Gharbi	0.801
14	Ostan Hamadan	0.805
15	Ostan Lorestan	0.825
16	Ostan Bushehr	0.832
17	Ostan Chaharmahal & Bakhtyari	0.843
18	Ostan Hormozgan	0.858
19	Ostan Kurdistan	0.861
20	Ostan Zanjan	0.876
21	Ostan Sistan & Baluchestan	0.876
22	Ostan Boyer Ahmad & Koheilouye	0.912
23	Ostan Ilam	0.923

is then obligated to take account of the interests of all generations in determining the rate of oil extraction. The model consists of two segments. The first is a welfare criterion, the second an input-output model. The oil-extraction policy is derived so that the welfare criterion is maximized and, at the same time, input-output constraints are satisfied.

The welfare criterion is formulated so that it takes into account the current welfare by incorporating the per capita consumption expenditure and the future welfare by deliberating the amount of factors left for the future production: the capital stock, accumulated foreign assets, and the oil reserves.

The input-output model is formulated by dividing economic activities into seven sectors: oil, agriculture, manufacturing and mining, construction, infrastructural services, other services, and noncompetitive imports. In addition to basic input-output relationships, a few macroequations are added to explain consumption, investment, taxes, and the depletion of oil reserves as well as the accumulation of foreign assets.

The optimal planning model, consisting of the welfare criterion and other constraining relationships, is solved by the dynamic programming technique to derive the foreign-trade policies that would maximize the utility of consumption during the planning period as well as the efficiency of the national portfolio at the end of the planning period.

The results of the model as solved for the years 1983 to 1992 are summarized in Table 6.2. The optimum pattern of oil export is critically dependent on the future trends of oil prices and the rate of return on foreign assets. The results in Table 6.2 are based on the assumption that oil price remains constant during the planning period and that the real rate of return on foreign assets stays around 5 percent. Accordingly, it becomes more profitable to keep the national wealth in the form of foreign assets rather than oil reserves. The optimal level of oil export then stays substantially above its target during the initial years of the plan in which there is a longer prospect of earning interest on the acquired foreign exchange.

To develop some sense about the effect of the rate of interest and oil price on the results, it would be useful to glance at the variations of the subsequent outcome as we alter the assumptions regarding the future trends of these variables. To this end, we first lower the rate of interest to 3 percent. This creates a downward rotation in oil exports such that the 1983 value decreases to 1,565 billion rials while the 1992 magnitude stays the same.

Changing the trend of oil price affects the level of oil exports in two distinct ways. First, it alters the pattern of physical amounts of oil exports in relation to the foreign-exchange requirements of the economy. Second, it changes the terminal price of oil, which determines the relative profitability of keeping the oil in the ground. The distinction of these two effects is important, especially if we utilize the more sophisticated approach of basing the shadow price of oil on the expected usefulness of this resource in the future (after the plan's period) rather than on the terminal price of oil. In our calculations, we first assumed that oil price would increase at an annual rate of 5 percent. For such a case, the level of oil export starts at 2.8 million barrels a day in 1983 and ends at 1.5 million barrels in 1993. Here, the shadow price of oil is taken as its terminal price, which is around 23,000 rials per barrel. We then utilize the same price trend but assign the value of 35,000 rials per barrel to the shadow price of oil. This is one way to implement the idea that the price of oil will continue to increase after the plan's period. This new price trend creates a substantial downward rotation in the pattern of oil exports, such that the starting volume in 1983 is around 2.2 million barrels a day and the terminal amount remains at 1.6 million barrels.

Clearly, the results described here constitute only a few examples of the possible application of the optimal planning model. As can be seen in the Appendix, the optimal planning model is actually quite flexible.

Table 6.2. Optimal Values of Policy and State Variables

Variable[a]	Sixth Development Plan						Seventh Development Plan			
	1983	1984	1985	1986	1987	1988	1989	1990	1991	1992
Exports										
Oil	1786	1725	1659	1585	1503	1411	1307	1189	1057	910
Agriculture	18.5	21.3	23.9	26.3	28.6	30.7	32.4	33.8	34.8	35.2
Manufacturing	7.7	10.9	14.1	17.4	20.7	24.0	27.2	30.1	32.5	34.4
Services	34.2	37.1	39.7	42.1	44.4	46.4	48.5	50.2	51.5	52.5
Imports										
Agriculture	26.4	28.7	30.5	31.9	32.8	33.4	33.5	33.2	32.4	31.1
Manufacturing	732	811	873	923	969	990	1007	1011	1001	967
Services	88.1	91.9	95.1	97.4	99.2	100.3	100.9	100.4	99.3	97.4
Noncompetitive	814	922	1009	1083	1148	1204	1250	1286	1308	1316
Output										
Oil	2228	2184	2133	2073	2002	1917	1817	1699	1561	1402
Agriculture	668	721	766	804	836	862	881	892	894	885
Manufacturing	1680	1864	2015	2144	2251	2338	2400	2436	2439	2401
Construction	621	716	792	858	915	964	1006	1039	1062	1073
Infrastructure	341	364	383	401	413	425	433	438	439	436
Services	1014	1070	1119	1161	1196	1224	1245	1257	1259	1250
GDP	4828	5001	5132	5337	5287	5309	5290	5224	5104	5083
Per capita consumption	46.5	47.9	48.8	49.3	49.4	49.2	48.7	47.7	46.5	45.1
Capital stock	7043	8412	9902	11479	13119	14801	16504	18207	19884	21510
Foreign assets	551	897	1318	1913	2163	2293	2285	2121	1778	1230
Oil reserves	51551	50082	48654	47272	45938	44651	43430	42298	41258	40324

[a]Per capita consumption is measured in thousands of 1974 rials; oil reserves are expressed in million barrels; all other variables are measured in billions of 1974 rials.

It can be used to derive trade policies that reduce the long-term dependency of the country on oil and can also provide a measure of tradeoffs between the current welfare versus the future welfare of the nation.

Role of the Information System

Information systems are certainly among the basic prerequisites of economic planning. It is therefore important to study the PBO's potential and endowments in this respect.

After the revolution of February 1979, the Informatics Division became the target of numerous political and professional attacks. On the political side, the division—being a symbol of Western technology and its personnel having been trained in Western countries—attracted a considerable amount of attention. On the professional side, many experts (including the division's personnel) believed that the Informatics Division had not produced an output worthy of the cost. A significant amount of time and effort was then spent on understanding the mistakes of the past, and the three most important mistakes were eventually diagnosed. First, the approach taken by the Informatics Division to persuade potential users to adopt computer services had been too aggressive and had caused a resistance on the part of the users. Second, the isolation of Informatics personnel from the employees of other divisions had been a significant obstacle that prohibited these personnel from understanding the PBO's tasks and activities. As a result, Informatics personnel had not acquired the professional background necessary to appreciate the practical issues and problems propounded in the national planning engagements. Third, the difference between the nature of data processing in the private sector and that of the public sector had not been realized. The general strategies to promote Informatics had been chosen based on the data-processing characteristics of the private sector and had been bound to fail when applied to the public sector.

Among the above reasons, the first and second points were discussed in Chapter 3, where we evaluated the organizational functions of the PBO. However, the third point needs some further explanation. To simplify the discussion, let us summarize the major steps of information flow as shown in Figure 6.4. Each step of this chart represents a general phase of information flow. The data-collection phase may include surveys, samplings, or compilation of documents. The analysis phase encompasses the design, development, and implementation of information systems. In addition, the analysis phase includes analytical efforts that may not be part of the standard activities normally faced in a data-processing environment. The final result of the analysis phase is the policy information provided to the decision makers. The decision makers then use

Figure 6.4 Flow of Information in the Public Sector

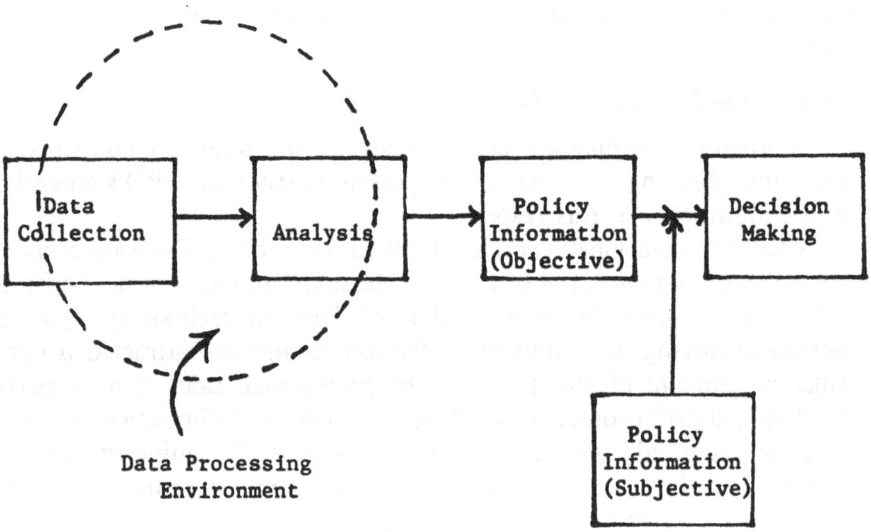

this information along with their own views of how things should work (the subjective policy information) to arrive at decisions.

It is customary for the data-processing involvement in the private sector to consist of some pieces of the first two phases. It usually covers some parts of data collection, leaving out the very evolved activities like field surveys. In the analysis phase, the data-processing department covers the portion of the task that can be done based on standard procedures.

No matter how much of the first two phases are covered by the data-processing unit, the views of the data-processing experts do not go beyond the analysis phase. That is, for a person who works in the data-processing department, it is almost immaterial to know how the eventual output affects the decision-making process. A normal consequence of this ignorance may be that the data-processing unit spends a considerable amount of resources to collect and analyze the data, yet the decision makers continue to base decisions on subjective information. In the private sector, this process cannot continue for a long time because there is an instrument inherent in the system that issues the appropriate signals regarding the eventual use of the information provided by the data-processing department. This instrument is, of course, the organization's additional revenue compared with the cost. Decision makers in the private sector are not ashamed of basing all their decisions on their own personal views regarding the operations of their firms. If these decision makers establish data-processing departments, it is because of the need for more comprehensive information. The extent of the data-processing activity will then be adjusted by the eventual use of the information generated by this activity. Therefore, in the private sector, the ignorance of later phases of information flow by the data-processing expert is not only justified but, in many cases, is required, because any attempt by this expert to understand how the real decisions are made may work as an undesired intervention in the management of the organization.

In the public sector, the data-processing unit has a different role and a different mission. In this sector, decision makers are not very proud to announce that they base their decisions on subjective information. In many instances, they are obligated to justify the basis for their decisions. To this end, they have a tendency to show that objective information, such as that produced by the data-processing unit, plays an important role in determining their policies. Nevertheless, the lack of a tangible criterion in the public sector for comparing the cost elements to the output creates the possibility that the data-processing department continues its work on the data collection and analysis while the decision makers continue to make decisions based on subjective information. This is a rather usual circumstance that one observes in many public organizations where a considerable amount of resources is devoted to the establishment and operation of data-processing units, and yet the effectiveness of the output of these units (in terms of affecting public policies) is insignificant.

In other words, the concept of data processing is considerably different in the public sector than it is in the private sector. Consequently, in the public sector a broader approach has to be employed with respect to both the conceptual and methodological issues. On the conceptual side, the data-processing framework has to be extended to an information-system approach in which the information system is interpreted in its broadest sense as the mechanism through which information flows from the stage at which the raw data is generated to the stage in which the final information is put into the decision-making process. Utilizing this approach has several implications regarding the policies that a data-processing unit of the public sector should pursue. First, the main mission of the data-processing unit (which we will from now on call the informatics unit) is to increase the role of objective information in the decision-making process. This is based on the generally accepted view that establishing policies according to subjective information will bias the decisions toward personal tastes and preferences that may not be in the best interest of the society. The aim of the informatics unit will then be to advocate procedures that can rely on the type of information that is independent of personal preferences and interpretations. To this end, the informatics unit should take a global view of the information flow. This does not mean that the informatics personnel should necessarily participate in the decision-making process. Rather, it means that the framework of informatics tasks should be designed in such a way that personnel can see how the generated information is translated into practical decisions.

The second implication of the information-system approach is that the informatics unit of the public sector should concentrate more on advocating new procedures and improving existing procedures than on providing data banks (the latter is normally the case). This is not to say that the provision of actual data systems should be neglected or given less emphasis. Instead, it means that the concept of information system (as we have defined it) is much broader than data systems (as known in the current literature). Provision of an information system deals with the whole mechanism through which the information flows, including the procedures utilized at different stages of the mechanism.

The third implication is that the informatics unit of the public sector should not limit its task to computerized systems. Manual information systems are indeed the best starting point for promoting the role of objective information in the decision-making process. Through the manual information systems, the informatics unit can persuade different sections of the public sector to decrease the bureaucratic frictions against the flow of information and can reveal the real need for information. In this way, the informatics unit's task is not limited to the use of computer services. It is, in fact, important that the informatics unit avoid computerizing information systems before the volume of data or computation reaches a level to justify the automation.

Obstacles to Economic Planning

Regardless of which political group rules in Iran in the future, the endeavor of economic planning will encounter more obstacles than facilities. The design of a planning system, like any other system, entails the following three steps: (1) identification of the system elements, (2) determination of the interrelationships among these elements, and (3) devising a mechanism that evokes an automatic interaction and prompts signals concerning where and when the system is not working properly.

In the case of the Iranian planning system, some efforts have been put into the identification of the system elements. However, steps 2 and

3 have not received much attention. As we explained in Chapter 3, there was no planning system, as such, during the shah's regime. In the 1950s and 1960s, PBO activities were limited to the coordination of some public projects that had not been chosen within a planning framework. In the late 1960s and early 1970s, the notion of development planning attracted the attention of government authorities, and theoretically it was put into practice. Nevertheless, the inherent conflict between planning and personal decision-making prevented the task from accomplishing anything. One consequence of this situation was that the development process did not engender much planning expertise.

Only a few scattered attempts were made to provide a framework for the planning activities, with one outcome being the emergence of a line of thought with regard to the design of a consistent planning system. After the revolution, this line of thought was interrupted for about two years. In 1981, the trial-and-error type of process used to arrive at a new planning system eventually converged with the pre-revolution line of thought, and a planning system was introduced. Although the Iranian planners' design of this initial system is, all things considered, admirable, there is still a long way to go. The present planning system is based on a sound identification of the system elements (step 1). It has also touched upon the determination of the interrelationships among the elements (step 2). However, it still needs an enormous effort to complete step 2 and to devise the mechanism of the system (step 3). What is needed to accomplish this huge task is planning expertise, and that is exactly what Iran has never had. It is true that the PBO has had a limited number of planners—mostly academic—capable of originating a planning system, but planning expertise requires much more than that. The expertise should encompass the whole planning community, which involves hundreds of individuals working at different capacities. The production of this expertise requires a long period of time, significant political support, considerable amount of resources, and a systematic plan.

The second obstacle to economic planning is the establishment of the required institution for preparation and implementation of development plans. Even though it is true that the planning system document has outlined the overall format of such an institution, two other steps must be taken. First, the details of this institution have to be worked out. How the microelements of the system at the sectoral and regional levels will interact should be determined. Second, the institution has to be implemented. These are greater tasks by far than the preparation of the initial outline of the planning institution. They require a careful examination and understanding of how the microelements work and how they should work. This task is made even more complicated by the fact that the present structure of the bureaucratic system entails an antiplan character: The functioning of microsegments of the bureaucratic system is based on rivalry rather than cooperation and coordination. This is an inherent characteristic in the Iranian bureaucracy. It has always been the case that personal (mostly political) competition among certain individuals is translated into functional rivalry among their corresponding organizations. This means that the establishment of the planning system should include the restructuring of the bureaucratic system, which again involves a considerable amount of effort and a systematic plan.

The third obstacle to economic planning is the establishment of a coordinating mechanism between the public and private sectors. The private sector of the economy is, despite its shrinking size, extremely political. Although the bazaar merchants are rather limited in number and small in size, traditionally they are an important political force. They have their own network of communication and penetration into the society. They helped the Khomeini movement against the shah and may help another group against Khomeini, should they be forced to do so.

Among various characteristics attributed to bazaar merchants is their resistance to any government intervention in their business affairs. This will, of course, impair the preparation and implementation of any comprehensive plan. Given that a comprehensive plan will necessarily involve cooperation between the public and private sectors of the economy, the designers of the planning system and institution are faced with the task of taking account of this characteristic and devising a mechanism to avoid alienating the private-sector entrepreneurs while at the same time ensuring coordination.

Finally, the fourth obstacle to economic planning in Iran is the result of some cultural characteristics of the Iranian society. Most Westerners who visit Iran will notice that Iranian people do not usually budget their time and money very carefully. In fact, the expenditure of both of these resources is based on habits rather than on accurate calculations of needs and availabilities. As a result, most people do not feel the obligation to follow the special guidelines required to implement a plan. From a technical point of view, this cultural inaccuracy will lower the efficiency of the economic system. At the same time, the relaxation and lack of constant tension may be an addition to the welfare of the society. That is, rather than debating the desirability or undesirability of the antiplan culture, one simply has to take account of this cultural characteristic. This is, of course, an issue that has not been effectively dealt with in the planning efforts of either the shah's period or the Islamic regime.

Conclusion

Considering the vast involvement of the government in the Iranian economy, planning will be an essential tool for managing the economy in the remainder of this decade, regardless of which political group rules the country. To summarize, the Islamic regime (or any other group that may take over) has to cope with some serious bottlenecks to planning: (1) lack (or insufficiency) of planning expertise, (2) difficulties in establishing the institution of planning, (3) design and implementation of a coordinating mechanism between the private and the public sectors of the economy, and (4) cultural characteristics of the Iranian society.

On the positive side, the planning efforts of the future may be able to benefit from a few facilitating factors available in the planning community. The most important is the line of thought—engendered through many years of experience—that PBO personnel have developed with regard to different aspects of planning. It does not represent an admirable accomplishment if compared with the amount of time and resources spent on this matter, but it is still an asset that should be used to facilitate the task of economic planning.

Finally, an important implication derived from our discussion of this chapter is that the Islamic regime wasted a considerable amount of time and effort because it did not answer in advance some fundamental questions with regard to the role of the private sector and the structure of the planning system. In this respect, the opposition groups that think of themselves as potential candidates for the future rulers of the country should devote more attention to answering these questions before they are caught up in the same circumstances as the Islamic regime.

Notes

1. This is in fact the way that mass media in Iran and the international community have described the conflict. However, Hojatieh is not really a political group with distinct political and economic positions. In the shah's period Hojatieh was some sort of gathering of different religious figures whose common characteristic was anti-Bahaeism. People who on and off were associated with Hojatieh include religious figures of completely different types. For example, President Ali Khameneii and Prime Minister Mousavi, both among the radical religious leaders, are known to have been associated with Hojatieh in the 1960s. The present conflict with regard to cooperation with the Soviet Union is due more to the political inclination of different individuals in the ruling party than

to Hojatieh versus Maktabis. See S. Akhavi, *Religion and Politics in Contemporary Iran: Clergy-State Relations in the Pahlavi Period* (New York: State University of New York Press, 1980).

2. People's Mojahedin Organization of Iran. *The History of the People's Mojahedin Organization* (Long Beach, Calif.: Moslem Students Society, 1981), p. 16.

3. Ibid., p. 5.

4. Ibid., p. 23.

5. See People's Mojahedin Organization of Iran, "Program of the Provisional Government of the Democratic Islamic Republic of Iran," *Iran Liberation* (occasional publication of PMOI), June 1982.

6. Ibid., p. 6.

7. Ibid., p. 2.

8. Ibid., p. 8.

9. Firouz Vakil, *A Twenty Year Macroeconomic Perspective for Iran, 1351–1371* (Tehran: Plan and Budget Organization, 1975b).

10. Farhad Noorbakhsh, "A Model for Determining the Priorities To Reduce the Regional Gaps in Iran" (Tehran: Plan and Budget Organization, 1977).

11. H. Razavi, "Optimal Rate of Oil Production for OPEC Member Countries, *Resources and Energy* 4, no. 4 (1982), pp. 291–305.

7
Conclusion: Planning and Dictatorship

From the viewpoint of economic theory, there is no fundamental conflict between planning and dictatorship. Indeed, dictatorship facilitates the task of planning because the characterization of the welfare preference does not have to face the so-called voting paradox. The dictator sets the targets, and the planner determines the appropriate strategies and efficient policies for achieving these targets.

In practice, however, things do not tie together so neatly. It is difficult to find a politician rigid enough to be a dictator and at the same time flexible enough to listen to what planners prescribe. Development of dictatorial manners in a person seems to coincide with the evolution of the feeling that the person "knows it all" and with increasing intolerance of disagreements. The dictator still may have advisers and technical counselors, but their role will gradually change from that of providing technical advice to that of listening to the lectures by the dictator on how wrong they are if they have an opinion that is contrary to the one expressed by the dictator. This process in turn leads to a change in the environment surrounding the dictator, as the individuals who choose to adhere to their principles and opinions or have strong personalities gradually leave the government. If they stay, they play a more passive role. Indeed, those who remain often lack both the capability to manage the economy and the ability to defend or justify the actions they take in following the dictator's commands. In order to stay in power, they use the dictator's position to protect themselves against objections from the people. This behavior permeates the entire bureaucratic system, resulting in a rigid top-down administration with little room for bottom-up corrective and innovative signals.

In such an environment, effective economic planning cannot take place. The planner's major task is to provide the decision maker with information about the efficiency of economic policies. If all the channels are constricted and information cannot flow, there is little to be gained from the planning exercise.

We exempt a group dictatorship from the process we have just described. The whole field of economic planning owes its strength and validity to the experiences of the centrally planned economies, most of which are managed by the so-called dictatorship of the proletariat. This type of dictatorship is an intentional and embedded part of the system. Thus, all elements of the system are designed to work under this discipline.

Iran's experience with economic planning under the two regimes provides an interesting example of the interactions between planning and dictatorship. The shah's period certainly falls in the category of evolving personal dictatorship. In October 1941, just after his accession to the throne, the shah stated that his intention was to "govern constitutionally,"[1] even though the constitution provided him with an opportunity to reign and no authority to rule.

For about a decade, the shah played a limited role in ruling the country. After his return from exile in 1954, however, he decided to actually rule the country. Initially, he made only the major political decisions of the country, but within a few years his involvement became very extensive. According to Khosrow Fatemi's analysis,

> . . . to operate his system, the Shah had effectively made himself the sole decisionmaking authority in every significant phase of Iran's political affairs. He regularly presided over the meetings of councils, commissions, and even ad hoc committees and gave specific orders on issues ranging from the price of eggs to the duration of medical education, from minimum wages for textile workers of Isfahan to the electrification of the Trans-Iranian Railroad System, and from the discount rate of the Central Bank to the use of natural gas as opposed to water for the secondary recovery of Khuzistan oil wells. In addition, more than 20 of his top aides who held the country's most important military and civilian positions had regular and frequent audiences with him—one to five times a week—to present their reports and receive instructions.[2]

The dynamics of personal dictatorship require that the ruler's role in the management of the country be intensified. This will force the dictator to get involved in increasingly detailed aspects of decision making—a trend that will eventually be limited by the capacity of the dictator to handle the task or by the capacity of people to tolerate the situation.

The shah's dictatorship was even more complicated because it was based on the politics of distrust. Khosrow Fatemi has stated that the shah's primary concern in the management of the country was to protect himself and his throne from potential threats (such as military coups) and political rivals. Fatemi described a few examples of the shah's involvement in the administration of the country.

1. His engagement in military affairs was so detailed that no military plane could take off from any airport without his permission; no officer above the rank of second lieutenant could be transferred from one branch of the military to another without his authorization; and no commissioned officer could be promoted without his approval.

2. His involvement in foreign affairs was as extensive. He had daily meetings with the minister of foreign affairs, who presented him with all confidential reports and coded telexes that Iranian ambassadors had sent to the Foreign Ministry during the preceding twenty-four hours. Moreover, he was furnished with intelligence reports on other countries, especially those in the region.

3. In the oil industry, the shah considered himself an expert on all aspects of international oil and was the sole decision maker in Iran's petroleum affairs, both in the policymaking and the operations sectors of the industry.[3]

The extensive involvement of the shah in political and economic affairs raises two questions. First, was he (or any other individual) capable of handling such increasing involvements? Second, did the subsequent policy environment lend itself to the practice of economic planning? Our interest in this book has been in the second question. We have discussed in various chapters the fundamental inconsistencies between the shah's manner of decision making and the practicability of economic planning.

Iran's period under Khomeini is more difficult to assess. It is true that the constitution of the Islamic Republic provides the leader with a great deal of power. According to the constitution, "the absolute ruler of the world and humanity is God and He alone has determined the social destiny of human beings." Further, "those who transgress the limits of God are oppressors. . . . There is no obedience in a creature who disobeys his creator."[4] The rule of God is then conveyed to people through the holy Imams: "God has chosen him above you and has imbued him abundantly with knowledge and strength. . . . God has given it to the Imams of justice to appoint themselves by the weakness of people." Since at the present time the last Imam is absent, he will be represented by the religious leader: "During the absence of the Glorious Lord of the Age [the missing twelfth Imam of the Shiite sect], may God grant him relief, he will be represented in the Islamic Republic of Iran as religious leader and imam of the people by an honest, virtuous, well-informed, courageous, efficient administrator and religious jurist, enjoying the confidence of the majority of the people as a leader."[5]

The general function of the leader is then translated into detailed duties and powers:

1. Appointing the jurists on the Council of Guardians.
2. Appointing the highest judical authorities of the country.
3. Commanding all the armed forces as follows:
   a. Appointing and dismissing the chief of the general staff;
   b. Appointing and dismissing the commander-in-chief of the Islamic Revolution Guards Corps;
   c. Organizing the High Council for National Defense, which will be composed of the following seven members: president of the republic, prime minister, minister of defense, chief of the general staff, the commander-in-chief of the Islamic Revolution Guards Corps, and two advisers specified by the leader;
   d. Naming the commander-in-chief of the three armed forces at the suggestion of the High Council for National Defense;
   e. Declaring war and mobilizing the armed forces at the suggestion of the High Council for National Defense.
4. Signing the order (formalizing) of the election of the president after he has been elected by the people. Approving the competence of candidates for the presidency with regard to the qualifications specified by this law. Confirming them before the Council of Guardians before the elections and confirming the president's first terms.
5. Dismissing the president of the republic in consideration of the good of the country after an order is issued by the Supreme Court charging him with violating his legal duties toward the National Legislative and Constituent Consultative Assembly and relieving him of his political competence.
6. Pardoning or reducing the sentences of convicts within the limits of Islamic standards, pursuant to the suggestions of the Supreme Court.

This religious leader at present (as written into the constitution) is the Great Ayatollah Imam Khomeini. Though a few qualifying clauses in the constitution impose some limitations on the power of the leader, for all practical purposes Khomeini has had the constitutional grounds to rule the country by a personal dictatorship. It is also true that he has used this privilege to make important global and political decisons, but he has avoided intervening in the detailed decision making, especially that related to economic affairs.

Though Khomeini has not (at least consistently) acted as a dictator, there is little ground for denying the existence of dictatorship in Iran.

Twenty thousand executions in two years do not characterize anything but a dictatorial rule. However, the dictatorship seems to be embedded in the system, being more a dictatorship by the ruling party rather than a dictatorship by an individual. This is basically the reason that the Islamic regime seems to offer better prospects for economic planning than did the previous regime.

The question frequently addressed these days is the one of what will happen after Khomeini. If we assume that the Islamic system will stay after Khomeini, then we still face at least three distinct alternatives. The first (but not necessarily the most likely) is the emergence of a new dictator. This is based on the speculation that the Islamic Revolution Guards Corps, with the cooperation of some factions of the armed forces, will initially take over the country in order to save the Islamic revolution. The military rule would then require a strong commander, and the country, including its economy, would be governed through personal dictatorship. This scenario is probably the worst that could happen in so far as the planning system is concerned, as it would result in a policy environment in which the role of economic planning would again be reduced to a tool for coping with administrative formalities. The official institution of planning would remain, but its input into the management of the economy would fade over time.

The second scenario (still assuming that the Islamic regime stays) is that a moderate Islamic government would rule the country. This would basically be a continuation of the present trends (given the perpetuation of recent moderations). The likelihood of such an occurrence depends on how well the present ruling group can establish itself and how successfully the rival individuals and wings of the ruling group can avoid conflicts. This scenario would be smooth on every aspect of the system including economic planning. The efforts to establish a planning system within the framework of a mixed economy would continue, and the private sector would be allowed to play a partial role in the economy.

The third alternative is that, although the Islamic regime would formally stay, a radical group would smoothly and gradually take over the management of the economy. This also can be viewed as the continuation of present trends, given that certain individuals in the ruling party can eliminate some others—a normal process in the Islamic regime. Clearly, under such circumstances the role of economic planning would expand to cover the major part of the economy. Private-sector involvement would, on the other hand, become more limited and consist of the activities of small industrial producers and small farmers.

The hypothesis that Islamic fundamentalists will take over the country does not develop an independent alternative. The rule by Islamic fundamentalists would not generate a stable government unless accompanied by a military-type control (eventually falling into the category of the first alternative) or by the dictatorship of the proletariat (the third alternative).

Finally, should the Islamic regime fall after Khomeini's death, there will not be many alternatives available. The opposition groups are so large in number and so diverse in their objectives and approaches that one cannot conceive of any feasible coalition among these groups, at least in the short run. The only viable alternative seems to be the National Council of Resistance, which encompasses several democratic, liberal, and socialist groups. Its main core is, however, the People's Mojahedin Organization of Iran. Should the council replace the Islamic regime after Khomeini's death, prospects for economic planning would not be fundamentally different from what they are in the Islamic regime. The framework of mixed economy would again be utilized in the planning approach, and the private sector's partial role in the economy would be preserved.

Notes

1. See Chapter 1.
2. Khosrow Fatemi, "Leadership by Distrust: The Shah's Modus Operandi," *The Middle East Journal* 36, no. 1 (1982).
3. Ibid.
4. Islamic Republic of Iran, *The Constitution of Islamic Republic.*
5. Ibid., p. 11.

Appendix: Planning Models

This appendix provides a technical discussion of the three planning models that were briefly described in Chapter 6.

The Macroeconometric Model

The macroeconometric model developed by Firouz Vakil[1] is a twenty-equation model consisting of:

1. Expenditure Identity
   $GNP = C + I + E - M$

2. Income Identity
   $GDP = GNP + T_f$

3. Consumption Identity
   $C = C_p(ur) + C_p(ru) + C_g$

4. Investment Identity
   $I = I_p(m) + I_p(c) + Ig$

5. Export Identity
   $E = E_o + E_{no}$

6. Import Identity
   $M = M_{k+1} + M_c$

7. Urban Consumption Function
   $C_p(ur) = a_{10} + a_{11}GNP + a_{12}M_{k+1(-1)}$

8. Rural Consumption Function
   $C_p(ru) = a_{20} + a_{21}VAA + a_{22}P_{rI}$

9. Government Consumption Function
   $C_g = a_{30} + a_{31}T_D + a_{32}T_A + A_{35}VA_{oil}$

10. Gross Private Investment in Machinery
    $I_p(m) = a_{40} + a_{41}GNP_{(-1)}$

11. Gross Private Investment in Construction
$I_p(c) = a_{50} + a_{51}CR_p + a_{52}\ WPI$

12. Government Investment
$I_g = a_{60} + a_{61}VA_{oil}$

13. Oil Exports
$E_o = a_{70} + a_{71}E_{o(-1)}$

14. Nonoil Exports
$E_{no} = a_{80} + a_{81}M_{k+1} + a_{82}VAA$

15. Capital and Intermediate Goods Imports
$M_{k+1} = a_{90} + a_{91}GNP + a_{92}VAM_{(-1)}$

16. Consumer Goods Imports
$M_c = a_{100} + a_{101}VA_{oil} + a_{102}GNP_{(-1)} + a_{103}VAM_{(-1)}$

17. Private Sector Credits
$CR_p = a_{111}VAM + a_{112}MSB_{(-1)}$

18. Net Factor Income from Abroad
$T_f = a_{120} + a_{121}E_o$

19. Direct Tax Equation
$T_D = a_{130} + a_{131}GNP$

20. Customs Tax Equation
$T_A = a_{140} + a_{141}M_c.$

The variables of the model are defined as:

GDP = Gross Domestic Product

GNP = Gross National Product

C = Total Consumption Expenditures

I = Gross Domestic Investment

E = Total Exports

M = Total Imports

T_f = Net Factor Income from Abroad

$C_p(ur)$ = Urban Private Consumption Expenditures

$C_p(ru)$ = Rural Private Consumption Expenditures

C_g = Government Consumption

$I_p(m)$ = Private Investment in Machinery

$I_p(c)$ = Private Investment in Construction

I_g = Government Investment

E_o = Oil Exports

E_{no} = Nonoil Exports

M_{k+1} = Capital and Intermediate Imports

M_c = Consumer Goods Imports

CR_p = Private Sector Credit

T_D = Direct Taxes

T_A = Customs Revenues

$M_{k+1(-1)}$ = Last Year's Capital Imports

VAA = Value Added in Agriculture

P_{rI} = Rural Population Index

VA_{oil} = Value Added in Oil

$GNP_{(-1)}$ = Last Year's Gross National Product

WPI = Change in Wholesale Price Index

$E_{o(-1)}$ = Last Year's Oil Exports

$VAM_{(-1)}$ = Last Year's Value Added in Manufacturing

VAM = Value Added in Manufacturing

$MSB_{(-1)}$ = Last Year's Money Supply.

There are thirty variables in all, twenty of which are endogenous. The latter have been chosen from the more important of the uncontrolled variables of the Iranian economy. The remaining ten are the exogenous variables, identified on the basis of certain theoretical considerations and isolated on the basis of their explanatory powers.

Estimation of the fourteen behavioral equations, 7 through 20, was performed with ordinary least squares regression techniques. Because at the time of this estimation consistent sets of data were only available for the period 1959–1971, it was not possible to use simultaneous estimation techniques, such as two stage least squares. The number of observations (thirteen), in some cases reduced by the inclusion of lagged variables (reduced to twelve), precluded the use of more sophisticated regression methods. Although some of the estimated coefficients may suffer from a simultaneity bias, because of the existing correlation between the error term and some of the independent variables (endogenous variables of the model) in a single equation estimation of a simultaneous equation model, it is hoped that the predictive abilities of the model will compensate for some of its statistical weaknesses.

The estimated model is shown in Table A.1. All variables are measured in billion rials of current prices. Thus, any projections based on the estimated structural equations of Table A.1 will of necessity include a price inflation factor.

The results are quite satisfactory considering both the very high values of the coefficients of determination (R^2's) and the size of the regression coefficients relative to their standard errors. Only two equations—10, gross private investment in machinery, and 18, net factor income from abroad—failed to achieve coefficients of determination above 0.900. This is to be expected in the case of 18 because the variations are to some extent up to the policymakers, reflecting world conditions for the supply and demand of oil[2] and until the last decade reflecting the relative political bargaining positions of underdeveloped countries vis-à-vis developed countries. In the case of equation 10, it is not unusual to expect lower coefficients of determination, since private investments in machinery contain an entrepreneurial evaluation of risk and climate for investment not easily quantified and thus not easily introduced as an explanatory variable of $I_p(m)$.

The consumption equations—7, 8, and 9—reflect the two basic dualities of the Iranian economy, the conventional duality as stipulated by Ranis and Fei[3] and the private sector–public sector duality that reflects the importance of the oil sector. The former is exemplified by the two different consumption equations used to describe urban and rural consumption expenditures; the latter is reflected in the fact that a major explanatory variable of government consumption is value added in the oil sector.

Turning to equation 7, urban consumption expenditures, we note that the two explanatory variables are gross national product (GNP) and imports of capital plus intermediate goods ($M_{k+1(-1)}$) lagged by one year. It is usually customary to use personal disposable income as an explanatory variable of consumption. Unfortunately the relevant data were not readily available and consequently GNP had to be used instead. This procedure is not very likely to lead to biases in the coefficients,

Table A.1. - Estimated Structural Equations

(1)	GDP	$= C + I + E - M$	
(2)	GNP	$= GDP - T_p$	
(3)	C	$= C_p(ur) + C_p(ru) + C_g$	
(4)	I	$= I_p(m) + I_p(c) + I_g$	
(5)	E	$= E_o + E_{no}$	
(6)	M	$= M_{k+1} + M_c$	
(7)	$C_p(ur)$	$= -9.276 + 0.358GNP + 0.591_{k+1(-1)}$	$R^2 = 0.997$
		(0.035) (0.241)	
(8)	$C_p(ru)$	$= -168.476 + 0.385VAA + 2.364P_{rI}$	$R^2 = 0.992$
		(0.137)	
(9)	C_g	$= 3.528 + 1.644T_D + 4.059T_A + 0.124VA_{oil}$	$R^2 = 0.997$
		(0.720) (1.122) (0.060)	
(10)	$I_p(m)$	$= 4.928 + 0.035GNP_{oil}$	$R^2 = 0.755$
		(0.006)	
(11)	$I_p(c)$	$= 15.610 + 0.108CR_p - 0.366\Delta WPI$	$R^2 = 0.945$
		(0.206)	
(12)	I_g	$= -15.301 + 0.623VA_{oil}$	$R^2 = 0.949$
		(0.010)	
(13)	E_o	$= 4.939 + 1.060E_{o(-1)}$	$R^2 = 0.994$
		(0.081)	
(14)	E_{no}	$= -3.919 + 0.045M_{k+1} + 0.118VAA$	$R^2 = 0.979$
		(0.018) (0.024)	
(15)	M_{k+1}	$= -64.917 + 0.698GNP - 3.723VAM_{(-1)}$	$R^2 = 0.977$
		(0.129) (0.999)	
(16)	M_c	$= -36.979 + 0.934VA_{oil} + 0.361GNP_{(-1)} - 2.949VAM_{(-1)}$	$R^2 = 0.991$
		(0.104) (0.202) (1.194)	
(17)	CR_p	$= -28.515 + 1.721VAM + 0.259MSB_{(-1)}$	$R^2 = 0.999$
		(0.255) (0.072)	
(18)	T_f	$= -10.109 + 0.569E_o$	$R^2 = 0.861$
		(0.072)	
(19)	T_D	$= -6.843 + 0.039GNP$	$R^2 = 0.986$
		(0.001)	
(20)	T_A	$= 1.304 + 0.162M_c$	$R^2 = 0.905$

since GNP and personal disposable income usually involve parallel movements over time. Imports of capital and intermediate goods, however, require greater justification. On a priori grounds it may seem that we tread on weak theoretical grounds by introducing this lagged variable into the urban consumption function. But in the words of Nurkse, "We are here in the classical world of Say's Law. In underdeveloped areas there is generally no deflationary gap through excessive savings. Production creates its own demand, and the size of the market depends on the volume of production. . . . Capacity to buy means capacity to produce."[4]

In developing areas, according to this hypothesis, we are likely to expect demand, and therefore consumption expenditures, to be a function of additional capacity. Since it is precisely the importation of capital and intermediate goods that has fueled the recent increases in capacity, we seem justified in suggesting that M_{k+1} is an explanatory variable of urban consumption.[5] The lag is introduced in response to the gestation periods associated with new investments, reflecting the time needed between the import of capital goods and their actual contribution to capacity expansion.[6]

The same cannot be said for equation 8, the rural consumption function. Indeed the different explanatory variables used in equation 8, *VAA* and P_rI, tend to reconfirm the essentially dual nature of the Iranian economy.[7] The results shown in Table A.1 indicate a rather good fit for equation 8: The $R^2=0.992$ and the standard errors are low relative to the estimated coefficients.

The relatively high correlation existing between value added in agriculture and rural consumption expenditures adds further credence to the notion of conventional duality in the Iranian economy. Thus nonagricultural activities in the rural sector accounted for nearly 30 percent of the employed labor force. Yet only the returns to the factors of production in agriculture (i.e., value added) and the rural population index seemed to be the relevant explanatory variables of rural consumption expenditures. This suggests that agricultural incomes in the rural sector set the base to which households relate their consumption expenditures.

Seeing that such incomes are primarily from labor inputs and that their per-worker equivalents relative to other sectors have not shown any significant increases over the period 1959–1967, it seems relatively safe to conclude that value added in agriculture, as a significant explanatory variable of rural consumption expenditures, indicates to what extent the agricultural economy is characterized by subsistence conditions, dependence on barter and in-kind transactions, and a lack of integration with other sectors of the economy. Were this conclusion invalid, we would more than likely expect rural consumption expenditures to be a function of rural incomes, which in itself would reflect a greater sectoral diversification as well as a higher component of profits. Two additional observations also tend to support this evidence: (1) the cost of living index included in the initial estimation was found to have a coefficient statistically insignificant at a 5 percent level and was consequently dropped from the equation, suggesting a certain degree of self-sufficiency in that the index includes the goods from all sectors; and (2) the rural population index was found to be significant at a 5 percent level, in turn indicating the high degree to which increases in consumption expenditures are a function of increases in population.[8]

Turning to the final consumption relationship equation 9, we note that the significant explanatory variables of government consumption expenditures are direct taxes (T_D), customs duties (T_A), and value added in the oil sector (VA_{oil}).

The results presented in Table A.1 suggest a very good fit in that the $R^2=0.997$ and the standard errors are low relative to their coefficients.

Equations 10, 11, and 12 represent the major investment relationships in the Iranian economy. As noted earlier, the careful delineation of private and public sectors is again exposed by virtue of the special role of the oil sector (the so-called oil duality). The contribution of oil revenues to capital formation need not be elaborated upon; the results of equation 12 shown in Table A.1 are adequate in reflecting both the crucial role of oil in the development process of Iran and the importance of the public sector as a vehicle for the channeling of economic resources from the oil sector (nationalized in this case) to the rest of the economy.

Equations 13 and 14 represent the major export relationships in the Iranian economy. Because of the importance of oil in the economy, the export sector has been appropriately divided into the two subsectors of oil and nonoil, each of which is specified as a function of its important determinants.

Equations 15 and 16 are the major estimated import equations for the Iranian economy. Total imports have been conveniently divided into consumer goods imports and capital and intermediate goods imports. From an economic development strategy viewpoint, this subdivision delineates those goods intended to presently increase the level of material welfare and those intended to further economic growth.

Equation 15, as shown in Table A.1, expresses imports of capital and intermediate goods as a function of gross national product and value added in manufacturing lagged by one year. The results suggest a good correlation between the dependent and the independent variables. The standard errors are quite low relative to the estimated coefficients and $R^2=0.997$.

Equation 16 expresses imports of consumer goods as a function of value added in the oil sector, GNP lagged by one year, and value added in manufacturing lagged by one year. Table A.1 indicates the regression results. The $R^2=0.991$ and the standard errors are quite low relative to the coefficients.

Equation 17 shows private-sector credits as a function of value added in the manufacturing sector and of the money supply lagged by one year. The results shown in Table A.1 are quite adequate: $R^2=0.999$ and the standard errors are very low relative to the coefficients. The money supply is traditionally regarded as one of the main explanatory variables of private-sector credits. This link is the basis for monetary policy, yet much discussion has centered around the fact that monetary policy acts with a lag. When decisions are taken to affect the money supply, there is usually a year's lag until the new credit conditions begin to affect the real sectors of the economy. Accordingly present credit conditions were postulated to be a function of last year's money supply. The good correlation between $MSB_{(-1)}$ and CR_p seems to indicate that the lag relationship observed in developed countries, such as the United States, also applies to developing countries such as Iran.

The remaining three equations are quite straightforward. Equation 18 is merely a linear approximation over time of net factor income from abroad. The relatively low determination coefficient ($R^2=0.861$) suggests the arbitrariness of tying this variable to oil exports. The two tax equations, 19 and 20, were included for use in a policymaking context.

The Regional Planning Model

This model, developed by Farhad Noorbakhsh,[9] makes use of fifty-five development indicators to measure the gaps in development among the twenty-three ostans (counties) of Iran. The fifty-five development indicators utilized by the model are as follows:

A. **Economic Indicators**

(A-1) **Industrial Indicators**

X_1 = Percentage of rural population (ages ten and above) employed by small rural industries

X_2 = Per capita value added in small rural industries

X_3 = Average wage rate in small rural industries

X_4 = Per capita investment in small rural industries

X_5 = Value of per capita electricity consumption by large industries

X_6 = Value of per capita production of capital goods by large industries

X_7 = Per capita capital formation in large industries

X_8 = Per capita share of large industries from GDP

X_9 = Per capita value added in large industries

(A-2) Agricultural Indicators

X_{10} = Per capita value added in the agricultural sector

X_{11} = Average daily wage rate for agricultural workers

X_{12} = The sum of loans during the past three years for each hectare of agricultural land

X_{13} = Index of modernization (of the agricultural sector)

X_{14} = Average assets held by agricultural coops

(A-3) Employment Indicators

X_{15} = Employment in rural areas

X_{16} = Employment in urban areas

X_{17} = Rate of employment

X_{18} = Rate of employment in manufacturing and mining

X_{19} = Rate of employment in services sector

X_{20} = Percentage of skilled worker employment

X_{21} = Average hourly wage rate

X_{22} = Distribution of migrant population with high school and university education

B. Social Indicators

(B-1) Urbanization and Migration

X_{23} = The ratio of inmigration over outmigration for each ostan

X_{24} = Percentage of urban population

(B-2) Living Facilities

X_{25} = Change in the number of families living in one unit during the last four years

X_{26} = Percentage of units having access to electricity

X_{27} = Percentage of units with water facilities

X_{28} = Percentage of households living in units with three bedrooms or larger

X_{29} = Per capita expenditure by municipalities

X_{30} = Per capita consumption of red meat per month

(B-3) Education Indicators

X_{31} = Number of students in elementary school (per 1,000 population)

X_{32} = Number of students in high school (per 1,000 population)

X_{33} = Number of students in vocational school (per 1,000 population)

X_{34} = Number of students in universities (per 10,000 population)

X_{35} = Ratio of female students in universities

X_{36} = Number of students in teacher-training schools (per 100,000 population)

X_{37} = The literacy rate (ages six and above)

X_{38} = The literacy rate for female population (ages six and above)

X_{39} = Number of books in libraries (per 10,000 urban literate population)

X_{40} = The inverse of "shortage of high school teachers for high school students"

(B-4) Health Indicators

X_{41} = Number of physicians (per 100,000 population)

X_{42} = Number of dentists (per 100,000 population)

X_{43} = Number of hospital beds (per 100,000 population)

X_{44} = Number of laboratories (per 100,000 population)

X_{45} = Number of health clinics (per 100,000 population)

X_{46} = Number of nurses (per 100,000 population)

X_{47} = Number of physicians (per 10,000 square kilometers)

X_{48} = Number of dentists (per 10,000 square kilometers)

X_{49} = Number of hospitals (per 10,000 square kilometers)

C. Political and Organizational Indicators

(C-1) Communication

X_{50} = Percentage of population covered by television networks

X_{51} = Number of telephones (per 1,000 urban population)

X_{52} = Number of mail boxes (per 10,000 square kilometers)

(C-2) Management Capabilities

X_{53} = Number of government employees (per 100 population)

X_{54} = Per capita (direct and indirect) taxes

(C-3) Participation in Political Affairs

X_{55} = Percentage of population (ages eighteen and above) participating in general elections.

The regional statistics for each year and each indicator are compiled. Then the model standardizes each indicator as

$$Z_{ij} = (X_{ij} - \overline{X}_j)/S_j \qquad \text{(A.1)}$$

$$i=1,2,\ldots,23 \quad \text{and} \quad j=1,2,\ldots,55$$

where Z_{ij} is the standardized value of indicators j for ostan i and X_j and S_j are the mean and standard deviation of the indicator j.

The simple distance between ostans p and q is measured as

$$Z_{pj} - Z_{qj}, \qquad j=1,\ldots,55. \qquad \text{(A.2)}$$

The composite distance between ostans p and q is calculated from

$$d_{pq} = \left[\sum_{j=1}^{55} (Z_{pj} - Z_{qj})^2 \right]^{\frac{1}{2}} \qquad \text{(A.3)}$$

The result of this calculation is a 23 × 23 symmetric matrix that shows the composite distances among the twenty-three ostans of Iran.

The next step is to choose the ideal ostan. For the indicator 1, we inspect all values of Z_{i1} and choose the highest value. This specific value is assigned to Z_{o1}. We then repeat the process for other indicators. The result is fifty-five values representing the best of everything, all assigned to the ideal ostan, *o*.

The model calculates the simple and composite distances of all ostans from the ideal ostan. This then shows, for each ostan, the extent and directions of underdevelopment. These distances are calculated as

$$Z_{oj} - Z_{ij} \qquad \text{(A.4)}$$

for the simple distance and

$$d_{oi} = \left[\sum_{j=1}^{55} (Z_{oj} - Z_{ij})^2 \right]^{\frac{1}{2}} \qquad \text{(A.5)}$$

for the composite distance.

Thus far, we have discussed how the model measures the distances and the development gaps among the regions of the country. The next module of the model utilizes these results to calculate the development targets of each ostan. In this module of the model, ostans are first grouped by their development patterns, then the target for each indicator and each ostan is calculated.

The grouping of ostans is done as follows. The matrix of composite distances [(d_{pq}), $p=1,\ldots,23$, $q=1,2,\ldots,23$] is utilized to observe the distance between each ostan and others. The average and standard deviations of these distances (for each ostan) are calculated. Then the upper and lower ranges for the development pattern of a specific ostan are calculated as

$$\begin{aligned} d_{(+)} &= d + 2\ SD \qquad \text{(upper range)} \\ d_{(-)} &= d - 2\ SD \qquad \text{(lower range)} \end{aligned} \qquad \text{(A.6)}$$

where d is the average distance and SD shows the standard deviation. That is,

$$\begin{aligned} \bar{d} &= (1/23) \sum_{i=1}^{23} d_i \\ SD &= \left[(1/23) \sum_{i=1}^{23} (d_i - \bar{d})^2\right]^{½} \end{aligned} \qquad \text{(A.7)}$$

Using the above ranges, the model determines a set of homogeneous groups, each corresponding with one ostan. Thus far, this grouping of ostans will show which ostans are homogeneous from a development-pattern point of view. However, the model utilizes this grouping to set the development targets for each ostan. To this end, the model takes, for each ostan, its homogeneous group and eliminates those ostans that are below this ostan from the development point of view. Then the model calculates the average value of each indicator for ostans above this ostan. The resultant value is announced as the target for this ostan. The process is repeated for all ostans and all indicators, resulting in a set of values

$$T_{ij}\ ,\quad i=1,2,\ldots,23,\quad j=1,2,\ldots,55 \qquad \text{(A.8)}$$

for each indicator and each ostan.

The next question the model tries to answer is what to do when resource availability does not match the requirements of all the calculated targets. The answer that the model suggests is that the target achievement should be adjusted in such a way that the burden of resource constraint would be imposed on the more advanced regions. The target achievement is the difference between the target value and the present status,

$$M_{ij} = T_{ij} - X_{ij} \tag{A.9}$$

This will actually show the required advancement to achieve the target. The adjusted targets are shown as

$$\hat{M}_{ij} = S_{ij}M_{ij} \tag{A.10}$$

where $\hat{M}_{ij}$ is the adjusted program and S_{ij} is the adjustment factor for region *i*, indicator *j*. The model suggests that S_{ij} should be calculated as follows. First, the simple distance between the ideal ostan and all twenty-three ostans for each indicator,

$$Z_{o,j} - Z_{i,j} \tag{A.11}$$

is used to determine which ostan is farthest from the ideal ostan. The distance between that ostan and the ideal ostan is defined to be 1 (unity). Then other distances are calculated in proportion to the above definition. In this way the model comes up with a set of values all between zero and one. These values show the extent of backwardness of each ostan and each indicator. The model then uses these values as the adjusted factor S_{ij} to modify the targets.

The Optimal Planning Model

As explained in Chapter 6, the optimal planning model for Iran should take account of oil-resource utilization to arrive at the long-term extraction rate of this resource. The desirable rate of depleting exhaustible resources in general, and oil resources in particular, has for a long time been the subject of a significant volume of economics literature. The traditional approach to this issue considers the producer as a business agent whose aim is to maximize the expected flow of profits. There are at least two reasons why this approach does not furnish an appropriate framework for analyzing Iran's oil-production policy. First, Iran utilizes oil exports to obtain the required foreign exchange for the importation of various capital, intermediate, and consumer goods. It is then more obligated to adhere to requirements related to the structure of its economy than to the implications of pure profit maximization. Second, Iran is faced with an increasing domestic political pressure to take account of the public ownership of oil resources and to choose depletion strategies that elevate the welfare of both the present and the future generations living in the country.

Faced with the above constraints, Iran is now attempting to devise its oil-extraction policy within a national planning framework in which it can relate this strategy to the economy's requirements of foreign exchange, on the one hand, and the national welfare, on the other. Here we present the methodology developed by H. Razavi[10] to derive Iran's optimal oil-extraction policy within a national planning framework. This model is based on a multisectoral specification of the economy and depicts the relationships between the oil-extraction policy and the welfare of the nation during the plan's period, as well as the portfolio of national wealth at the end of this horizon.

Iran, like most oil-producing countries, is presently searching for the foreign-trade policies that will provide: (1) a satisfactory level of well-being for the nation during the plan's period, (2) an optimum portfolio of assets (including oil reserves) at the end of the plan, and (3) a possibility of decreasing the dependency of the economy on the oil revenues in the long run. One objective function capable of implementing all of the above goals is

$$W = \sum_{t=1}^{T} \{1/(1+\delta)^{t-1}[U_t(C_t)POP_t] - \tfrac{1}{2}\sum_{i=1}^{n-1} q_i(E_{it} - \bar{e}_{it}X_{it})^2 \tag{A.12}$$

$$-\tfrac{1}{2}\sum_{i=1}^{n-1} p_i(MC_{it} - \bar{m}_{it}X_{it})^2 + s_{k,T}K_T + s_{f,T}F_T + s_{r,T}R_T,$$

where C_t shows the real per capita consumption expenditure; POP stands for population; E_i, MC_i, and X_i are the exports, the competitive imports (i.e., those that can be substituted by the domestic production), and the output of sector i; K_T, F_T, and R_T designate the accumulated stock of capital, the holdings of foreign assets, and the oil reserves at the end of the planning period. Parameters q_i, p_i, $s_{k,T}$, $s_{f,T}$, and $s_{r,T}$ are the objective function parameters.

The first term of this objective function measures the current welfare of the nation that is intended to be maximized. The utility index $U_t(C_t)$ can be expressed in a variety of mathematical forms. The specification utilized here is a quadratic form such as

$$U_t(C_t) = -\tfrac{1}{2}q_{ct}C_t^2 + s_{ct}C_t. \tag{A.13}$$

This form, chosen here because of its mathematical tractability, is also a reasonable approximation to many other utility functions. One way to interpret this function is to assume that utility is measured in monetary units (e.g., constant dollars). The term $s_{ct}C_t$, with s_{ct} equal to unity, then would measure the utility of current consumption if the marginal utility stayed constant. The term $-\tfrac{1}{2}q_{ct}C_t^2$ measures the deduction from this utility due to the actually diminishing marginal utility. The planner, however, may feel more comfortable in viewing this function as a tool to minimize the deviations of C_t from a predetermined target trend for per capita consumption, usually chosen based on political considerations. This target trend is easily shown to be $\overline{C}_t = s_{ct}/q_{ct}$. It is then possible to assign an ascending trend to s_{ct} to indicate a continuous upward shift in the planner's view of standards of living.

The second term of the objective function (equation A.12) represents the policymaker's desire to keep the amount of export from each sector close to a specific target. These targets are set such that the importance of the nonoil exports in the provision of foreign exchange is increased over time. A simple way in which to incorporate this idea is to take the export targets as a set of predetermined trends.[11] However, it is more realistic to relate the target for each sector's export to the output of that sector. The term $\hat{e}_{it}X_{it}$ shows the target for the ith sector's export, and $\hat{e}_{it}$ is the desirable ratio of this export to x_{it}. The values of q_i will then show the relative weights that the planner wishes to assign to obtaining the export targets.

The third term of the objective function (equation A.12) serves a similar purpose to that of the second term except that it keeps competitive imports close to a desired proportion of the sectoral output. Complementary imports are left without hindrance to satisfy the requirements of the national production.[12]

The last three terms of the objective function (equation A.12) show the portfolio of national wealth at the end of the planning period. The parameters $s_{k,T}$, $s_{f,T}$, and $s_{r,T}$ are then the shadow prices of various types of assets. Given that K_T, F_T, and R_T are considered as pure assets, the values of $s_{k,T}$ and $s_{f,T}$ can be taken as simple discount factors; the expected price of oil in year T may be chosen as the proper value for $s_{r,T}$. It is, however, noted that if the planner utilizes a broader view of K_T, F_T, and R_T and considers them as the future factors of production, the assignment of values to $s_{k,T}$, $s_{f,T}$, and $s_{r,T}$ should be based on the expected future services of these factors, which is clearly a more complicated procedure.

Utilizing the objective function A.12, Iranian planners derive the optimal values of E_{it}, MC_{it} for $t = 1,2, \ldots, T$ such that this function is maximized. Before doing this, however, it is necessary to determine the relationships between these policy variables and the relevant endogenous variables (C_t, X_{it}, K_T, F_T, and R_T). The primary requirement in writing these relationships is to separate the output of the oil sector from that of the nonoil sector. Planners, however, find a general multisectoral specification of the economic activities more useful in studying the effect of policy variables on the state of the economy. The domestic production is thus separated into $(n-1)$ sectors, the first of which is oil, with the noncompetitive import treated as the *n*th sector. The required relationships make a simple multisectoral model such as

$$X_{it} = \sum_{j=1}^{n-1} a_{ij}X_{jt}+c_iPC_t+g_i\bar{G}_t+\sum_{j=1}^{n-1} b_{ij}I_{jt}+E_{it}-MC_{it}, \tag{A.14}$$

$$I_{jt} = \beta_j I_{j,t-1}+\gamma_j \Delta X_{jt}+\epsilon_{jt}, \quad j=1,2,\ldots,n-1, \tag{A.15}$$

$$PC_t = \alpha_{n+1}+\beta_{n+1}PC_{t-1}+\gamma_{n+1}YD_t+\epsilon_{(n+1),t}, \tag{A.16}$$

$$YD_t = GNP_t-TD_t-\upsilon_1 X_{1t}, \tag{A.17}$$

$$TD_t = \alpha_{n+2}+\beta_{n+2}GNP_t+\epsilon_{(n+2),t}, \tag{A.18}$$

$$GNP_t = GDP_t+\overline{NFI}_t, \tag{A.19}$$

$$GDP_t = \sum_{j=1}^{n-1} \upsilon_j X_{jt}, \tag{A.20}$$

$$K_t = (1-\lambda)K_{t-1}+\sum_{j=1}^{n-1} I_{jt}, \tag{A.21}$$

$$F_t = (1+r_t)F_{t-1}+\sum_{j=1}^{n-1} (E_{jt}-MC_{jt})-X_{nt}+\overline{NFI}_t-\overline{NCO}_t, \tag{A.22}$$

$$R_t = R_{t-1}-(1/\bar{P}_t)X_{1,t}. \tag{A.23}$$

Equation A.14 is the balance relationship where *PC* and *G* are private and government consumption expenditures, and I_j shows the investment expenditure in sector *j* (investment by destination). Equation A.15 is Koyck's specification for investment function; ΔX_j stands for change in the output of sector *j*.

Equation A.16 specifies the private consumption expenditure as a function of disposable income *YD*, where *YD* is determined as the net nonoil income. This definition of the disposable income is based on the fact that in the case of Iran the oil income (except for a minor part distributed as wages) is received by the government and then charged into the economy in the form of public (current and development) expenditures.

Equation A.18 specifies the direct tax (*TD*) as a function of GNP; Equation A.19 determines the gross national product where NFI stands for the net factor income from abroad, taken as an exogenous variable. Equation A.20 defines GDP as the sum of value added in $(n-1)$ sectors, where v_i stands for the ratio of value added to the output in sector i.

Equation A.22 determines the holdings of foreign assets (including gold), where r_t is the real rate of return to these assets and $\overline{NCO}$ stands for the net capital outflow. $\overline{NCO}$ includes discrepancies in the balance of payment and is taken as an exogenous variable. Equation A.23 measures the stock of oil reserves R_t, where P_t is defined as the weighted average of the domestic and the international price of oil.

Equations A.14 through A.23 constitute a set of linear relationships that depict the effect of policy variables on the state of economy. After eliminating *YD*, *TD*, GNP, and GDP, we may solve these equations to obtain the following reduced form

$$y_t = A_t^* y_{t-1} + B_t^* U_t + C_t^* Z_t, \tag{A.24}$$

where

$$y_t' = [X_{1t}, \ldots, X_{nt}, I_{1t}, \ldots, I_{n-1,t}, PC_t, K_t, F_t, R_t],$$

$$U_t' = [E_{1t}, \ldots, E_{n-1,t}, MC_{1t}, \ldots, MC_{n-1,t}], \tag{A.25}$$

$$Z_t' = [\bar{G}_t, \overline{NFI}_t, \overline{NCO}_t, 1.0].$$

Following G.C. Chow's formulation of the control problem,[13] we write

$$\begin{pmatrix} y_t \\ U_t \end{pmatrix} = \begin{pmatrix} A_t^* & 0 \\ 0 & 0 \end{pmatrix} \begin{pmatrix} y_{t-1} \\ U_{t-1} \end{pmatrix} + \begin{pmatrix} B_t^* \\ I \end{pmatrix} U_t + \begin{pmatrix} C_t^* \\ 0 \end{pmatrix} Z_t, \tag{A.26}$$

where I is a $2n-2$ identity matrix and **0** stands for a null matrix of the same size. We then define

$$Y_t = \begin{bmatrix} y_t \\ U_t \end{bmatrix}$$

which includes $4n+1$ elements, and rewrite the above equation as

$$Y_t = A_t Y_{t-1} + B_t U_t + C_t Z_t. \tag{A.27}$$

This relationship represents our state equation where Y_t, U_t, and Z_t are treated as the vectors of state, control, and exogenous variables respectively.

To complete the formulation of our control problem, we should express the objective function (equation A.12) in the matrix notation of equation A.27. To this end, we first substitute A.13 into A.12 and manipulate the function to obtain

$$\begin{aligned} W = \sum_{t=1}^{T} \{ & - \tfrac{1}{2} [q_{ct}/(1+\delta)^{t-1}] (1/POP_t) PC_t^2 + [s_{ct}/(1+\delta)^{t-1}] PC_t \\ & + \sum_{i=1}^{n-1} [- \tfrac{1}{2}(q_i \bar{e}_{it}^{2} + p_i \bar{m}_{it}^{2}) X_{it}^2 - \tfrac{1}{2} q_i E_{it}^2 - \tfrac{1}{2} p_i MC_{it}^2] \\ & + [q_i \overline{e_{it}} X_{it} E_{it} + p_i \overline{m_{it}} X_{it} MC_{it}] \} + s_{k,T} K_T + s_{f,T} F_T + s_{r,T} R_T. \end{aligned} \tag{A.28}$$

We then write this function as

$$W = \sum_{t=1}^{T} [\tfrac{1}{2} Y_t' Q_t Y_t + Y_t' s_t] , \tag{A.29}$$

where the matrix Q_t and the vector s_t contain the objective function parameters. Q_t is a square matrix of dimension $4n+1$, which is displayed in Figure A.1, and the vector s_t contains $4n+1$ elements such that

$$s_t' = [\underbrace{0,\ldots,0}_{n},\underbrace{0,\ldots,0}_{n-1}, s_c/(1+\delta)^{t-1}, s_{k,t}, s_{f,t}, s_{r,t}, \underbrace{0,\ldots,0}_{2n-2}] \tag{A.30}$$

where

$$s_{k,t} = s_{f,t} = s_{r,t} = 0 \quad \text{for} \quad t=1,2,,\ldots,T=1,$$

and

$$s_{k,t} = s_{k,T}, \quad s_{f,t} = s_{f,T}, \quad s_{r,t} = s_{r,T} \quad \text{for} \quad t=T.$$

Figure A.1. Matrix Q_t

X_1	X_2	X_{n-1}	X_n	I_1	I_{n-1}	PC	K	FA	R	E_1	E_2	E_{n-1}	MC_1	MC_2	MC_{n-1}	
$-(q_1e_1^2+p_1m_1^2)$	0	0	0	0	0	0	0	0	0	q_1e_1	0	0	0	0	0	X_1
0	$-(q_2e_2^2+p_2m_2^2)$	0	0	0	0	0	0	0	0	0	q_2e_2	0	0	p_2m_2	0	X_2
0	0	$-(q_{n-1}e_{n-1}^2+p_{n-1}m_{n-1}^2)$	0	0	0	0	0	0	0	0	0	$q_{n-1}e_{n-1}$	0	0	$p_{n-1}m_{n-1}$	X_{n-1}
0	0	0	0	0	0	0	0	0	0	0	0	0	0	0	0	X_n
0	0	0	0	0	0	0	0	0	0	0	0	0	0	0	0	I_1
0	0	0	0	0	0	0	0	0	0	0	0	0	0	0	0	I_{n-1}
0	0	0	0	0	0	$-[q_c/(1+\delta)^{t-1}](1/POP_t)$	0	0	0	0	0	0	0	0	0	PC
0	0	0	0	0	0	0	0	0	0	0	0	0	0	0	0	K
0	0	0	0	0	0	0	0	0	0	0	0	0	0	0	0	FA
0	0	0	0	0	0	0	0	0	0	0	0	0	0	0	0	R
q_1e_1	0	0	0	0	0	0	0	0	0	$-q_1$	0	0	0	0	0	E_1
0	q_2e_2	0	0	0	0	0	0	0	0	0	$-q_2$	0	0	0	0	E_2
0	0	$q_{n-1}e_{n-1}$	0	0	0	0	0	0	0	0	0	$-q_{n-1}$	0	0	0	E_{n-1}
p_1m_1	0	0	0	0	0	0	0	0	0	0	0	0	$-p_1$	0	0	MC_1
0	p_2m_2	0	0	0	0	0	0	0	0	0	0	0	0	$-p_2$	0	MC_2
0	0	$p_{n-1}m_{n-1}$	0	0	0	0	0	0	0	0	0	0	0	0	$-p_{n-1}$	MC_{n-1}

* Parameters q_i, p_i, e_i and m_i carry a subscript "t" which is eliminated here to save space.

Objective function A.29 and state equation A.27 constitute a linear-quadratic dynamic programming problem that can be solved[14] to result in the optimal values of policy variables as

$$U_t = (B_t' H_t B_t)^{-1} (B_t' H_t A_t Y_{t-1} + B_t' H_t C_t Z_t + B_t' h_t), \qquad \text{(A.31)}$$

where arrays H_t and h_t are defined recursively by

$$H_{t-1} = Q_{t-1} - A_t' H_t' Bt (B_t' H_t B_t)^{-1} B_t' H_t A_t + A_t' H_t A_t,$$

$$\text{(A.32)}$$

$$h_{t-1} = s_{t-1} + A_t' h_t + A_t' H_t C_t Z_t - A_t' H_t B_t (B_t' H_t B_t)^{-1}$$

$$X (B_t' H_t C_t Z_t + B_t' h_t),$$

$$\text{(A.33)}$$

$$H_T = Q_T \text{ and } h_T = s_T.$$

To summarize, the application of the methodology discussed in this section requires taking the following steps. First, estimate equations A.15, A.16, and A.18 and the input-output ratios a_{ij}, b_{ij}. Second, calculate the reduced form (A.27). Third, choose the values for $\bar{e}_{it}$, $\overline{m}_{it}$, q_i, and p_i and construct the arrays Q_t and s_t. Fourth, utilize equations A.32 and A.33 to calculate H_t and h_t for $t=T, T-1, \ldots, 1$. Fifth, use equation A.31 to compute the optimal values of policy variables for $t=1,2,\ldots, T$.

To implement the above procedure, we first separate the economic activities into the following sectors: oil, agriculture, manufacturing and mining, construction, infrastructure (water, power, and communications), services, and noncompetitive imports. Coefficients a_{ij}, b_{ij}, v_i, c_i, and g_i are calculated based on Iran's 1974 input-output table.[15] Equations A.15, A.16, and A.18 are estimated based on the time series statistics for the period of 1959 to 1978, with all values deflated to constant 1974 rials (1 US\$ = 70.6 rials). The results of the ordinary least squares (OLS) estimation of these equations are summarized in Table A.2.[16]

Utilizing the above results, we set out the system of equations A.14 to A.23. After eliminating *YD, TD,* GNP, and GDP, we solve[17] this system to obtain the reduced form A.24 where the vector y consists of seventeen elements ($X_1, X_2, \ldots, X_7, I_1, I_2, \ldots, I_6, PC, K, FA$, and R), the vector U contains seven elements ($E_1, E_2, E_3, E_6, MC_2, MC_3$, and MC_6), and the vector Z involves four elements (G, NFI, NCO, and 1.0). The final state vector Y_t is then of the dimension 24 x 1.

Table A.2. Estimation Results of Equations A.15, A.16, and A.18*

Eq.	Dependent variable	$\hat{\alpha}$	$\hat{\beta}$	$\hat{\gamma}$	R^2	D.W.
(A.15)	I_1	—	0.963 [19.1]	0.008 [1.6]	0.91	2.81
	I_2	—	0.918 [12.3]	0.049 [0.9]	0.87	1.68
	I_3	—	0.752 [6.5]	0.896 [2.2]	0.94	2.70
	I_4	—	0.901 [23.0]	1.788 [4.7]	0.96	2.53
	I_5	—	0.838 [14.6]	2.44 [4.3]	0.95	1.76
	I_6	—	0.882 [10.4]	0.177 [2.4]	0.92	2.64
(A.16)	PC	12.767 [0.4]	0.659 [2.9]	0.292 [2.0]	0.98	2.04
(A.18)	TD	-14.789 [-2.7]	0.0454 [14.7]	—	0.93	1.68

*Figures in brackets are t ratios.

In order to specify the objective function A.29, we need to determine the elements of the matrix Q_t and the vector s_t, which are calculated based on the values of e_{it}, m_{it}, q_i, and p_i. These values are, in turn, related to the trade targets and the weights assigned to obtaining these targets. The planner utilizes alternative values for these parameters and examines their efforts on the state of the economy. Before doing this, however, a set of initial values should be chosen to establish a base case. In this application, the set of initial values for these parameters is chosen as

$$\overline{e}_{1t} = 0.813 - 0.01t \qquad \overline{m}_{2t} = 0.039 - 0.001t$$

$$\overline{e}_{2t} = 0.333 + 0.001t \qquad \overline{m}_{3t} = 0.308 - 0.005t$$

$$\overline{e}_{3t} = 0.006 + 0.0002t \qquad \overline{m}_{6t} = 0.0879 - 0.001t$$

$$\overline{e}_{6t} = 0.038 + 0.001t \qquad t = 1,2,\ldots,T$$

where the constant terms represent the current situation. In addition to the above values, we take the following magnitudes for the objective function parameters:

$$s_{ct} = s_{co}(1+0.05)^{t-1}, \quad s_{c0} = 1.0, \quad q_{ct} = 0.02,$$

$$s_{k,T} = s_{f,T} = 1/(1+\delta)^{T-1}, \quad s_{r,T} = P_T/(1+\delta)^{T-1},$$

$$q_1 = 4.50, \quad q_2 = 0.001, \quad q_3 = 28.10, \quad q_6 = 1.38,$$

$$P_2 = 1.87, \quad P_3 = 0.005, \quad P_6 = 0.149,$$

where s_{ct} and q_{ct} are set such that the target for per capita consumption expenditure starts at 50,000 rials (US$710.00) and increases by an annual rate of 5 percent. The shadow price of oil is taken as its expected price at the end of the planning horizon. The values of parameters q_i and p_i are chosen such that a rather standard penalty is imposed on the deviation of each variable from its target.[18]

Notes

1. Firouz Vakil, *A Twenty Year Macroeconomic Perspective for Iran, 1351–1371* (Tehran: Plan and Budget Organization, 1975b).

2. Payments to the oil consortium are shown as net factor income from abroad in the national accounts of Iran. Thus, T_f contains a very large policy element and should have been, by all rights, treated as an exogenous variable. The only reason for including it as endogenous was the good correlation between

T_f and oil exports (E_o) as shown in (18) of Table A.1. However, future predictions based on (18) should be viewed with caution.

3. G. Ranis and J. Fei, "A Theory of Economic Development," *American Economic Review* 51, no. 2 (September 1961).

4. R. Nurkse, *Problems of Capital Formation in Underdeveloped Countries* (New York: Oxford University Press, 1953), pp. 8–9.

5. Rural consumption is precluded from this hypothesis precisely because of the dual nature of the Iranian economy. It is unlikely that the processes we have described reach all the way down to the village level.

6. M. K. Evans, *Macroeconomic Activity: Theory, Forecasting and Control* (New York: Harper and Row, 1969), pp. 100–101.

7. Jahangir Amuzegar and M. Ali Fekrat, *Iran: Economic Development Under Dualistic Conditions* (Chicago: University of Chicago Press, 1971).

8. The consumption expenditures of dynamic, nonsubsistence sectors are more likely related to income or their proxies (such as GNP) in that income growth by far outpaces population growth. Thus, we would expect population to be significant only in low-productivity sectors.

9. Farhad Noorbakhsh, "A Model for Determining the Priorities to Reduce the Regional Gaps in Iran" (Tehran: Plan and Budget Organization, 1977).

10. H. Razavi, "Optimal Rate of Oil Production for OPEC Member Countries," *Resources and Energy* 4, no. 4 (1982).

11. H. Razavi, "National Welfare Versus Economic Independence," *Optimal Control Methods and Applications* 4, no. 3 (1983).

12. The heavy cost of restricting complementary imports is discussed in ibid.

13. G. C. Chow, *Analysis and Control of Dynamic Economic Systems* (New York: John Wiley, 1975).

14. Ibid.

15. Input-output tables for the Iranian economy were obtained from the Plan and Budget Organization in 1977.

16. The OLS estimates of the investment equations suffer from the problem of serial correlation. Application of the Cochrane-Orcutt procedure improved the results. However, we utilized the OLS results to avoid the complications in the optimization model that are created by the lag structure of the Cochrane-Orcutt estimates.

17. Since the last two equations involve r_t and P_t as coefficients, the system of equations A.14 to A.21 is first solved, and then the results for X_7 and X_1 are substituted in A.22 and A.23.

18. As mentioned previously, the values of q_i and p_i should be chosen based on relative weights that the planner wishes to assign to obtaining different targets. If we assign the same value to all these parameters, any variable that is larger will be more strongly forced to follow its target because its deviation is penalized more heavily. The values of q_i and p_i chosen for the objective function parameters are such that a 1 percent deviation from the target is penalized equally for all policy variables.

Bibliography

Abdul-Rauf, M. *The Islamic Doctrine of Economics and Contemporary Economic Thought.* Washington, D.C.: American Enterprise Institute, 1979.

Abrahamian, E. *Iran Between Two Revolutions.* Princeton: Princeton University Press, 1982.

Ahmad, Eqbal. "The Iranian Revolution: A Landmark for the Future." *Race and Class* (London) 21, no. 1 (Summer 1979).

Akhavi, S. *Religion and Politics in Contemporary Iran: Clergy-State Relations in the Pahlavi Period.* New York: State University of New York Press, 1980.

Albert, D. H. *Tell the American People: Perspectives on the Iranian Revolution.* Philadelphia: Movements for a New Society, 1980.

Amuzegar, Jahangir. "Iran's Economic Planning Once Again." *Middle East Economic Papers,* Occasional Papers, 1957.

———. *Iran: An Economic Profile.* Washington, D.C.: The Middle East Institute, 1977.

———. "Oil Wealth: A Very Mixed Blessing." *Foreign Affairs* 60, no. 4 (Spring 1982), pp. 814–835.

Amuzegar, Jahangir and M. Ali Fekrat. *Iran: Economic Development Under Dualistic Conditions.* Chicago: University of Chicago Press, 1971.

Aresvick, O. *The Agricultural Development of Iran.* New York: Praeger, 1976.

Askari, Hossein; J. Cummings; and B. Harik. "Land Reform in the Middle East: A Note on Its Redistributive Effect." *Iranian Studies* 10, no. 2 (Autumn 1977).

Baldwin, George. *Planning and Development in Iran.* Baltimore: Johns Hopkins University Press, 1967.

Banani, A. *The Modernization of Iran: 1921–1941.* Stanford, Calif.: Stanford University Press, 1961.

Bank Markazi Iran. *Annual Report, 1974/1975* (Tehran: Bank Markazi Iran, 1975).

Benedick, Richard. *Industrial Finance in Iran.* Cambridge: Harvard University Press, 1964.

Bharier, Julian. *Economic Development in Iran 1900–1970.* London: Oxford University Press, 1971.

Bill, James A. *The Politics of Iran: Groups, Classes and Modernization.* Columbus, Ohio: Charles Merrill, 1972.

______. "Iran and the Crisis of 1978." *Foreign Affairs* 57, no. 2 (1978), pp. 323–342.

______. "Power and Religion in Revolutionary Iran." *The Middle East Journal* 36, no. 1 (1982), pp. 22–47.

Blitzer, C.; A. Mearaus; and A. Stoutjesdijk. "A Dynamic Model of OPEC Trade and Production." *Journal of Development Economics* 2, no. 3 (Fall 1975), pp. 319–335.

Bohi, D. R., and M. Russell. *U.S. Energy Policy.* Baltimore: Johns Hopkins University Press, 1975.

Bozeman, A. B. "Iran: U.S. Foreign Policy and the Tradition of Persian Statecraft." *Orbis* 23, no. 2 (Summer 1979), pp. 387–402.

Burris, V. "Capital Accumulation and the Rise of the New Middle Class." *Revolutionary Radical Political Economy,* Spring 1980, pp. 387–402.

Carswell, R. "Economic Sanctions and the Iran Experience." *Foreign Affairs* 60, no. 2 (1981), pp. 247–265.

Chow, G. C. *Analysis and Control of Dynamic Economic Systems.* New York: John Wiley, 1975.

Craig, D. "The Impact of Land Reform on an Iranian Village." *The Middle East Journal* 32, no. 2 (1978), pp. 141–154.

Cudsi, A. (ed.). *Islam and Power.* Baltimore: Johns Hopkins University Press, 1981.

Daftary, Farhad. "The Balance of Payments Deficit and the Problem of Inflation in Iran, 1955–1962." *Iranian Studies* 5 (Winter 1972).

______. "Development Planning in Iran: A Historical Survey." *Iranian Studies* 6 (Autumn 1973).

Dasgupta, P.; R. Eastwood; and G. Heal. "Resource Management in a Trading Economy." *Quarterly Journal of Economics* 92, no. 297 (1978).

Dellafar, W. A., and J. K. Shirazi. "An Analysis of the Dynamics of Growth in Iran: 1959–73." *Journal of Economic Development* 3, no. 2 (July 1979).

Deshmukh, S. D., and S. R. Pliska. "Optimal Consumption and Exploration of Non-Renewable Resources Under Uncertainty." *Econometrica* 48, no. 1 (January 1980), pp. 177–200.

Donohue, J. *Islam in Transition.* New York: Oxford University Press, 1982.

Evans, M. K. *Macroeconomic Activity: Theory, Forecasting and Control.* New York: Harper and Row, 1969.

Fatemi, Khosrow. "Leadership by Distrust: The Shah's Modus Operandi." *The Middle East Journal* 36, no. 1 (1982), pp. 48–62.

Fesharaki, F. *Revolution and Energy Policy in Iran.* London: The Economist Intelligence Unit, July 1980.

Fischer, D.; D. Gately; and J. F. Kyle. "The Prospect for OPEC: A Critical Survey of Models of the World Oil Market." *Journal of Development Economics* 2, no. 3 (Fall 1975), pp. 363–386.

Fischer, M. J. *Iran: From Religious Dispute to Revolution.* Cambridge: Harvard University Press, 1980.

Forbis, W. *Fall of the Peacock Throne: The Story of Iran.* New York: Harper and Row, 1980.

Fouad, M. H. "Petrodollars and Economic Development in the Middle East." *The Middle East Journal* 34, no. 2 (1980), pp. 307–321.

Friedman, M. R., and A. Schwartz. *A Monetary History of the United States.* New York: The National Bureau of Economic Research, 1963.

Graham, Robert. *Iran, The Illusion of Power.* London: Croom Helm; New York: St. Martin's Press, 1978.

Grayson, B. L. *United States Iranian Relations.* Washington, D.C.: University Press of America, 1981.

Halliday, F. *Iran: Dictatorship and Development.* New York: Penguin Books, 1979.

———. *After the Shah.* Washington, D.C.: Institute for Policy Studies, 1981.

Hirschfeld, Y. P. "Moscow and Khomeini: Soviet-Iranian Relations in Historical Perspective." *Orbis* 24, no. 2 (Summer 1980), pp. 219–240.

Hotelling, H. "The Economics of Exhaustible Resources." *Journal of Political Economy* 39, no. 2 (April 1931), pp. 137–175.

International Labour Office. *Employment and Income Policies for Iran.* Geneva: International Labour Office, 1973.

Jazani, B. *The Socio-Economic Analysis of a Dependent Capitalist State.* Tehran: Organization of the Iranian People's Fedaei Guerrillas, 1973.

Johnson, G. C. *High-Level Manpower in Iran: From Hidden Conflict to Crisis.* New York: Praeger, 1980.

Kaldor, M. *Strategic Factors in Economic Development.* New York: Cornell University Press. 1967.

Katouzian, H. *The Political Economy of Modern Iran: Despotism and Pseudo-Modernism.* New York: New York University Press, 1981a.

———. *The Political Economy of Modern Iran, 1926–1979.* London: Macmillan, 1981b.

Kazemi, F. *Poverty and Revolution in Iran: The Migrant Poor, Urban Marginality and Politics.* New York: New York University Press, 1980.

Keddie, Nikki R. *Roots of Revolution, An Interpretive History of Modern Iran.* New Haven: Yale University Press, 1981.

Labanon, B. "An Oligopolistic Model of the World Supply of Crude Petroleum." *Applied Economics* 7, no. 2 (April 1975), pp. 134–149.

Lambton, A.K.S. *The Persian Land Reform: 1962–1966.* Oxford: Oxford University Press, 1969.

Ledeen, M., and W. Lewis. *Debacle: The American Failure in Iran.* New York: Alfred A. Knopf, 1981.

Lenczowski, George. *Iran under the Pahlavis.* Stanford, Calif.: Hoover Institution Press, Stanford University, 1978.

Lewis, B. "The Return of Islam." *Middle East Review* 12, no. 1 (Fall 1979), pp. 17–30.

Liberman, S. "Development and Population Growth in Iran." *Population and Development Review* 5, no. 2 (June 1979), pp. 293–318.

Looney, Robert E. *Iran at the End of the Century.* Lexington, Mass.: Lexington Books, 1977.

———. *Economic Origins of the Iranian Revolution.* New York: Pergamon Press, 1982.

MacLachlan, Keith. "The Iranian Economy 1960–1976," in *Twentieth Century Iran*, edited by H. Amirsadeghi and R. W. Ferrier. London: Heineman, 1977.

Mehran, F. *Income Distribution in Iran: The Statistics of Inequality.* Geneva: International Labour Office, October 1975.

Moran, T. H. "Iranian Defense Expenditures and the Social Crisis." *International Security* 3, no. 3 (Winter 1978).

Motamen, H. *Expenditure of Oil Revenue: An Optimal Control Approach with Application to the Iranian Economy.* New York: St. Martin's Press, 1979.

Noorbakhsh, Farhad. "A Model for Determining the Priorities to Reduce the Regional Gaps in Iran." Tehran: Plan and Budget Organization, 1977.

Noorzoy, N. S. "Islamic Laws on Riba and Their Economic Implications." *International Journal of Middle East* 14, no. 1 (1982), pp. 3–17.

Nuske, R. *Problems of Capital Formation in Underdeveloped Countries.* New York: Oxford University Press, 1953.

People's Mojahedin Organization of Iran (PMOI). *An Analysis of Political Events in the Period of June 1978 to January 1979.* Tehran: People's Mojahedin Organization of Iran, 1979.

______. *The History of the People's Mojahedin Organization.* Long Beach, Calif.: Moslem Students Society, 1981.

______. "Program of the Provisional Government of the Democratic Islamic Republic of Iran." *Iran Liberation* (occasional publication of PMOI). June 1982, pp. 3–6.

Pesaran, M. H. *Income Distribution Trends in Rural and Urban Iran.* Tehran: Bank Markazi Iran, March 1974.

Pesaran, M. H., and F. Gahvary. "Growth and Income Distribution in Iran." in *Econometric Contributions to Public Policy,* edited by R. Stone. New York: St. Martin's Press, 1978.

Pindyck, R. S. "Gains to Producers from the Cartelization of Exhaustible Resources." *Review of Economics and Statistics* 60, no. 2 (May 1978), pp. 238–251.

Pipes, D. "This World is Political: The Islamic Revival of the Seventies." *Orbis* 24, no. 1 (Spring 1980), pp. 9–37.

Plan and Budget Organization. *Iran's Fifth Development Plan 1973–78, Revised: A Summary.* Tehran: Plan and Budget Organization, 1975.

______. *Annual Report on the Performance of the Economy: 1981–1982.* Tehran: Plan and Budget Organization, 1982a.

______. *The Planning System.* Tehran: Plan and Budget Organization, 1982b.

Ramazani, R. K. "Iran and the Arab-Israeli Conflict." *The Middle East Journal* 33, no. 4 (1979), pp. 413–428.

______. "The Constitution of the Islamic Republic of Iran." *The Middle East Journal* 34, no. 2 (1980), pp. 182–196.

______. "Who Lost America? The Case of Iran." *The Middle East Journal* 36, no. 1 (1982), pp. 5–21.

Ranis, G., and J. Fei. "A Theory of Economic Development." *American Economic Review* 51, no. 2 (September 1961).

Razavi, H. "Optimal Rate of Oil Production for OPEC Member Countries," *Resources and Energy* 4, no. 4 (1982), pp. 291–305.

______. "An Analysis of Iran's Oil Production Policy." *Applied Economics* 15, no. 2 (April 1983), pp. 243–254.

______. "National Welfare Versus Economic Independence." *Optimal Control Methods and Applications* 4, no. 3 (1983), pp. 227–238.

______. "Optimal Adjustment in Manpower-Requirement Forecasts: A Case Study in Iran." *Mathematical Social Sciences* 6, no. 3 (December 1983).

Rizvi, A. *Iran: Royalty, Religion and Revolution.* Melbourne: Marfat Publishing House, 1980.

Rodan, P. Rosenstein. *Capital Formation and Economic Development.* Cambridge: Massachusetts Institute of Technology Press, 1964.

Rouleau, E. "Khomeini's Iran." *Foreign Affairs* 59, no. 1 (1981), pp. 1–20.

Saikal, A. *The Rise and Fall of the Shah.* Princeton: Princeton University Press, 1980.

Shahshahani, A., and T. M. Dowling. "An Econometric Model Forecast of Iran 1965–1985." *Journal of Energy and Development* 1, no. 2 (Autumn 1976).

Stiglitz, J. E. "Monopoly and the Rate of Extraction of Exhaustible Resources." *American Economic Review* 66, no. 3 (September 1976), pp. 655–661.

Sweeney, J. L. "Economics of Depletable Resources: Market Forces and Intertemporal Bias." *Review of Economic Studies* 44, no. 1 (February 1977), pp. 125–141.

Tinbergen, Jan. *Development Planning.* New York: McGraw-Hill Book Co., 1967.

Vakil, Firouz. *Determining Iran's Financial Surplus 1352–1371: Some Management Concepts.* Tehran Papers No. 2. Tehran: The Institute for International Political and Economic Studies, 1975a.

______. *A Twenty Year Macroeconomic Perspective for Iran, 1351–1371.* Tehran: Plan and Budget Organization, 1975b.

______. "Iran's Basic Macroeconomic Problems: A Twenty Year Horizon." *Economic Development and Cultural Change* 25, no. 4 (July 1977), pp. 713–730.

Walton, T. "Economic Development and Revolutionary Upheavals in Iran." *Cambridge Journal of Economics* 4, no. 3 (September 1980), pp. 271–302.

Waterston, Albert. *Development Planning: Lessons of Experience.* Baltimore: Johns Hopkins University Press, 1956.

Watkins, M. H. "The Staple Theory Revisited." *Journal of Canadian Studies* 12, no. 5 (Winter 1977), pp. 83–93.

Wilber, D. N. *Iran, Past and Present: From Monarchy to Islamic Republic.* Princeton: Princeton University Press, 1982.

Wright, C. "Implications of the Iran-Iraq War." *Foreign Affairs* 59, no. 2 (1981), pp. 276–303.

Index

For Product Safety Concerns and Information please contact our EU representative GPSR@taylorandfrancis.com Taylor & Francis Verlag GmbH, Kaufingerstraße 24, 80331 München, Germany

Batch number: 10758210

Printed by Printforce, the Netherlands